PATERNOSTER THEOLOGICA

What is Economic Justice?

Biblical and Secular Perspectives Contrasted

PATERNOSTER THEOLOGICAL MONOGRAPHS

A full listing of titles in this series and
Paternoster Biblical Monographs appears at the end
of this book

Series Preface

In the West the churches may be declining, but theology—serious, academic (mostly doctoral level) and mainstream orthodox in evaluative commitment—shows no sign of withering on the vine. This series of *Paternoster Theological Monographs* extends the expertise of the Press especially to first-time authors whose work stands broadly within the parameters created by fidelity to Scripture and has satisfied the critical scrutiny of respected assessors in the academy. Such theology may come in several distinct intellectual disciplines—historical, dogmatic, pastoral, apologetic, missional, aesthetic and no doubt others also. The series will be particularly hospitable to promising constructive theology within an evangelical frame, for it is of this that the church's need seems to be greatest. Quality writing will be published across the confessions—Anabaptist, Episcopalian, Reformed, Arminian and Orthodox—across the ages—patristic, medieval, reformation, modern and counter-modern—and across the continents. The aim of the series is theology written in the twofold conviction that the church needs theology and theology needs the church—which in reality means theology done for the glory of God.

Series Editors

David F. Wright, Emeritus Professor of Patristic and Reformed Christianity, University of Edinburgh, Scotland, UK

Trevor A. Hart, Head of School and Principal of St Mary's College School of Divinity, University of St Andrews, Scotland, UK

Anthony N.S. Lane, Professor of Historical Theology and Director of Research, London School of Theology, UK

Anthony C. Thiselton, Emeritus Professor of Christian Theology, University of Nottingham, Research Professor in Christian Theology, University College Chester, and Canon Theologian of Leicester Cathedral and Southwell Minster, UK

Kevin J. Vanhoozer, Research Professor of Systematic Theology, Trinity Evangelical Divinity School, Deerfield, Illinois, USA

*To Claire, my lovely wife and faithful friend,
and to Daniel, Rosanna, Bryony and Joseph,
my wonderful and inspiring children*

Contents

Acknowledgements

I am glad to express my warm appreciation to Michael Banner, who supervised my PhD studies at Kings College, London; to the staff and my fellow students at Oak Hill Theological College who encouraged me along this road; to numerous others who supported me in various ways; and to Anthony R. Cross who has helped me prepare the text for publication with painstaking care.

Andrew Hartropp
Watford
July 2007

CHAPTER 1

Introduction

One of the arguments developed in this book is that the contemporary Western world is presented with such a confusing array of accounts of economic justice that the prospects for achieving a significant degree of consensus regarding the nature and conception of justice in economic life, on the basis of some or all of those accounts, are now remote. The argument is not solely that different views about justice exist, but also that these differences involve incompatibilities at a fundamental level.

A second major argument of the book is that, whilst a biblical conception of economic justice ought to be able to address this contemporary setting with considerable effectiveness, existing treatments from Christian quarters are in practice seriously lacking in authority in this regard. These Christian contributions, it is argued, are insufficiently based on the Gospel, and thus on biblical revelation; and they do not engage adequately with other accounts, either in learning from them or in offering rigorous critical appraisal of them. Consequently, there is ample scope for a treatment of economic justice that is rooted thoroughly in the biblical revelation to make a significant contribution. The main task of this short introductory chapter is to outline the case for the validity of these two arguments.

References in economics textbooks nowadays to 'justice' are rare.[1] There is extensive analysis of equity and equality, at least in the welfare economics branch of the discipline,[2] but these concepts are necessarily restricted to one or

---

[1] And have been, it may be argued, at least since the academic discipline of economics shed its formal interest in broader matters of 'political economy' and attempted to focus instead on being a purely analytical discipline. At the same time, any consensus regarding what 'justice' actually consists of was fading away. Thus, regarding justice, economists would have been able to offer only personal opinions and judgments, which would in turn appear to be incompatible with the requirements of an analytical discipline.

[2] A brief introductory survey is provided in chapter 6 of Amartya Sen, *Inequality Reexamined* (Oxford: Clarendon, 1992); fuller and critical surveys may be found in, e.g.: Y.-K. Ng, *Welfare Economics* (London: Macmillan, 1979); Donald Hay, *Economics Today: A Christian Critique* (Leicester: Apollos, 1989), pp125-142. A recent textbook which offers analysis of equity-efficiency trade-offs is Joseph E. Stiglitz, *Economics of the Public Sector*, 3rd ed. (New York/London: Norton, 2000).

another *quantifiable* measure (of, for example, income, wealth or utility). Substantial treatments of justice, whilst of major interest to some economists, are generally regarded as topics for other disciplines, such as political or moral philosophy.[3] Thus economists typically have little to say, as economists, about justice in economic life.

In political and moral philosophy, there is of course a vast literature on justice, and a substantial part of it is addressed to questions of justice in social and economic life. One frequently used term here is 'social justice'. As Miller suggests, the concept of social justice is best understood as a subset of the broader concept of justice in general.[4] With regard to the latter, Miller makes use of the fruitful distinction between *aggregative* and *distributive* political principles, with the former referring only to 'the total amount of good enjoyed by a particular group', but the latter referring 'to the share of that good which different members of the group have for themselves'.[5] This fits well with the classical conceptualization of justice as 'to each his due'. For, in terms of the aggregative/distributive distinction, 'principles of justice are distributive principles... Indeed, the most valuable general definition of justice is that which brings out its distributive character most plainly: justice is *suum cuique*, to each his due. The just state of affairs is that in which each individual has exactly those benefits and burdens which are due to him by virtue of his personal characteristics and circumstances.'[6]

Miller proceeds to suggest helpfully that, with regard to the relation between justice in general and social justice in particular, the most important contrast is between, on the one hand, legal justice and, on the other, social justice. Legal justice, being concerned with customs and practices recognized by a

---

[3]Hausman and McPherson (Daniel M. Hausman and Michael S. McPherson, *Economic Analaysis and Moral Philosophy,* Cambridge: CUP, 1996, especially pp 150-61) indicate that there has, more recently, been a growing interest by some economists in ideas of justice, and in particular the libertarian, utilitarian and contractualist approaches (which will each be addressed here in chapter 4). These diverse approaches, however, are unlikely to lead to any consensus amongst economists as to the nature and application of justice. The overall tone of Hausman and McPherson's argument is more to persuade economists to take a greater interest in justice than to claim that such interest is already widespread.

[4]David Miller, *Social Justice* (Oxford: Clarendon, 1976; repr. 1998), p17. Miller's conceptual framework, being clear and fruitful, is utilized here. Later chapters in this book, of course, introduce additional perspectives on the nature of justice in social and economic life.

[5]*Ibid.*, p19.

[6]*Ibid.*, p20. This is a formal, not a material, definition. As Miller, points out, this definition, whilst conceptually fruitful, says nothing about the actual content of justice, i.e. about what those 'characteristics and circumstances' may consist in. Here, it is argued below, there is much confusion.

community as binding, will include such matters as the punishment of wrongdoing and the compensation of injury through the creation and enforcement of a public set of rules. 'Social justice, on the other hand, concerns the distribution of benefits and burdens throughout a society, as it results from the major social institutions - property systems, public organizations, etc.'[7] This understanding of the term 'social justice' clearly incorporates *economic* burdens and benefits within its scope: thus justice in economic life is part of this social justice.

Given this definitional framework, the question of the substantial confusion regarding existing treatments of economic justice - as claimed by the first major argument developed in this book - can be briefly addressed. It should be noted that the line of argument indicated here will be fully developed, especially with reference to some particular treatments of economic justice, in later chapters. At this introductory stage, the first point is to recognize not only that a large number of different understandings exist regarding the nature and content of economic and social justice, but also that major and insoluble conflicts exist between them. For example, MacIntyre, who addresses issues both of justice in general and also of social and economic justice in particular, considers the responses given to questions about, say, whether justice permits gross income inequality. He observes that contending individuals and groups in contemporary societies offer 'alternative and incompatible answers'.[8] There is no consensus about what economic justice consists in. He proceeds to show that the conflicts exist not only at the level of what justice requires in specific situations, but at the foundational level of the very conception of justice. Thus, 'underlying this wide diversity of judgments upon particular types of issue are a set of conflicting conceptions of justice, conceptions which are strikingly at odds with one another in a number of ways.' He continues:

> Some conceptions appeal to inalienable human rights, others to some notion of human contract, and others again to a standard of utility. Moreover, the rival theories of justice which embody these rival conceptions also give expression to disagreements about the relationship of justice to other human goods, about the kind of equality which justice requires, about the range of transactions and persons to which considerations of justice are relevant, and about whether or not a knowledge of justice is possible without a knowledge of God's law.[9]

One consequence for a given society, as a whole, is a very substantial measure of confusion regarding justice and everyday economic life. With no consensus about what social and economic justice are, people cannot appeal to any agreed standard or norm for justice. The word 'justice' is still used in debate and

---

[7]*Ibid.*, p22.
[8]Alasdair MacIntyre, *Whose Justice? Which Rationality?* (London: Duckworth, 1988), p1.
[9]*Ibid.*

discussion, but as soon as it becomes clear that one person disagrees with the someone else's claim that a given state of affairs is (say) unjust, then the scope for a resolution can be seen to be extremely limited.

The same type of conflict and confusion is demonstrated by Miller, who shows that, in the literature on social justice, three different principles of justice are put forward: 'to each according to his rights; to each according to his deserts; to each according to his needs'.[10] Crucially, he proceeds from there to demonstrate briefly - reinforcing this in detail in the following three chapters - that these three principles (rights, deserts and need) are, unavoidably, *conflicting* principles. Conflicts between any two of these principles - and between all three - exist, essentially, because rights, desert and needs are not, in general, identical with one another. For example, rights (on any mainstream view of the scope and nature of rights) and needs, whilst sharing some sense of givenness in any given setting, are in principle different from each other.[11] And desert is an entirely distinct basis for justice compared with either rights or needs, with issues of merit affecting desert but playing no part at all for the other two principles.

In similar terms to MacIntyre and Miller, Forrester argues that, in modern times, there are profound uncertainties about what justice is. Consequently, because 'understandings of justice are so varied, volatile and confusing, administering justice and attempting to frame and apply policies that are just become perplexing and systematically confusing operations.'[12] And this is serious not only for policy-makers:

> In many areas of life...the problems for people on the ground who feel a calling to act justly and dispense justice are acute. Different and sometimes incompatible ideas of justice are presented to them as having claims on their allegiance, and in a situation where 'nobody knows what justice is', often enough it is the self-interest of the powerful that prevails because the trumpet-call for justice makes an uncertain sound.[13]

So the confusion regarding justice - including economic justice - is not a matter only for academic debate, but has very serious consequences for daily life, not least for those who struggle in the face of what at least some people still regard as, in some sense, injustice. Moreover, the confusion, and the very serious practical consequences, are not at all likely to fade. Forrester argues that, despite the clarifications and insights offered by recent 'grand theories of justice', not only do fundamental and irreducible incompatibilities remain, but

---

[10]Miller, *Social Justice, op.cit.*, p27.

[11]If rights were *defined* as equivalent to some definition of need – such as minimum subsistence need – such that the two were thus identical, then such an understanding of justice would not be recognized as an authentically rights-based approach.

[12]Duncan Forrester, *Christian Justice and Public Policy* (Cambridge: CUP, 1997), p1.

[13]*Ibid.*, pp1-2.

no serious resolution is in sight. For, 'in the absence of *some agreed standard*, the choice between differing positions appears to be largely arbitrary. Only very rarely is an account of justice presented as resting on an ontology, or the nature of things, or as being in some sense "true".'[14]

This bleak appraisal brings the discussion directly to the second major argument developed in this book. For Forrester's convincing assessment would seem to offer an open invitation to those who do believe in an ontologically true standard for justice. The invitation is surely to seek to put forward an account of justice that is, therefore, based on a definite, given and true standard. And the invitation is offered in particular to Christians who are convinced that God is real, that God is a God who speaks to human beings, and that God is himself a God of love and justice who is therefore by his own character and being the measure of love and justice.

To accept this invitation would be no easy thing. Any Christians who might take up this challenge are themselves, necessarily, already part of the confusion, at least to some degree: they are already influenced by at least some of the conflicting conceptions of economic justice. A further difficulty is that attempts to communicate a distinctively Christian understanding of justice - if it can be developed - to the pluralistic contemporary audience are likely to be in some measure misunderstood. It is all too easy, in a cacophony of rival voices, to misinterpret a new, unfamiliar sound as simply a variant upon some existing sound. To take up Forrester's trumpet-call idiom, it is also all too easy for those who have grown weary of uncertain trumpet-sounds to fail to hear a more authentic call.

Nevertheless, the challenge for Christian believers in a true, just and communicating God ought not to be shirked. Those who need to hear the Christian gospel - the good news - will undoubtedly hear nothing unless those who know the good news tell them.[15] Yet the second major argument of this book is that the challenge to articulate a clearly Gospel-based and contemporary account of economic justice does not seem, at least in the present day, to have been *adequately* taken up.

The qualifying term 'adequately' is important here. It is not being claimed that Christians have in general said nothing, or even said too little, about economic justice. Indeed, there are a number of influential Christian contributions in this field, and chapter 4 below considers three of them. The claim that *is* made is twofold. First, the existing Christian contributions are inadequate in that they are insufficiently based on the Gospel, and thus on the biblical revelation. Consequently they are at odds (to a lesser or greater extent) with what Scripture teaches. Secondly, the existing Christian contributions, taken together, are inadequate in that they do not grapple sufficiently with the rival and conflicting conceptions of economic justice offered by others: hence

---

[14]*Ibid.*, p2 [emphasis added].
[15]Rom. 10:14.

they are not thorough enough to meet the challenge.

These two claims require at least some brief justification at this point, although the following chapters are intended, amongst other things, to demonstrate the validity of these claims more fully. The first claim is that many treatments of economic and social justice by Christians - and certainly the more extensive treatments - do not have an adequate foundation upon the Gospel and upon biblical truth. These treatments typically pay *some*, but only some, attention to Scripture in their method of discussion. Thus they typically do not claim to have any means of offering a basis for an *agreed standard* for a conception of economic justice, founded upon ontological truth. These accounts contain many helpful insights, and they repay careful study. But they do not offer a conception of economic justice that, ultimately, derives from the Gospel and biblical revelation.[16] It must be emphasized here, then, that the position of the present book - essentially no different from that of historic Christian faith down the ages, and rearticulated by the Reformers - is that the truth of Scripture, being the word of God written, and the truth of the Gospel of the Lord Jesus Christ, to which Scripture points throughout, hold together.[17] Here, therefore - or so this book claims - is the foundation of truth on which an agreed standard for a conception of economic justice can be sought. Thus the central question addressed by this book is the following: what would it be for an account of economic justice to take the Bible seriously?

The second claim made above is that the existing Christian contributions to an understanding of economic justice do not grapple sufficiently with the contemporary treatments offered by those who are not Christians. Such engagement, however - both in learning from other accounts and in offering critical appraisals of them - is essential if Christian contributions are to be of

---

[16]Consequently, an account of justice that understands exploitation on the basis, say, of Marxist analysis, whilst perhaps providing important insights, will, unless this analysis is itself subject to the ultimate scrutiny of Scripture, necessarily be to some degree unsound.

[17]A slightly more detailed restatement of this position is offered by Richard B. Hays, *The Moral Vision of the New Testament* (Edinburgh: T&T Clark, 1996), pp1-10. Acknowledging the diversity within Scripture and the consequent challenges regarding interpretation, Hays nevertheless states that his aim is 'to articulate as clearly as possible a framework within which we might pursue New Testament ethics as a normative theological discipline: ...to clarify how the church can read Scripture in a faithful and disciplined manner so that Scripture might come to shape the life of the church' (p3). A confident and detailed restatement of the nature of Scriptural truth, and an engagement with liberal critics, is provided in the two volumes edited by D. A. Carson and John D. Woodbridge, *Scripture and Truth* (Grand Rapids, MI: Zondervan, 1983; repr. Grand Rapids, MI: Baker/Carlisle: Paternoster, 1995). Contemporary interpreters are, of course, fallible, and must therefore approach their task in humility, constantly seeking the enlightenment provided by the Holy Spirit. They are, nevertheless, engaging with ontological truth.

contemporary relevance. The proposition that existing contributions do not engage sufficiently in this task appears to be true both of Christians who do have a Reformed-type commitment to Scriptural truth, and to those who do not.[18] The recent literature in political and moral philosophy regarding economic and social justice will be searched in vain for any kind of detailed and thorough contribution from a Christian perspective, or an extensive engagement with that literature from a Christian perspective.

Indeed, Forrester is wary of even attempting to construct any kind of 'grand theory' of justice on a Christian basis, not least because of what he regards as the methodological disarray in theology.[19] He argues instead for the bringing together of 'theological fragments' which have been 'illuminating, instructive or provocative in grappling with policy issues "on the ground"'. Christians should, he says, reflect on these fragments, and on their 'embeddedness in the structure of Christian faith', and enquire 'whether this gives clues as to a constructive theological contribution in the public realm today'.[20]

A grand or comprehensive theory would indeed seem to be over-ambitious, and is not a concern of the Scriptures: the New Testament does command Christian believers to be transformed by the renewing of their minds,[21] but a fully worked-out theory of, say, economic justice, is not required. Nevertheless, the conviction underlying this book is that something more coherent and detailed than a set of fragments is both called for, and can be given. The appeal, following the apostle Paul's example, to 'take every thought captive to obey Christ',[22] requires a thoroughness and attention to detail that, at least in terms of

---

[18]Beisner and Mott, both building on Reformed-type commitments, debate the nature and content of economic justice in the Scriptures. See E. Calvin Beisner, 'Justice and Poverty: Two Views Contrasted', and Stephen Charles Mott, 'The Partiality of Biblical Justice: A reply to Calvin Beisner', in Herbert Schlossberg *et al*, eds., *Christianity and Economics in the Post-Cold War Era: The Oxford Declaration and Beyond* (Grand Rapids, MI: Eerdmans, 1994). However, they are unable to reach significant agreement either on a conceptual definition of justice, or on what biblical economic justice consists in. For another debate between authors from a Reformed perspective, see John A. Beversluis, ed., *Economic Justice and the State: A Debate Between Ronald H. Nash and Eric H. Beversluis* (Grand Rapids, MI: Baker, 1986). There are a number of hints in all these contributions that suggest that at least part of the problem is that it has been difficult to discern how existing conceptions of economic justice may be influencing the authors' interpretations of Scripture as regards justice. This is a difficulty faced by all would-be contributors – as already noted in the text – including this one. However, one way of helping to overcome this difficulty is to attempt both a thorough examination of the Scriptural material and a thorough engagement with other treatments. This is what this book aims to provide.

[19]Forrester, *Christian Justice*, pp198-199.

[20]*Ibid.*, p204.

[21]Rom. 12:1-2.

[22]2 Cor. 10:5.

engaging with conceptions of economic justice, has recently been distinctly lacking. What this book seeks to offer, then, is an indication of the character and shape of a conception of economic justice that attempts to be rooted thoroughly in the biblical revelation.[23]

The structure of the book is as follows. Chapter 2 offers a theological framework for justice, a framework that seeks to reflect the character of God in his love and justice, and to set out the demands and promises made by God to humankind with regard to justice. The following chapter proceeds on the basis of that framework to focus specifically on *economic* justice: the chapter provides a survey of the biblical material relevant to justice in economic life, and does so with the intention of giving a sense of the whole, in terms of the biblical conception of economic justice.

The remaining chapters turn to a detailed engagement with some other treatments of the conception of economic justice. Chapter 4 provides an account of six of them. Three of these are secular treatments, and the other three are offered within Christian thought. The main aim in chapter 4 is to recognize and highlight the challenges that these treatments pose for the attempt to develop a conception of economic justice that is both biblically rooted and of contemporary relevance. Chapter 5 then seeks to engage the theological and biblical perspectives of chapters 2 and 3 with these challenges: that is, it aims to examine how the earlier theological-biblical account must be further developed and sharpened if it is to be of *contemporary* relevance. The focus is on the specifically socio-economic dimension. The final chapter continues this process of engagement and sharpening, with the aim particularly of highlighting the distinctiveness of a biblically-rooted understanding of justice in economic life. Thus chapter 6 compares that understanding, especially in its moral, political and theological dimensions, with some other approaches. This process of highlighting and comparing is conducted in part by means of a conversation with the highly influential contribution offered by the U.S. Roman Catholic Bishops in their 1986 Pastoral Letter, *Economic Justice For All.*[24]

---

[23]It should be noted at this point that all references in these chapters to 'a' (or 'the') 'biblically-rooted conception of economic justice' – and the like – are to be understood as carrying the two riders already mentioned: first, what is offered is no more than an *indication* of what a biblically-rooted conception consists in; and secondly, that indication is only something of the character and shape of such a conception. Further, it is greatly to be desired that the inadequacies that doubtless run through this account are not left unattended by others.

[24]National Conference of Catholic Bishops, *Economic Justice For All: Pastoral Letter on Catholic Social Teaching and the U.S. Economy* (Washington, D.C.: United States Catholic Conference, 1986).

CHAPTER 2

A Theological Framework for Economic Justice

Introduction

The task of this and the following chapter is to offer a theological account of economic justice and, in particular, to develop a conception of economic justice that is rooted firmly in the teaching of the Scriptures. This task will involve a survey of the relevant Scriptural material - of which there is a substantial amount - with an emphasis on giving a sense of the whole, with regard to a biblical conception of justice in economic life. In seeking that overall understanding, a particular hypothesis is considered in the present chapter. The hypothesis is that a vital key to interpreting the biblical material on economic justice concerns the righteousness and justice of God: that is, the righteousness and justice of God's own being and character. If this hypothesis is valid, then it follows that it would be helpful to carry out a survey of that Scriptural material with - rather than without - some initial understanding of the righteousness and justice of God. In other words, rather than conducting that survey in a purely inductive manner (if that were possible) - simply looking to see what is there, without any explicit prior expectation or knowledge - it would be better to have that initial framework of understanding already in place.[1] As the survey proceeds in detail, the framework of understanding can itself be revised and amended, in the light of that detail. Thus there is an iterative process to the quest for a biblical conception, with both the overall framework and the detailed understanding open to continual revision in the light of each other. Nevertheless, it is helpful to begin with an explicit framework of understanding, especially if that framework can be shown to provide important clues to particular aspects of the Scriptural material. That this can indeed be shown is part of the hypothesis presented here regarding the righteousness and justice of God.

---

[1] A purely inductive approach may well be impractical: for it is likely that all students of Scripture commence any particular survey with *some* kind of initial framework of understanding – which may be relatively more, or relatively less, consistent with the teaching of Scripture as a whole. The argument in the text is, in part, that it is more helpful to conduct a survey of Scripture with (rather than without) an explicitly acknowledged framework of understanding, *if* that framework itself reflects at least to a significant extent the teaching of the Scriptures.

The presentation of the biblical material on economic justice in these two chapters will also proceed on the understanding that the Old Testament (OT) is fulfilled in the New Testament (NT) - especially in the person and work of the Lord Jesus Christ. Although it is accepted, then, that the NT makes full sense only in the context of the OT, it is a central principle here that the OT should be interpreted in the light of the NT. In the present chapter this principle is applied to the Scriptural material on the righteousness of God. Thus the OT material on God's righteousness is presented first - with an emphasis on obtaining a sense of the whole - and then this is considered in the light of the fuller revelation to be found in the NT. In the following chapter, the biblical material on all other aspects which relate to justice, especially with regard to economic life, is examined.

The present chapter proceeds by arguing, in the first section, that the righteousness of God refers centrally to God's acts of faithfulness to his own justice and mercy in his relationship to humanity. It is argued that, according to the testimony of Scripture, righteousness and justice are not only thus displayed by God, but are also demanded by God of humanity. The second section focuses on the righteousness expected of believers in response to God. The first two sections include careful examination of the vocabulary of righteousness and justice in the OT and NT, and a proposed understanding of the close link between righteousness and justice in the Scriptures. Given the theological framework developed in those two sections, the third section seeks to locate the place of human justice within that framework. It is suggested that human justice means practical righteousness in relationships, conforming to the norms of appropriate treatment that God has set and commanded. The final section briefly describes and explains the hermeneutical and interpretative principles employed by the present book in the movement from biblical text to contemporary application.

Righteousness and Justice: Displayed by God and Demanded by God

There are many occurrences of the word righteousness in the OT,[2] but one of the distinct categories included among them is 'the righteousness of God', and (the equivalent) 'his/your/my righteousness', in instances where it is clearly *God's* righteousness to which reference is made. This category of usage is found particularly, although by no means exclusively, in the Psalms and in the prophet Isaiah.[3] In investigating the meaning of this language, it is of course important to accept that vocabulary is often used - notably in the OT - with

---

[2]Translating two more or less interchangeable Hebrew words (from the same root), namely *sedeq*/צדק and *sedaqah*/צדקה.

[3]An overview of some of the relevant occurrences, and discussion of their meaning, is given on pp260-3 of Sam K. Williams,'The "Righteousness of God" in Romans', *Journal of Biblical Literature*, 99(2), 1980, 241-290.

considerable flexibility. Thus the purpose of such investigation is not to identify some common core meaning for particular phrases, but rather to discover whether there are similarities, or family resemblances, in the usage of particular words and phrases.[4]

On a number of occasions in Isaiah 'my righteousness' parallels 'my salvation' (46:13; 51:5,6,8; 56:1). In 59:16 the parallel seems to be more with God's power which lies behind his salvation. The significance of a parallel should not be overstated. It is not automatically the case that the terms used in parallel are to be considered as identical in meaning. But they are at least to be taken together, so that there is mutual reinforcement of meaning. Thus the salvation/righteousness parallel in these Isaianic references is likely to mean that God's righteousness here has an aspect relating to salvation; and, similarly, that his salvation has an aspect relating to righteousness. It should certainly not be assumed that one of the parallel terms is merely used as a technical term to mean precisely the same thing as the other term. Thus 'God's righteousness' in Isaiah cannot mean *only* God's salvation - not, at least, unless further aspects of the text (besides the mere existence of parallelism) point to that conclusion.

In the Psalms - where references to 'God's righteousness' are the most numerous - there are again some occurrences where there is a parallel between God's righteousness and his deliverance or salvation (e.g. 40:10 [Heb: 11]; 51:14 [Heb: 16], and also with his judgment and justice (e.g. Ps. 9:4,8 [Heb: 5,9]; 33:5). Often there is a parallel with an aspect of God's *character*, especially his name in general (7:17 [Heb: 18]), his steadfast or covenant love/*hesed* (e.g. 5:7f [Heb: 8f]; 36:5f [Heb: 6f]), his faithfulness/*emunah* (143:1), his trustworthiness/*emet* (143:1), or his goodness/*tub* (145:7). God's character has been experienced by his people, individually and corporately, in his dealings with them: it is on the basis of God's acts and revelation, especially in the context of his covenant with his people, that they know him.

The parallels with God's character as experienced make it unlikely that 'God's righteousness' in the Psalms simply means salvation from distress, or God's saving power, or God's acts and judgments which bestow salvation.[5] Nor, on the other hand, is it sufficient to say that 'God's righteousness' in the Psalms refers to God's displayed character which works out in acts of salvation or deliverance: in other words, to say that it refers to 'a readiness on God's part to help and save his creatures'.[6] Whilst that account is part of the truth, such a characterization does not reflect the emphasis on the *judging* (i.e. condemnatory) aspect of God's righteousness (e.g. Ps. 50:6). It is better to suggest that the various references to God's righteousness, in both Isaiah and the Psalms, and elsewhere, share a family resemblance in that they generally

---

[4]For further comment on lexical studies and their dangers, see the following sub-section.
[5]Williams, 'Righteousness', p262, refers to some scholars who do propose such meanings.
[6]*Ibid.*

refer to God acting in a way that is consistent with what his covenant people already know of him. Thus God's righteousness involves both his mercy and his judgment: that is, faithfulness both to his own covenant promises, and also to his own absolute intolerance of sin and evil. And God's people know what he is like, because he has displayed himself to them. Thus in Psalm 7, which refers both to God as one who saves (vv1,10 [Heb: 2,11]) and one who judges (vv6-11 [Heb:7-12]), the psalmist's confidence and joy is in the righteousness of God, which he parallels with God's name (v17 [Heb: 18]). And the name of Yahweh, as recorded in Exodus chapter 34, was proclaimed to Moses as follows (vv6-7):

> The LORD passed before him, and proclaimed, 'The LORD, the LORD, a God merciful and gracious, slow to anger, and abounding in steadfast love and faithfulness, keeping steadfast love for the thousandth generation, forgiving iniquity and transgression and sin, yet by no means clearing the guilty, but visiting the iniquity of the parents upon the children and the children's children, to the third and the fourth generation.'

Thus this name of God embraces, as does the righteousness of God, his mercy and his judgment.[7]

Whilst this language of the righteousness of God is found, within the OT, particularly in Isaiah and the Psalms, the relationship between God's mercy and God's judgment is, of course, central to the OT. Whenever God's judgment is proclaimed, his mercy is also at hand. This is seen particularly in the books of Jeremiah, Ezekiel, Hosea, Amos, Jonah and Micah. Yet the pages and events of the OT do not themselves contain any ultimate resolution of the tension between God's judgment and mercy. Rather, they look ahead to the dawning of salvation, to the total fulfilment of God's promises, which, with NT eyes, is

---

[7]In the epistle to the Romans, the notion of the righteousness of God is central to Paul's exposition of the gospel. It would be surprising if the above OT background were not relevant to this exposition. What has been much debated, however, is the precise meaning in Paul's hands, and especially in Romans, of the phrase 'the righteousness of God' (δικαιοσύνη τοῦ θεοῦ). This ongoing debate is tangential to the present book, and therefore is not analysed further here. Significant contributions to the debate include the following: Ernst Käsemann, '"The Righteousness of God" in Paul', in his *New Testament Questions of Today* (Philadelphia: Fortress, 1969), 168-82; Williams, 'Righteousness', who offers a survey of Käsemann's article and the ensuing literature; Charles E. B. Cranfield, *A Critical and Exegetical Commentary on the Epistle to the Romans*, Volume I, The International Critical Commentary series (Edinburgh: T & T Clark, 1975), 91-100; E. P. Sanders, *Paul and Palestinian Judaism: A Comparison of Patterns of Religion* (Philadelphia: Fortress, 1977); James D. G. Dunn, *Romans 1-8*, Word Biblical Commentary, (Dallas, TX: Word, 1988), 40-42; Mark A. Seifrid, *Christ, our Righteousness: Paul's Theology of Justification* (Leicester: Apollos, 2000).

seen to have arrived in the person of the Lord Jesus Christ.[8]

'Righteousness' as a More General Notion

It was noted earlier that the particular nuance of the term 'the righteousness of God' is only one of the uses of the word 'righteousness' in the Bible. It is important to ascertain what the relationship is, if any, between that particular nuance and the other uses of the word 'righteousness' in the Scriptures. Only then can the link between God's righteousness and human righteousness, for example, be assessed.

Lexical studies of Scripture carry dangers. On the one hand, they can lead to an excessive emphasis on the occurrences of particular words, and a neglect of the *range* of meaning of these words. On the other hand, they can also lead to a lack of emphasis on the development of *themes*, in cases where those themes are not always accompanied by particular words.[9] Nevertheless, bearing in mind these dangers, word studies have the potential to demonstrate important links within the Scriptures. The particular focus here will be on whether the word 'righteousness', as used in the Bible, has a *central meaning* - along the lines of a family resemblance - i.e. a meaning which relates to, and helps to explain, various shades of meaning in the usage of that word.[10]

It is proposed here that 'righteousness', both in the OT and the NT, has a central meaning of conformity to a norm; and that it is usually a relational word (i.e. it is to do with relationships, such as those between members of God's people). However, the precise content of the norm - i.e. of what is required - may vary from case to case.[11] The case-specific content of the norms of righteousness is brought out by Hill: he defines the fundamental idea of righteousness as 'conformity to a norm which requires to be defined in each

---

[8]For this recognition see, for example, the testimony of Simeon in Luke 2:29-32 (the 'Nunc Dimittis'), the response of the Samaritans in John 4:16-42, Paul's gospel proclamation in Acts 13:16-47, and Peter's words in 1 Pet. 1:1-12.

[9]James Barr, *The Semantics of Biblical Language* (Oxford: OUP, 1961), provides a trenchant critique of poor quality linguistic studies. Moises Silva argues that, to the question of whether Barr's contributions have since been incorporated by biblical scholars, the answer is a qualified 'yes'. See Silva, *Biblical Words and Their Meaning: An Introduction to Lexical Semantics*, revised and expanded edition (Grand Rapids, MI: Zondervan, 1994), pp20ff.

[10]There is no suggestion that, for example, the Hebrew noun *sedeq* always has the same meaning, nor that it has any *essential* meaning. The question, rather, is how particular words are used. The notion of 'central meaning' or 'family resemblance' relates to the pattern of usage of a given word.

[11]Later chapters explore the content of the norms relevant for *economic* life.

particular case'.[12] Nevertheless, the argument here is that Hill's definition, whilst helpful, needs to be supplemented by an emphasis on a relational understanding of righteousness, at least in most cases. Without a relational emphasis, 'righteousness' would seem somewhat arid and static, which would in turn fail to reflect the biblical usage of the word. The proposition, then, is that righteousness has two aspects: it generally conveys the idea of conformity to a norm; and it usually has a relational meaning (i.e. it concerns relationships).[13] Thus what righteousness actually means in any given context depends on the relational norm(s) appropriate to that context.

An initial defence of this proposition will require an appraisal of the use of the language of righteousness in both the OT and the NT, and therefore of the relevant words in both the Hebrew and Greek originals and of the links between them. Such an appraisal is offered below. Before that, however, the potential significance of this proposition for our understanding of the importance of 'the righteousness of God' will be briefly indicated. The two proposed aspects of righteousness - a relational setting (typically), and conformity to norm - will be examined in turn.

As argued in the previous sub-section, God's righteousness involves both his mercy and his judgment. Is this consistent with the emphasis on a relational meaning for righteousness? It is clear from the Scriptures considered above that the righteousness of God is not something dwelling in a vacuum, but rather is expressed and demonstrated, in action. And it is demonstrated, in particular, towards human beings. God's righteousness is demonstrated, then, in his relationship to humanity, and is revealed especially in his covenant relationship with his people. The righteousness of God clearly does have a relational meaning.

The other aspect of the proposed central meaning for righteousness is conformity to a norm. Is this also consistent with the above discussion of God's righteousness? Theology has to be careful when speaking of God 'conforming' to a norm. There are no norms external to God's own character and being and action. Nevertheless it is possible to speak of God determining to act in faithfulness to himself. With regard to 'the righteousness of God', therefore, as used in the OT, it may be suggested that the emphasis of this phrase, in terms of norms, is on God acting in faithfulness both to his own mercy and his own justice - and thus in faithfulness to his covenant promises which are a display and demonstration of his mercy and justice. God determines to act in line with his mercy and justice; and this action displays the righteousness of God.

---

[12]David Hill, *Greek Words and Hebrew Meanings: Studies in the Semantics of Soteriological Terms*, Society for the New Testament Studies, Monograph series, no.5 (Cambridge: CUP, 1967), p83.
[13]This (amended) working definition will be defended further in chapter 3.

Old Testament Terminology for Righteousness and Justice

It is now appropriate, as indicated earlier, to appraise the use of the language of righteousness and justice in the OT, in both the Hebrew MT and the Greek LXX. Since the themes of righteousness and *justice* are very closely related, especially in the OT[14], it will be helpful to consider together the Hebrew and Greek words for both 'righteousness' and 'justice'.

In English translations of the OT, the word 'justice' is typically a translation of the Hebrew word *mishpat*/ משפט. (That Hebrew word is by no means always translated as 'justice': 'justice' is one of a range of particular meanings; others include judgment, statute and, more rarely, pattern.) The word 'righteousness' is normally used, as noted earlier, to translate two more or less interchangeable Hebrew words (from the same root), namely *sedeq*/צדק and *sedaqah*/צדקה.[15] The Greek Septuagint (LXX) translation of the OT normally translates the two *s-d-q* words (*sedeq/sedaqah*) as δικαιοσύνη and normally translates *mishpat* as either κρίσις or κρίμα.[16]

These patterns of usage and translation may be briefly demonstrated, first from Gen. 18:19, where Yahweh ('the LORD') refers to his choosing of Abraham:

> "For I have chosen him, in order that he may command his children and his household after him to keep the way of the LORD by doing righteousness and justice; in order that the LORD may bring upon Abraham what he has spoken about him."

Here 'righteousness' (δικαιοσύνη in the LXX) translates *sedaqah*, and 'justice' translates *mishpat* (in this case, κρίσις in the LXX). A second example is 2 Sam. 8:15, which describes David's rule:

> So David reigned over all Israel; and David administered justice and righteousness for all his people.

The pattern is the same as in Gen. 18:19, except that here the LXX has κρίμα instead of κρίσις.

The Close Link between Justice and Righteousness

Brief substantiation now follows of the claim that - especially in the OT - justice and righteousness are closely related and overlapping terms. Justice and

---

[14]For example, they are coupled in the form of a hendiadys some 35 times in the OT.. For more analysis of this, see chapter 3.

[15]For convenience these two words will sometimes be referred to as the *s-d-q* words.

[16]Note, however, that in the NT (compared with the LXX), κρίσις and κρίμα rarely have the sense of 'justice'; rather, they usually mean 'sentence', 'condemnation' or 'judgment'. This is discussed further in section 2 below.

righteousness are frequently used in close parallel. Where this is so, then the two *s-d-q* words are typically used to describe the more foundational aspects - relational rightness as a *root* reality and notion - whereas *mishpat* refers more to the outworkings of this.[17] Put another way, *mishpat* is what is done, whereas *s-d-q* is the quality that fills what is done. Thus *s-d-q* is more a living thing, whereas *mishpat* is more a doing thing. Neither is static: rather, both are dynamic ideas; but within that similarity, a living/doing distinction seems to be present. Thus the OT can say, 'let the skies rain down righteousness/*sedeq*' (Is. 45:8), and 'the throne is established by righteousness/*sedaqah*' (Pr. 16:12) - references which bring out righteousness as a living *quality* - whereas it uses *mishpat* in teaching that the LORD requires people 'to do justice' (Mic. 6:8) and in observing that the wicked 'refuse to do what is just' (Pr. 21:7).

To note the above nuances, however, should not detract from the substantial degree of overlap between the two themes.[18] For many OT references it might well be foolish to seek to dissect the meanings of righteousness and justice. This is especially so when they are used in direct parallel. One of many such instances is Ps. 37:6 (NKJ):

> He [the Lord] shall bring forth your righteousness/*sedeq* as the light, and your justice/*mishpat* as the noonday.

Similarly, in relation to God's own righteousness and justice, Ps. 48:10f [Heb: 11f] says (RV):

> As is thy name, O God, so is thy praise unto the ends of the earth: Thy right hand is full of righteousness/*sedeq*. Let Mount Zion be glad, let the daughters of Judah rejoice, because of thy judgments/*mishpatim*.

---

[17]As R. Schultz argues, righteousness emphasizes 'being or acting in conformity with the norm', whereas *mishpat* emphasizes 'the act itself' ('Justice', *New International Dictionary of Old Testament Theology and Exegesis*, Willem A. VanGemeren (ed.) (Carlisle: Paternoster, 1997, vol.4, p838). Similarly Alec Motyer comments (in the context of Is. 5:16): '*Righteousness* is holiness expressed in moral principles; *justice* is the application of the principles of righteousness...' (*The Prophecy of Isaiah*, Leicester: IVP, 1993, p72).

[18]On the basis of his survey of the OT material on justice and righteousness, Paul Ramsey concludes that 'it cannot be denied that the idea of justice, and precisely that sort of justice secured through political and other institutions, has been invaded by what righteousness on God's part means... These qualities, justice (*mishpat*), righteousness (*tsedeq*), and mercy (*hesed*), which are to be distinguished on first beginning to understand the Bible, prove on closer inspection not at all clearly distinguishable in their meaning and never separable in fact. Perhaps their meanings never entirely coalesce into bare identity, but they infect one another, and this influence in the direction *from* God *manward*' (*Basic Christian Ethics* (London: SCM, 1950), pp8-9). Section 3 below discusses the link in the NT between justice and (to a large extent the NT equivalent of *hesed*) love.

language regarding righteousness requires attention. It has already been argued that the uses of the term 'righteousness' share a family resemblance - a central meaning - throughout Scripture, namely that of conformity to norm; typically within a relational context. However, the pattern of usage in the NT is slightly different from that of the OT. One significant difference between the two Testaments is that (unlike the OT) the NT never parallels 'justice' and 'righteousness'.[20] Furthermore, in the NT the words κρίμα and κρίσις are rarely used in the sense of either 'justice' or 'righteousness' (the few such cases are examined below); rather, they normally mean 'judgment', 'sentence' or 'condemnation'. Thus the word most commonly used, in the NT, to convey some idea of justice and/or righteousness is δικαιοσύνη. An important issue, therefore, concerns the central meaning, and also the range of meaning, associated particularly with δικαιοσύνη in the NT. In the present chapter the focus in this regard will be on the use of δικαιοσύνη in Matthew's gospel.[21] Thus part of the aim here is to shed light on the relationship between (on the one hand) δικαιοσύνη in the NT and, on the other hand, *mishpat* and the two *s-d-q* words (*sedeq* and *sedaqah*) in the OT. The analysis is also intended to clarify the meaning and importance of the theme of δικαιοσύνη, particularly in Matthew, and therefore the link between believers' 'righteousness' and God's righteousness.

Δικαιοσύνη (dikaiosune) in Matthew's Gospel

The meaning of righteousness in Matthew is not a matter on which there is full scholarly consensus.[22] Przybylski argues that there are essentially two diametrically opposed views: some hold that δικαιοσύνη refers to God's gift to humankind, whilst others claim that it is God's demand upon humankind. In addition there are mediating positions.[23] It will be argued here that, in terms of the believers' side of their relationship with God, it is vital to see righteousness as first and foremost God's gift or provision, which is to be received by faith.

The word δικαιοσύνη occurs seven times in Matthew, five of them in the 'Sermon on the Mount'. The first is in the context of Jesus' baptism by John the

---

[20]Even if this is partly because the NT typically does not engage in parallelism, careful analysis of the actual pattern of usage will aid accurate interpretation of the texts.

[21]To conduct an examination of this issue for the whole NT is beyond the scope of this book.

[22]See Norvald Yri, 'Seek God's Righteousness: Righteousness in the Gospel of Matthew', in D. A. Carson (ed), *Right With God: Justification in the Bible and in the World* (Carlisle: Paternoster, 1992).

[23]Benno Przybylski, *Righteousness in Matthew and His World of Thought* (Cambridge: CUP, 1980), pp160-170. It may be that the scholarly dispute here has been unhelpfully influenced by the post- Käsemann debate, referred to earlier, concerning the meaning of 'the righteousness of God' in Romans. At any rate it is argued here that the meaning of δικαιοσύνη is relatively easy to discern.

Baptist. John initially sought to prevent this baptism from happening, but Jesus insisted, saying, 'Let it be so now; for thus it is fitting for us to fulfil all righteousness.' Then John consented (Mt. 3:15). This seems clearly to be a programmatic statement for the whole gospel, and so it is clear that righteousness - whatever the intended meaning here - is a central concept in Matthew.

The next occurrence is in the fourth 'beatitude' (Mt. 5:6):

> Blessed are those who hunger and thirst for righteousness, for they shall be satisfied.

This again places great significance on the notion of righteousness in Matthew's gospel account. Four verses later, Jesus states (5:10):

> Blessed are those who are persecuted for righteousness' sake, for theirs is the kingdom of heaven.

In verse 20 of the same chapter, Jesus says:

> For I tell you, unless your righteousness exceeds that of the scribes and Pharisees, you will never enter the kingdom of heaven.

In 6:1 Jesus warns his followers against practising their 'acts of righteousness' before men, lest they receive no reward from their Father in heaven who sees in secret. Then, in 6:33, Jesus says:

> For the Gentiles seek all these things; and your heavenly Father knows that you need them all. But seek first his kingdom and his righteousness, and all these things shall be yours as well.

This reference to *God's* righteousness makes this a key verse in understanding the link between 'righteousness' in Matthew and the OT usage of 'righteousness' and 'God's righteousness'.

The final reference is in 21:32, where Jesus chides the chief priests and elders of the people for not believing John the Baptist, who came 'in the way of righteousness'.

Of these seven Matthean references to 'righteousness' (δικαιοσύνη), two of the most significant - in terms of establishing how Matthew's use of δικαιοσύνη relates to the terminology of 'righteousness' and 'justice' in the OT - are 5:6 and 6:33. For, as will be shown below, these are two references for which there is a clear OT background. Furthermore, each of these references occupies a central place in the Sermon on the Mount, which in turn is one of the central sections of Jesus' teaching in the whole Gospel account. Thus the following discussion will focus particularly on Mt. 6:33 and 5:6.

Mt. 6:33 refers explicitly to 'his [i.e. God's] righteousness'. In section I above, it was shown that, especially in Isaiah and the Psalms, the notion of God's righteousness tends to have a particular meaning, which can be summarized as God's determination to be faithful to his own character and covenant promises - a meaning consistent with a more general central meaning for 'righteousness'. It seems very likely that this OT background is in view in Mt. 6:33[24] (as will be confirmed shortly). What, then, does it mean to 'seek' God's kingdom and God's righteousness? Are his kingdom and his righteousness synonymous, or do they carry different emphases or shades of meaning? Further questions arise with regard to 5:6, where there is no possessive pronoun, simply the statement, 'Blessed are those who hunger and thirst for righteousness'. What is the meaning of 'righteousness' here? And what does it mean to hunger and thirst for it?

To 'hunger' or 'thirst' is a straightforward OT metaphor for seeking and desiring something: e.g. Ps. 42:2f; 63:1; 143:6; Am. 8:11. In addition, however, Mt. 5:6 seems clearly to allude to Is. 55:1 - 56:2, in which thirst, hunger and seeking the LORD are combined with an emphasis on justice/*mishpat* and righteousness/*s-d-q*.

Isaiah 55 begins (vv1-2):

> Ho, every one who thirsts, come to the waters; and he who has no money, come, buy and eat! Come, buy wine and milk without money and without price. Why do you spend your money for that which is not bread, and your labour for that which does not satisfy? Hearken diligently to me, and eat what is good, and delight yourselves in fatness.

The thirst/hunger metaphor is central here. Verse 3 continues:

> Incline your ear, and come to me; hear, that your soul may live; and I will make with you an everlasting covenant, my steadfast, sure love for David.

This is an important pledge on God's part to re-establish the Davidic covenant. In verses 6-7 the metaphor of thirst is dropped, and a straightforward summons is given:

> Seek the LORD while he may be found, call upon him while he is near; let the wicked forsake his way, and the unrighteous man his thoughts; let him return to the LORD, that he may have mercy on him, and to our God, for he will abundantly pardon.

This 'seeking' is clearly not a passively pious thing, something with no consequence in people's lives. To seek the LORD entails repentance, a turning

---

[24]Matthew's gospel is addressed, at least in the first instance, to a Jewish audience which, we may confidently assume, would have some understanding of the OT notion of God's righteousness.

from wickedness and unrighteousness; and, therefore (implicitly) a turning to walk in God's way (as, e.g., in Is. 56:2).

Verses 8-11 make it clear that what is to happen will be God's doing, done in his way; and v11 stresses that God's word will accomplish that which he purposes. Verses 12-13 give the promise of great joy and of peace. The prophet then continues (56:1-2):

> Thus says the LORD: "Keep justice, and do righteousness, for soon my salvation will come, and my deliverance be revealed. Blessed is the man who does this, and the son of man who holds it fast, who keeps the sabbath, not profaning it, and keeps his hand from doing any evil."

The RSV does not reflect the Hebrew's double usage of righteousness/*sedaqah* here; the NASB is more helpful (56:1):

> Thus says the LORD, "Preserve justice, and do righteousness, For My salvation is about to come and My righteousness to be revealed."

The LORD's pledge is described this time in terms of his salvation and his righteousness; but it clearly refers to the same action promised by him in the previous verses (chapter 55). Thus the LORD's pledged action, comprising his righteousness and salvation, is the response to those who are thirsty and hungry (55:1-2). And this is, at least in part, the OT background for Jesus' reference to people who hunger and thirst for righteousness: for this is what those described in Is. 55:1 - 56:2 were seeking.

There is a further observation to be made from Is. 56:1. In the light of God's soon-to-come salvation and righteousness, what are those who hear his word to do? They are to 'preserve justice and do righteousness'. In view of *God's* righteousness, they themselves are to do righteousness. What does this mean? The two things cannot, of course, be equivalent: it would be meaningless to do something now if that identical thing is yet to come. However, we have already seen (in section 1) the close salvation-righteousness link in Isaiah. Taking on board also the parallels in the Psalms between God's righteousness and his faithfulness, steadfast love, trustworthiness and goodness, we can (as suggested earlier) speak of God's righteousness as his righteous and saving character, or, similarly, the display or revelation of his saving character in righteous acts of salvation. It is only in anticipation of *God's* saving righteousness that Isaiah makes the call to do righteousness now; the latter does not *cause* the former (we have already seen that it is only on God's initiative that the new thing will happen). Nevertheless the double usage of *sedaqah* is highly significant (and it is repeated elsewhere in Isaiah, e.g. Is. 5:7 cf. 5:16; and 45:13 cf. 45:19,21). Isaiah's message here is that those who hear God's word must act now in the light of what is to come. Eschatology leads to ethics. The knowledge that God's saving righteousness is soon coming is to lead people to produce righteousness now.[25]

There is still more to the linkage between God's righteousness and that righteousness required of his people ('human righteousness', for short). For God's decision to act in saving righteousness comes as the answer to the *lack* of righteousness among the people. This is crystal clear in Is. 59:9-20. Take v9, for example:

> Therefore justice is far from us, and righteousness does not overtake us; we look for light, and behold, darkness, and for brightness, but we walk in gloom.

The *lack* of justice and righteousness is restated in v14. The other verses in this section refer to the *absence* of truth, uprightness, and justice (e.g. vv11, 16) and the absence of light and brightness. It is precisely into this context that the LORD announces his decisive action, which is described, in vv16f, in terms of righteousness (twice), victory, salvation and vengeance. The lack of human justice and righteousness is countered and overcome by God's own righteousness.

Can the coming of God's righteousness, in this context (or any other context, for that matter) *not* involve human response in terms of righteousness? Isaiah chapter 59 sees the matter clearly enough, as v20 shows:

> And he will come to Zion as Redeemer, to those in Jacob who turn from transgression, says the LORD.

So it is required of those who are to be redeemed that they turn from transgression. This is very similar to the way in which Jesus proclaimed, at the beginning of his ministry (and prior, of course, to the 'Sermon on the Mount'): 'repent, for the kingdom of heaven is at hand' (Mt. 4:17). Again there is a close link between Isaiah and Matthew's gospel, regarding the meaning of righteousness.

It seems clear, then, that chapters 55 and 56 of Isaiah are, at least in part, the relevant OT background for Jesus' references in Mt. 5:6 and 6:33 to righteousness. However, further questions now arise. In 6:33, does the seeking of God's righteousness mean simply watching or 'looking out' for it, or does it entail action on the part of Jesus' followers? In 5:6, does Jesus refer to hungering for *God's* righteousness - for the demonstration of his righteousness in salvific acts - or for the righteousness required by God of his people? The two verses, with their associated questions, will be addressed in turn.

---

[25]What this righteousness is to consist of is examined further below: it will be argued that, as with God's righteousness, humanity's righteousness has a relational context and involves conformity to norm.

Matthew 6:33

The language of 'seeking', as already noted, is very close to that of hunger and thirst; and it is not a passively pious thing, but, rather, entails changes in one's life. In Matthew chapter 6, verse 33 brings to a climax some very practical teaching on riches. Someone who is seeking God's kingdom and God's righteousness can have neither the same attitude nor the same lifestyle as 'the pagans'. Moreover the word 'seek', which is used in this same passage to describe how the Gentiles 'seek' material things ('all these things', v32), clearly involves practice, not mere passivity.

How, then, are Jesus' followers to 'seek' the kingdom and righteousness of God? The context gives no indication of a restricted meaning (solely regarding, say, prayer for God's kingdom, or the giving of money for the sake of God's kingdom and righteousness). The meaning must therefore include, at the least, all of the aspects of discipleship taught by Jesus in the surrounding context, i.e. in the 'Sermon on the Mount' - and, quite possibly, all of his teaching recorded elsewhere in Matthew's gospel.

This is not salvation by human works. The above discussion, and the background in Isaiah, make it plain that God alone brings about salvation (e.g. Is. 56:1). But the particular point here in Matthew chapter 6 is that the seeking of God's righteousness must involve some doing of righteousness on the part of Christian believers. Their righteousness cannot produce God's, nor can it cause it to come. And their righteousness can never equate to the saving righteousness that is God's alone. Nevertheless, believers cannot truly be seeking God's righteousness if their lives do not begin to demonstrate something of that righteousness that he requires of them.

Matthew 5:6

The question here is the nature of the righteousness to which Jesus refers when he says, 'Blessed are those who hunger and thirst for righteousness, for they shall be satisfied'. Is this God's righteousness, or human righteousness? It seems unlikely that Jesus refers solely to *God's* righteousness, since he simply says 'righteousness', without specifying that he means that of God. On the other hand, given the close link in Isaiah 55-59 (discussed earlier) between thirsting/hungering and God's righteousness, it is extremely unlikely that there is no reference at all to God's righteousness. The nature of that link, however, may hold the answer to the question posed. In Is. 55-56, it is the coming of God's righteousness - in the context of the current lack of righteousness and justice - which satisfies thirst and hunger. The implication is that the hungering and thirsting to which Jesus refers is the yearning for the full demonstration of righteousness in the world, both in people's own personal lives, and in the community as a whole: and yet this is in the recognition that such righteousness can come fully only with the coming of God's saving righteousness.

This leads to a very significant conclusion. It is inappropriate to drive a wedge between God's righteousness and human righteousness, for they are closely related. God's righteousness comes as the answer to the lack of human righteousness; and it also requires righteousness from believers. As in Isaiah 55, then - where the people were to seek God, and turn from wrong - so in Mt. 5:6: hungering and thirsting for righteousness includes both an earnest desire for righteousness, both personally and socially, *and* dissatisfaction with anything less. And the thirsty recognize that full satisfaction comes only with God's righteousness.

Further, the above analysis may be a pointer concerning the NT's usage of OT 'justice and righteousness'. It seems clear that, in Matthew's gospel at least - and especially in Mt. 5:6 and 6:33 - the one word δικαιοσύνη is used to 'cover', as it were, the OT's combination of *mishpat* and *s-d-q*. For in Is. 56:1a, the two Hebrew words are used in parallel, referring to the responsibility upon those who hear God's word, whereas Jesus' similar call to his followers uses the one word δικαιοσύνη. It appears from this evidence that, in Matthew at least, the full meaning of the two Hebrew words as used in Isaiah 55-56 can be intended when the one Greek word is utilized.

The references in Isaiah 59, discussed earlier, also support this claim. It is into a society which lacks justice and righteousness that God's righteousness will come. This suggests that the meaning of 'God's righteousness' in Matthew is likely to include the same range of meaning as that which is included in the OT parallelling of justice and righteousness, notably in Isaiah. It is more than this, of course (as already noted[26]), but it must include this.[27]

The above argument can be summarized by posing the following question: does the use of the word righteousness/δικαιοσύνη in Matthew include the sense of 'justice' as well as 'righteousness'? The answer is yes, for the following three reasons, as argued in the last few pages. First, in the relevant background chapters in Isaiah (especially chapters 55-59), 'God's righteousness' clearly embraces both justice and righteousness, in that it supplies what is lacking in terms of justice and righteousness in personal and social life. Secondly, in Mt. 6:33, to 'seek God's righteousness' does not mean solely a pious passivity: rather, it includes the demonstration of God's righteousness in the life of the believers, by the grace of God; and since God's righteousness includes justice, then this demonstration must include both justice and righteousness. Thirdly, in Mt. 5:6, to hunger and thirst for

---

[26]In particular, a salvific dimension is also included.

[27]It seems at least plausible, then, that Isaiah has already laid some of the foundations for the NT's primary linguistic focus upon righteousness (δικαιοσύνη), with relatively less usage of the word cluster justice/*mishpat*/κρίμα/κρίσις. As indicated earlier, however, it is beyond the scope of this book to provide a thorough examination of the use of δικαιοσύνη in the NT, and so it is not appropriate to draw firm conclusions regarding the NT as a whole from the above analysis.

righteousness includes dissatisfaction with any lack of justice and righteousness (see the background in Is. 55-56, and 59).

As well as clarifying the content of 'righteousness', as used in Matthew, in terms of justice, the analysis of the last few pages also sheds light on the question of whether righteousness in Matthew is God's gift or God's demand. Matthew makes it plain that Jesus is requiring 'a righteousness that goes beyond what human beings are able to achieve'.[28] The good news, however, is that Jesus is the one who fulfils all righteousness - symbolized in his baptism in the River Jordan - for he died in the place of sinners to accomplish redemption. Through Jesus, then, God provides the righteousness which he demands. It is people who receive this righteousness by faith in Jesus - and only those people - who are then freed to begin to display righteousness in their own lives and communities.

Justice as Part of the Outworking of Righteousness

Having developed a theological framework in the first two sections, it is now possible to locate the particular place of justice within it (bearing in mind the partial distinction in the OT, assessed above, between the words 'righteousness' and 'justice'). It will also now be appropriate to propose a more precise central meaning for the biblical notion of justice. The first part of the framework developed above focuses upon the righteousness of God: that is, his determination to be faithful to his own mercy and justice in his relationship with human beings. With NT eyes, this is seen to include God's gift to believers of righteousness in and through the Lord Jesus Christ. The second part of the framework focuses on the response of believers to God's righteousness: this response is, first and foremost, that of faith, the correlate of which is a loving obedience, the practical outworking of righteousness, 'faith working through love' (Gal. 5:6). The third part of the framework applies the first two parts, with particular respect to justice. Thus justice is one aspect of that obedient, loving righteousness.

Justice in its Central Meaning: A Proposed Definition

It has already been shown that, in the OT, the words for righteousness (*s-d-q*) and justice (*mishpat*) are very closely related. It has also been shown that, in the NT, the one word δικαιοσύνη involves - at least on occasions - both of these aspects: both the quality, the root reality, of relational rightness, and its outworking in justice. In this framework, the foundation is the righteousness of God. On that basis, the righteousness imputed to believers can be understood. That is the setting for a theological understanding of the outworking of righteousness.

---

[28]Norvald Yri, 'Seek God's Righteousness', p98.

It is now necessary, however, to be more precise about 'justice', as distinct from - though never far removed from - righteousness. First, it is proposed here that the central meaning of justice is *appropriate treatment*, especially of human beings. Secondly, it is proposed here that justice, like righteousness, is a relational term. It does not dwell in a vacuum, in the abstract, but is to do with relationships.[29] As argued in the first two sections, righteousness and justice in the Scriptures are both dynamic, they overlap one another, and are often coupled as a hendiadys. Nevertheless, again as argued earlier, the pattern of usage (especially in the OT) also suggests some distinction between the two: righteousness (*sedeq/sedaqah*), centrally, is a living quality of conformity to norm, whereas justice (*mishpat*) refers more to what is actually done. Thirdly, it is proposed that the norms required in terms of appropriate treatment - justice - have to be defined in each particular case. In the same way that righteousness was defined as conformity to norm, with the norm requiring definition in each particular case, so too the content of justice depends on the particular case. It is God, Creator and Redeemer, who declares by his word what is required in each particular case. Moreover, precisely because this world's Creator is the God who is good and holy, the norms which he sets for human behaviour are the norms which best enable human flourishing. There is a match between that which God wills and that which leads to human flourishing.

Thus the proposed definition is that justice is appropriate treatment, especially of human beings, and usually in a relational setting, according to the norms commanded and set by God in each particular case. This definition, amongst other features, seems to reflect the close link in the OT between righteousness/*s-d-q* and justice/*mishpat*, but without suggesting that the two are identical.

A full defence of this definition, especially in terms of the OT material, must await the next chapter. However, some initial arguments will be offered here, in the context of seeking to demonstrate where the proposed conception of justice differs from some other conceptions.

Justice is not only about the Poor and Needy

Some authors argue that the OT notion of justice is primarily an egalitarian one. According to the *Anchor Bible Dictionary*, for example, God 'establishes justice in the world by eliminating inequalities (Ps. 113:4-9)'. 'God's justice', it is said, 'aims at creating an egalitarian community in which all classes of people maintain their basic human rights.'[30] This suggests that the key thing

---

[29]Compared with righteousness – which involves relationship to God as much as to other human beings – one aspect of the proposed definition of justice is that the latter is primarily a matter of relationships and behaviour *in relation to human beings*.

[30]Temba L. J. Mafico, 'Just, Justice' in *Anchor Bible Dictionary*, D. N. Freedman, ed. (New York: Doubleday, 1992), Vol.3, p1129.

about justice is that it concerns justice for the poor and needy.

It will be argued in the following chapter that appropriate treatment of the poor and needy is indeed a major aspect of justice.[31] According to the definition proposed in this chapter, however, that aspect is not the core of justice. In this regard, the essential defence for the proposed definition is that, while there are many OT references to justice for the poor and needy, there are also many which do not have this feature. In particular, since righteousness and justice are the foundation of God's throne (Ps. 89:14), then it would appear that, even before *injustice* to the poor and needy came into the world, justice was a reality. This is not to detract from the importance of justice for the poor, but rather to place it in an appropriate framework.

Justice is not only Allocational but also Relational

In a tradition extending back to Aristotle,[32] justice is understood as 'to each his due'. Whilst this does not by definition exclude a relational conception of justice, in practice it often does so. In his Nicomachean Ethics, Aristotle has a lengthy discussion of justice in terms of apportioning resources, in the context of reciprocal transactions, in a way that gives each his approximately equal share.[33] The emphasis here is on getting the allocation right, in almost a mathematical sense. There is little or no sense of mutual obligation within a meaningful relationship, whereas a relational notion of justice would place substantial emphasis on this.[34]

Emil Brunner[35] explicitly adopts the narrower of Aristotle's conceptions of justice, as 'to each his due'. This is a very restricted understanding compared with the notion whereby 'all virtue is subsumed in justice' (Brunner, p13, quoting the ancient sage Theognis), or the similarly broad and rich biblical understanding of justice as 'real devoutness, confidence based on faith in the grace of God' (p13). Brunner argues that since Aristotle's time this broader notion has almost vanished from our minds. And so he sets it to one side, and restricts himself (as he argues Aristotle also chose so to do) to the narrower sense. This leaves him with a conception of justice in terms only of claims (p19), which therefore disregards any personal dimension.

---

[31]It is not difficult to see that the proposed definition of justice – that justice is relational, and means appropriate treatment according to the appropriate norms – offers plenty of room for justice in relation to the poor and needy.

[32]Aristotle, *The Nicomachean Ethics*, tr. J. A. K. Thompson (Harmondsworth: Penguin, 1955); see especially Book Five.

[33]Aristotle, *The Nicomachean Ethics*, Book Five, Chapter Five (Penguin edition, pp151-155).

[34]In the first two chapters of Book Five Aristotle does discuss justice as a virtue, before commencing his study of justice in a narrower sense.

[35]*Justice and the Social Order*, tr. Mary Hottinger (London: Harper, 1945).

Justice is more than 'Fairness'

Aristotle is also the inspiration for John Rawls' proposal for 'justice as fairness'.[36] In a sense Rawls' book is one version of the above allocational conception, although Rawls' emphasis on the least well-off persons is clearly distinct from Aristotle's approach. However, one key difference between the definition of justice proposed in this chapter and that offered by Rawls concerns again the relational aspect. Justice as fairness is essentially a detached, impersonal understanding of justice. By contrast, relational justice - biblical justice, it is argued here - is an involved, highly personal conception. This is clearly seen in God's proclamation to Moses in Exodus 3:7-9, in response to the suffering of the Israelites in Egypt:

> Then the LORD said, 'I have seen the affliction of my people who are in Egypt, and have heard their cry because of their taskmasters; I know their sufferings, and I have come down to deliver them out of the hand of the Egyptians, and to bring them up out of that land to a good and broad land, a land flowing with milk and honey, to the place of the Canaanites, the Hittites, the Amorites, the Perizzites, the Hivites, and the Jebusites. And now, behold, the cry of the people of Israel has come to me, and I have seen the oppression with which the Egyptians oppress them...'

The Content of Justice is Proclaimed by the Word of God

To say that the norm for what appropriate treatment means has to be defined in each particular case is by no means to make justice morally relative rather than absolute. And it does not mean that it is essentially for human beings to decide for themselves what is just. Rather, it is to acknowledge that God has not only created the world but also orders it, and that human beings are to seek to live in accord with his word and will. It is also to recognize that the created world is one of variety and complexity, so that what is required in terms of justice in one relational context is not necessarily identical to what is just in another. For example, the content of the justice required in the OT of rulers towards the people (e.g. Deut. 16:18) is not precisely the same as the content of the justice with which the aliens and orphans are to be treated (Deut. 24:17).

As noted earlier, however, Christian believers are not left on their own to try to decide what justice requires. Rather, God has revealed his mind and will in and by his word, especially in and by his written word of Scripture. In order to find out what it is to do justice, Christians must study the whole counsel of God, both the NT and, as interpreted by the NT, the OT. Here the place of the

---

[36]Rawls, *A Theory of Justice* (Oxford: OUP, 1972/Cambridge, Mass.: Harvard University Press, 1971), pp10-11. Particular details of Rawls' approach are assessed in chapter 4 below.

OT can be seen. Christian believers are under grace, not under the Law (e.g. Rom. 6:14f); they are bound neither by the demands of the Law as Law, nor by its detail. Nevertheless, through the OT God reveals to his people his mind[37]; and his mind does not change.[38] What this means in practice, in terms of the teaching in the OT on justice, is to seek to discern, from the pages of the OT - in the light of the whole of Scripture - key lessons regarding justice. For example, the OT material concerned with the treatment of the poor and needy has much to say about what God requires in relation to the poor and needy.

Justice is Dynamic, not Static

Over and over again in the OT *mishpat* is commanded and regarded as something to be *done*.[39] Justice is *treating* people in the way God desires and requires: appropriate treatment. This dynamic notion of justice contrasts sharply with conceptions of justice as, primarily, impartiality, or an abstract notion, or a state of affairs. The ultimate foundation of justice is, of course, God's being and character; and since God is not abstract or static but active and dynamic,[40] it comes as no surprise that, for the God who is 'a God of justice' (Is. 30:18) and who loves justice (Is. 61:8; Ps. 37:28), justice is a matter of doing. This is seen, for example, in Deut. 32:4 ('all his ways are just') and in Ps. 111:7 ('the works of his hands are faithful and just.).[41] And God sets the standard for human beings.

Hermeneutical Principles in the Movement from Text to Application

The definition of economic justice proposed in this chapter speaks of appropriate treatment of human beings – usually in a relational setting –

---

[37]In chapter 3 it is emphasized that there is an *unfolding* of divine revelation throughout the Scriptures: thus the truth disclosed by God in the OT regarding, for example, his character and purposes, can be understood more fully in the light of what is later revealed in the NT (Heb. 1:1-2).

[38]'Mind' here is used in the sense of will, purpose and valuation. In these respects God is unchanging. This does not exclude the reality that God's ways of dealing can alter, as taught, for example, in Acts 17:30: 'The times of ignorance God overlooked, but now he commands all men everywhere to repent...'

[39]In Hebrew, 'to do' is the verb *'asah*. For example, Gen. 18:19,25; Deut. 10:18; 2 Sam. 8:15. A similar emphasis on 'doing' comes with righteousness, as the earlier material on God's righteousness as an active thing sought to convey.

[40]His 'being' and 'action' cannot be absolutely divorced.

[41]It may be noted in passing that the above analysis raises a question about the treatment of justice (by Nicholas Wolterstorff) in the *New Dictionary of Christian Ethics and Pastoral Theology*, D. J. Atkinson and D. H. Field, eds. (Leicester: IVP, 1995) in which love is said to be a trait of character, whereas (in contrast) justice is seen as a feature of social arrangements and interactions (p20).

according to the norms commanded and set by God. It has also been suggested that the content of justice is proclaimed by the word of God, especially in God's written word of Scripture. It follows, therefore, that Christians should both study Scripture carefully in order to learn what justice means, and seek to apply this teaching in practice. Clearly these activities involve a movement from the text of Scripture to its application today, and thus there is a central and important hermeneutical issue concerning this movement: how can any attempt to derive contemporary principles of application from the biblical text be explained and justified?

It is therefore appropriate (before embarking on more detailed biblical study in the following chapter) briefly to describe and explain the hermeneutical and interpretative principles employed by the present book in this movement from text to application. It is important to give some attention to biblical hermeneutics, but – in the space available – what can be offered here is only a modest treatment of a complex issue.[42]

The same central hermeneutical issue would arise with *any* piece of literature written at some former date – whether the writings concerned were, for example, religious, historical, or fictional – if it were being proposed that contemporary moral principles were to be derived from that literature. For any of these writings the issue would be that of moving from text to application. There are three essential stages in this movement – exegesis, synthesis and application – and together these provide the central hermeneutical logic. With particular regard to the biblical writings, regarded as moral statements or commands, these three stages may be summarised as follows: (a) exegesis – trying to understand accurately the meaning of the particular Scriptural texts in their own right and context; (b) synthesis – setting those particular biblical texts in the context of other biblical texts, and indeed of the whole of Scripture, and thus reaching a more general understanding; (c) application – relating that general understanding and overall picture to the concerns of today.[43]

The task of this short section is to indicate how the essential hermeneutical

---

[42]Given the major concern and thrust of this book in developing a biblical conception of economic justice and engaging with secular treatments, there is space here only to sketch the hermeneutical principles being employed, and not to defend them at length or debate the various issues involved. Goldingay offers a thorough treatment of these issues and of recent literature on biblical hermeneutics (John Goldingay, *Models for Interpretation of Scripture*, Grand Rapids, MI: Eerdmans/Carlisle: Paternoster, 1995), and the present section draws upon this work.

[43]Cf. Goldingay, *Models for Interpretation*, p251. Goldingay adds two additional stages: *appropriation* – the person's own response (not exclusively cerebral) to the text: a response which involves faith and the willingness to obey; and *communication* – sharing the results of interpretation with other people. In the context of the present book – and without wishing to downgrade the general importance of those additional stages – significance attaches especially to exegesis, synthesis and application. Herein lies the central logic of the argument.

logic – sketched above – can be implemented in practice, with particular regard to the search for biblically-based moral principles for economic justice. On the assumption that the Scriptural texts carry authority as moral teaching, then it is logically possible to proceed from exegesis through synthesis to application, and thus reach conclusions about moral conduct – with regard to economic life and justice in particular – in the contemporary world.

Whilst the three stages identified are by no means independent of one another,[44] they will here be taken in turn.[45] It must also be acknowledged that, although the hermeneutical logic already spelt out is clear, the practice may involve difficulties. Some of these will be referred to in the brief outline which follows.

Exegesis

The first task in the hermeneutical process is to understand particular texts as clearly and precisely as possible, in order to discern their original meaning. With particular regard to the Scriptural texts which bear on economic justice, careful exegesis will require attention to, for example, the original languages in which the texts were given, the historical and theological setting of those texts, and also their geographical and socio-economic context.

Much of the Scriptural exegetical work in the present book is conducted in chapter 3, although some has already been done in the present chapter. The exegesis seeks to examine closely, for example, the semantic meaning – including the range of meaning – of words (both Hebrew and Greek) which are particularly important in the Scriptural teaching with regard to justice in economic life. Similarly attention is paid to the particular historical setting of individual texts: some of the OT material, for example, is given before Israel had become a *people*, some is given in the context of the Israelites' slavery in Egypt, and some is given whilst they were ruled by a monarchy. The theological setting is also important, and so distinctions are made between teaching given in the OT and that given in the rather different – e.g. the explicitly Christological – setting of the NT. Sound exegesis of material relevant to economic justice also requires careful attention to the geographical and socio-economic context, and so the treatment offered in this book attempts

---

[44]Goldingay, *ibid.*, pp256-62.

[45]The above three-stage framework is similar to that offered by Hays (Richard B. Hays, *The Moral Vision of the New Testament*, Edinburgh: T&T Clark, 1996) who – in the context of NT ethics in particular – distinguishes these four tasks (pp3-7): descriptive; synthetic – seeking to describe a unity of ethical perspective within the diversity of the canon of Scripture; hermeneutic – by which Hays means 'relating the text to our situation' (p5); and pragmatic – 'living the text' (p7). The considerable overlap between the frameworks offered by Hays and by Goldingay, *Models for Interpretation*, is evident.

to understand particular texts in that light also: for example, the teaching given in the Mosaic law about economic life is examined carefully with regard to its particular meaning in an agrarian setting.

Part of the motivation for hermeneutics, of course, is the application of the text to our own day, but this must not cloud or confuse the exegetical task. The two horizons – that of the Scriptural text and that of our contemporary world – need always to be distinguished, as far as possible.[46] With regard to biblical material on economic life, then, it is important *not* to assume that practices such as slavery and the charging of interest meant precisely the same in the original context as they have meant in, for example, the Western context in more recent or contemporary times. It is not always easy or straightforward to distinguish the two sets of horizons, but it is vital to seek to do so.

One additional difficulty that has recently been suggested, with regard to the exegetical stage of the hermeneutic task, concerns, first, whether it is in reality possible for any exegete to know the intention of the original author in writing a text, and secondly whether it is possible to discern a given, determinate meaning in a text. The attacks on the notions of both authorial intention and determinate meaning have been applied to a range of types of literature, but their application to the biblical texts raises particular problems for any attempt – such as that of the present book – to study Scripture on the assumption that it is the word of God written. The church has traditionally turned to the Scriptures in order to discern the mind of God. If in reality, however, it is not possible to gain an understanding either of the authorial intention with regard to any given biblical text – and especially the intention of the divine author – or of a text's actual meaning, then exegesis of Scriptural texts can never achieve the desired goal of discerning with any degree of confidence the mind of God in those texts.[47]

One recent response by Christian writers to these attacks on the concepts of determinate meaning and authorial intention has been to apply speech-act theory[48] to the written word of Scripture. It is not possible here to assess this approach in any depth or to offer anything other than a brief outline, but the

---

[46]Goldingay, *Models for Interpretation*, p257.

[47]The attack against determinate meaning and authorial intention is both explained and criticised in, for example, Anthony C. Thiselton, *New Horizons in Hermeneutics: The Theory and Practice of Transforming Bible Reading* (London: HarperCollins, 1992) and Francis Watson, *Text and Truth: Redefining Biblical Theology* (Edinburgh: T&T Clark, 1997). With regard to biblical and theological studies, Watson argues that this attack has elevated useful insights into 'hermeneutical dogmas' (pp96-7), and in turn that these dogmas are to be rejected, both '*because they conflict with the dogmas held to be foundational to orthodox Christian faith, and because, in the light of that conflict, certain inherent problems and implausibilities rapidly come to light*' (p97; emphasis in the original).

[48]A key text here is J. L. Austin, *How To Do Things With Words*, 2nd ed. (Cambridge, Mass: Harvard University Press, 1985).

essence of the argument is that if the words *spoken* by someone can in principle be understood with regard to their meaning, then the same claim can apply to *written* words.[49] Using Austin's terminology, when someone performs the 'locutionary' act of uttering a particular sentence, they also typically perform two other acts. One is the 'illocutionary' act that occurs *in* (*il-*) the act of locution – e.g. asking a question, or giving information. The other is the 'perlocutionary' act: that is, 'we intend, *by means of* (*per-*) the locutionary and illocutionary act, to bring about some effect – e.g. convincing, persuading, deterring, surprising or misleading'.[50] Watson argues that 'the category of the speech-act can be extended to include written communications' and that, therefore, 'current hostility to the concepts of determinate meaning and authorial intention is unjustified'.[51]

A further difficulty that has been raised with regard to this first stage of the hermeneutic process concerns the notion of at least some degree of objectivity in exegesis, and this problem in turn suggests an important practical conclusion concerning the conduct of exegesis. The concept of objectivity has come under heavy attack in recent years (along with the ideas of literal sense and authorial intent). Nevertheless it can be argued that, whilst absolute objectivity is not available to any mortal being, some notion of objectivity is both feasible and vital in the study of texts. Thus Watson argues that 'there is an "objectivity" which is indispensable for all textual interpretation'.[52] This objectivity has to be considered, however – especially with regard to study of the Scriptures – alongside the presuppositions, perspectives and values which are present in the mind of this, as any other, exegete, and which to a greater or lesser extent are in conflict with the teachings and values of Scripture itself. It is important, therefore, that there is a community of scholars who can assist one another in helping, through discussion and debate, to make each other aware of their presuppositions. But it is only and precisely through careful attention to the

---

[49]The case for the use of speech-act theory in relation to Scripture has been made by, in particular, Thiselton, *New Horizons*, and Watson, *Text and Truth*.

[50]Watson, *ibid.*, p124, footnote 3 (emphasis in the original).

[51]*Ibid.*, p103. Further, Thiselton suggests the following with regard to some of the effects intended by various Scriptural communications: 'The biblical writings, it may be argued, embody an institutional framework of covenant in which commitments and effects become operative in acts of promise, acts of blessing, acts of forgiveness, acts of pronouncing judgment, acts of repentance, acts of worship, acts of authorization, acts of communion, and acts of love' (*New Horizons*, pp17-18).

[52]Watson, *Text and Truth*, p113. He presents three reasons for the indispensability of 'objectivity' (pp113-4): first, it implies a relative freedom from particular local interests; secondly, it implies 'that some of the questions which interpreters ask about texts have a single right answer', which is in line with the widespread concern (in general) to reduce ambiguity and avoid misunderstanding; thirdly, it implies 'the existence of criteria which enable interpreters to assess the relative merits of the various proposed solutions to a problem'.

Scriptural text that this process will take place. This process, in other words, is part of the exegetical step within biblical hermeneutics – rather than being some separate or independent step.[53]

Synthesis

The second logical stage in the hermeneutic process is synthesis: that is, setting particular biblical texts in the context of other Scriptural texts, and indeed of Scripture as a whole, and thus reaching a more general understanding. Synthesis is a necessary stage in biblical hermeneutics, because any particular texts which may be exegeted are, by definition, part of the Bible as a whole, and thus their full biblical meaning cannot be discerned without consideration of their place in the whole of Scripture. This synthetic stage is similarly necessary for any other body of literature (such as the works of a particular human author): if one is seeking an understanding of the *general* conception, within that body of literature, of a given topic, then it is necessary not only to exegete particular texts, but also to seek to synthesise them with other texts from that overall body of material.

One possible objection to the synthetic stage of biblical hermeneutics would be to claim that the biblical material – on some or all topics – is not actually cohesive, but rather internally contradictory. If this were the case, then the search for a *general* biblical understanding would be a vain quest: the different voices in Scripture would be irreconcilable and instead would be a 'chaotic cacophony'.[54] However, this objection to any attempted synthesis is only *a posteriori*, not *a priori*: it is an argument that synthesis may fail, not that it is impossible. If there is in practice, on one or all topics, no such thing as 'the teaching of Scripture as a whole', then the synthetic exercise will be shown to have been in vain – but that lesson could have been learned only through engaging in the practical attempt at synthesis. On the other hand, it might conceivably be the case that the teaching of the Scriptures on one or more issues *is* harmonious and cohesive, in which case the synthetic exercise would be shown to be not only necessary but also highly worthwhile. The church has traditionally sought to understand what the Scriptures as a whole say on a range of topics, working from the initial conviction that there is indeed such a thing as the teaching of the whole of Scripture.

It is also important to emphasise the validity of synthesis, in the sense that it is appropriate for ordinary human beings – despite all their limitations – to engage in this quest. As was said earlier with regard to the exegetical process, the efforts of any individual interpreter – or indeed any group of interpreters – to conduct this synthetic process are necessarily provisional, and should be

---

[53]Within the present book, some exegetical work has been offered in this chapter, although the bulk of it is contained in chapter 3.

[54]Hays, *Moral Vision*, p188.

open to constructive critique from others, under the searchlight of Scripture itself. In Hays' words: '…we cannot escape acknowledging that any synthetic account of the unity of the New Testament's moral vision will be a product of our artifice… Of course, this acknowledgment in no way denies the necessity or legitimacy of the synthetic judgment; it merely alerts us to exercise due modesty about our own synthetic proposals.'[55] Thus our efforts to conduct the synthetic stage of the hermeneutic process are always provisional, but they remain a valid activity.[56]

With regard to the biblical teaching on economic justice, the synthetic stage of the hermeneutic process requires that, as well as conducting an exegesis of relevant particular texts – in both Testaments – in their geographical, historical and theological context, these texts are also considered in the context of the Bible as a whole, and this will involve comparing and weighing different strands of biblical teaching against one another. It will also involve placing the material on economic justice in the wider context of the overall message of the Scriptures in terms of salvation history. Within the present book, these aspects of the synthetic process are conducted primarily in chapter 3, where the burden of my argument will be that, given an appropriate theological framework, the different strands of biblical teaching on justice in economic life can be clearly shown – in a Christological context, ultimately – to hold together.[57]

---

[55]*Ibid.*, p189.

[56]With regard to the synthetic stage of the hermeneutic process, Timothy Ward (*Word and Supplement: Speech Acts, Biblical Texts, and the Sufficiency of Scripture*, Oxford: OUP, 2002) emphasizes both the canonical harmony of Scripture, and the need for our differing interpretative frameworks to be continually and mutually subjected to the bar of Scripture: 'The more the Bible is read through a variety of interpretative frameworks, and the more those frameworks are revised in light of the texts, the more what is and is not there in the canon as a whole will be discerned' (p295)… Further: 'Dialogue with Bible-readers from other communities is a crucial part of "careful reading", and a vital means for becoming rightly suspicious of one's own prior readings' (p295, footnote 276).

[57]With regard to this synthetic aspect of hermeneutics, the importance of interpreting the Old Testament (OT) Christologically is emphasized by Watson - although this by no means diminishes the significance of the OT or any of the detail therein: 'Christian confession of Jesus as the Christ ascribes to him a universal and ultimate significance. [But it] should not therefore be assumed that a christologically-oriented Old Testament interpretation will inevitably reduce the polyphony of the Old Testament texts to monotony. If the scope of the Christ-event is the whole of reality, then there is no danger that any of the breadth and depth of the experience reflected in the Old Testament will be lost… A christological interpretation that impoverished the Old Testament could only stem from an impoverished christology' (Watson, *Text and Truth*, pp217-8).

Application

The third and final stage in the hermeneutic process, following on from the exegesis and synthesis of the Scriptures (in both their particularity and generality), is to move the Scriptural material outside its original context and consider how it applies in the contemporary context. Again there are practical difficulties with this stage (some of which are mentioned below), but the essential logic is plain, and would be relevant for *any* kind of literature relating to moral norms and principles: moral statements and norms which were given some time ago can, after careful exegesis and synthesis, still apply in the contemporary world. The precise way in which these moral norms and teachings apply in the contemporary context will require careful consideration, but moral standards apply in principle to any context.

Synthesis is an inductive process: examining how particular texts can legitimately be synthesized into a framework of general biblical principles. Application – the final step in the hermeneutical exercise – is a deductive process: studying how these general principles can be applied with some moral authority to particular situations in the contemporary context.[58] Clearly there are significant differences between the context of the Scriptures and the context of the contemporary world. These include cultural differences (e.g. language, patterns of family and communal relationships); theological differences (e.g. OT Israel was formed as a theocracy – God was their God, and they his people – which cannot, it is assumed here, be argued for any nation today);[59] technological differences (e.g. much of the Scriptural material addresses a largely agrarian socio-economy, which evidently the West is not); and political differences (e.g. the development of democratic institutions in the contemporary world).

It follows from these differences between the context then and the context now that care must be taken in applying a general framework of moral norms and principles. To take account of the kinds of differences mentioned in the previous paragraph, for example, is not always a simple or straightforward matter. Nevertheless the practical difficulties raised here are by no means insurmountable, and it can be argued that a faithful and intelligent transposition of general biblical principles into the contemporary context is perfectly feasible. As Goldingay points out, most of the direct commands in Scripture 'are not universal absolutes but enactments made to fit concrete situations. Yet they are hardly random enactments but concrete expressions of principles. They are thus of use to us in their concreteness, because they show principles applied in concrete ways; but in interpreting them we need to move behind the concrete

---

[58]The need for deduction as such is not controversial, nor does it in itself raise any fundamental issues.

[59]The exegesis and application of material within the Mosaic law of the OT which relates to economic justice raises some particular hermeneutical questions, apart from the more general issues mentioned in this section. Chapter 3 addresses these questions.

command to the principles which underlie it, *not so as to stop there but so as to turn these principles back into concrete commands applicable to our own situations.*[60]

A separate point to be made, with regard to application, concerns the moral authority of the biblical material and principles. It is assumed here that Scripture, being the word of God written (and written also by a wide range of human authors), discloses to us the mind and will of God. Thus the moral norms and principles found in the Bible are not mere human opinion, but express the mind of God. This understanding is in line, of course, with the way in which the church traditionally turns to Scripture in order to discern the will of God. Further, it is understood here that God's mind and will, and therefore God's moral norms and standards, do not change, and thus they apply to the people of today's world with the same underlying moral authority with which they applied when they were first spoken and revealed; for every human being, now as then, is made in the image of God and lives under the moral rule of God. Moreover, it is claimed that it always was and is *intended* by God that his written word should have this ongoing revelatory and authoritative significance. In the language of speech-act theory, the perlocutionary force of God's word in Scripture – whether to rebuke, teach or encourage (amongst other intended effects) – is part of God's communicative act.[61]

Given the assumption, outlined in the previous paragraph, concerning the moral authority of Scripture, it is clear that the hermeneutical task of exegeting, synthesising and applying Scripture is *important*. Combining this with the argument – presented over the previous few pages – that the hermeneutical task is in principle *valid and feasible*, it follows that there is a sound basis for the assertion put forward in this book (e.g. the present chapter) that Scripture discloses and teaches moral norms which are commanded and set by God, and which can, given careful hermeneutical work, be applied in the contemporary world.

It is not being claimed that everyone knows and comprehends the moral will of God, nor that sinful human beings are at present capable of fully obeying the moral will of God. Nevertheless, human beings live in a world which is

---

[60]Goldingay, *Models for Interpretation*, p92 (emphasis added).

[61]Thus Watson, in the context of his account and defence of the literal sense and verbal meaning of Scripture (see above), argues as follows: 'As communicative actions, the texts seek to convey a meaning in order to provoke a particular response. To concern oneself with the literal sense is therefore to reflect on "application" as well as verbal meaning, for without this dimension the texts are no longer understood as communicative actions' (*Text and Truth*, p123). Not least amongst the perlocutionary effects of Scripture are rebuke and correction, as Thiselton points out: 'Luther and Calvin argued that the word of God encounters readers most sharply when it addresses us as adversary, to correct and change our prior wishes and expectations. This corresponds at a formal level to the correction of a tradition. Grace and judgment, holiness and love, may recall us to new and better paths' (*New Horizons*, p9).

governed by God, in which right and wrong really exist, and in which the lives of human beings – even though they always fall short of God's standards – really matter in moral terms. As Goldingay argues, the mission and pastoral strategies recorded in the Bible 'may thus involve starting where people are as sinners and in their cultural context. The presence of this element of condescension in biblical injunctions and their background in the fact of creation as well as the fact of redemption point to the possibility of applying God's standards to our own real world.'[62]

This should remind biblical exegetes to be aware that the words of Scripture are addressed to sinful human beings, living in a world where the 'very good' creation (Gen. 1:31) has been flawed by sin. But it certainly does not follow that the perfect moral will of God is thereby compromised, nor that it is thereby hidden. As Jesus taught the Pharisees (with regard to marriage and divorce): 'Moses permitted you to divorce your wives because your hearts were hard. But it was not this way from the beginning' (Mt. 19:8). Here, then, is an example of starting where people are as sinners (with the permitting of divorce), yet without God's perfect moral standards being obscured. Given this revelation of God's moral will, albeit in the context of a fallen world, it is still feasible for human beings to learn, by faithful study of Scripture, what is pleasing to God. As Goldingay argues, the mission and pastoral strategy recorded in the Scripture 'thus offers us a paradigm for our own application *of God's ultimate standards* to the situations of sinful humanity that we encounter'.[63]

It should also be emphasized that the paradigm offered by the biblical material is a framework of principles, not a blueprint.[64] Thus it is argued in this book – with regard to ethical norms for economic justice – that Scripture does not give principles that are independent of one another, but rather a framework or package of principles. This is hardly surprising, given that justice in economic life involves (for example) the decisions of individuals, firms and communities, in a wide range of different situations, with implications both for how economic wealth is generated and for how it is distributed. Clearly many interconnections are involved, and thus it is important to recognize that the moral principles relevant to economic justice must be held together in a framework, rather than treated as isolated norms.

At the same time, it is important to appreciate that this Scriptural framework

---

[62]Goldingay, *Models for Interpretation*, p116.

[63]*Ibid.* (emphasis added).

[64]For discussion by evangelical writers of the relative merits of paradigms, frameworks, norms and blueprints – with regard to Christian social ethics – see C. J. H Wright, *Living as the People of God: The Relevance of Old Testament Ethics* (Leicester: IVP, 1983); Michael Schluter and Roy Clements, 'Jubilee Institutional Norms: A Middle Way between Creation Ethics and Kingdom Ethics as the Basis for Christian Political Action', *Evangelical Quarterly*, 1990, 62:1, 37-62; and Michael Schluter and John Ashcroft (eds.), *Jubilee Manifesto: a framework, agenda and strategy for Christian social reform* (Leicester: IVP, 2005).

of principles is given as a guide to be followed rather than a blueprint to be copied. This is clear from the biblical teaching itself, especially that of the New Testament. For example, when moving from doctrine to ethical application, the typical strategy within the epistles is not to teach a rigid obedience to a detailed (e.g. Old Testament) package of commands, but rather a faithful obedience to a pattern of principles perhaps illustrated with reference to one or more specific OT commands. In Ephesians, for example, chapter 6 teaches a framework of principles for the mutual relationships between slaves and masters, instructs children to obey their parents (with reference to the fifth commandment), and instructs fathers not to exasperate their children. Ethical teaching in the Scriptures gives a framework of principles, rather than a blueprint to be copied.[65]

There are still practical difficulties, of course, in applying the Scriptural teaching and principles, not least with regard to economic justice. For example, the OT teaching regarding debt and interest – from which it is conceivable that some general moral principles can be drawn – should not naively be applied to contemporary matters of debt and interest without carefully addressing the contextual differences (e.g. socio-economic) between then and now.[66] Nevertheless – as will be argued in chapters 5 and 6 – the Scriptural material, handled in a balanced way within a careful framework, opens up important and fruitful lines of thought and application.[67]

---

[65]Hays notes that, with regard to ethical argument in general, four modes of appeal to the Scriptural text may usefully be distinguished (*Moral Vision*, p209): rules; principles ('general frameworks of moral consideration'); 'paradigms' - by which he means accounts of *characters* in the Bible; and a more general 'symbolic world', especially the human condition and the character of God. There is no claim that any one of these is superior to the others. But it should by now be clear that the present book focuses primarily on the second of these modes of appeal, namely that of a framework of principles.

[66]There is also the possible danger that, especially with regard to economic, social and political issues, the reader's prior perceptions and social values predispose a particular reading of Scripture, and thus the pre-existing political norms – however wrong they might be – are actually upheld and reinforced. As Vanhoozer puts it: 'The postmodern suspicion of hermeneutics assumes that all organizing principles are socio-political constructions and thus so many expressions of the will to power' (Kevin J. Vanhoozer, *Is There a Meaning in This Text? The Bible, the Reader and the Morality of Literary Knowledge*, Leicester: Apollos, 1998, p435). Ultimately, however, this radical reader-response critique becomes nihilistic anarchy: 'If the truth-stating function of language cannot be taken seriously, and if all language can be reduced to rhetoric, then the self is ultimately unable to reach understanding of the world, of others, or of texts' (p433). He argues instead that, before and under God, true freedom in interpretation 'means subordinating all human concepts and ideas to the biblical witness. True freedom is freedom *under* the Word' (p437; emphasis in the original).

[67]The hermeneutical process described in these pages – including the importance of both inductive and deductive steps (as recognized by Goldingay, *Models for Interpretation*,

Conclusion

This chapter has explored the hypothesis that the righteousness of God is the foundation for a theological consideration of human justice. The insights that have been gained, and the consistency with the Scriptural material thus far considered, suggest that this foundation is both valid and helpful. In the theological framework offered above, the righteousness of God has been argued to mean his acts of faithfulness to his own justice and mercy in his relationship with humanity, and his gift to believers of righteousness in Christ. This righteousness in Christ secures Christian believers in a right relationship with God, and it is received by faith. But this righteousness is to be worked out in practice, in terms of loving obedience. It is here that this theological framework locates the place of human justice: actions which work for righteousness in human relationships, conforming in general to the norm of appropriate treatment, and conforming in particular to the norms appropriate, within God's created order, to each given relationship. These norms are commanded and set by the Creator-Redeemer God who himself is a God of justice.

---

e.g. chapter 7) – does not preclude, however, the possibility that *particular* words in Scripture can speak into *particular* circumstances today with remarkable power and clarity, under the work of the Holy Spirit. Effectively the process involving induction and deduction can on occasions be short-circuited. This is not a licence for lazy thinking, but a reminder that – *as with the careful hermeneutical work as well* – what we are dealing with is (as confessed regularly by Church of England and other congregations) 'the word of the Lord', and that obedience to this word involves submission to the guiding and over-ruling of the Holy Spirit.

CHAPTER 3

The Unfolding of Economic Justice in the Bible

Introduction

This chapter continues the task, begun in the previous chapter, of offering a theological account of economic justice. Chapter 2 sought to locate, in theological terms, the *place* of justice, including economic justice, and ended (in section 3) with some initial claims concerning the content of such justice. In terms of the biblical material, the focus of chapter 2 was on the righteousness *of God* - the foundation of the theological framework developed - and on proposing central meanings for righteousness and justice in Scripture. This chapter proceeds from there to provide an overview of all other aspects of the biblical teaching on justice, especially justice in economic life, with the aim of further defining and understanding the *content* of justice, especially economic justice. This chapter also aims - as indicated in the introduction to chapter 2 - to examine further the validity and helpfulness of the hypothesis that a vital key to interpreting the biblical material on economic justice is the righteousness of God. As this chapter's overview of biblical material proceeds, therefore, the theological framework offered in the previous chapter is examined further.[1]

There are several other aspects of this overview that require emphasis at this point. First, the treatment of biblical justice here is not intended to be exhaustive. Rather, it aims to give a sense of the whole, as regards the biblical conception of justice. Secondly, the account of the biblical teaching will build upon two conclusions from chapter 2: namely that, in the OT, 'justice' and 'righteousness' are very closely related (though not normally synonymous); and that, in the NT, the use of the word δικαιοσύνη can include both 'justice' aspects and 'righteousness' aspects. Thus the treatment does not seek to isolate 'justice' from 'righteousness', but rather to understand the thrust of all the

---

[1]Given the substantial scope of the overview to be presented here, and the methodology (as just explained in the text) of exploring and testing out the hypothesis proposed in chapter 2, it is neither feasible nor appropriate for this chapter to engage in a systematic way with the kind of questions raised by textual, form, source and redaction criticism. Instead this thesis adopts a canonical perspective to the Scriptures (as is explained further below). Brevard S. Childs offers a defence of this kind of approach in his *Introduction to the Old Testament as Scripture* (Philadelphia: Fortress, 1979).

teaching on 'justice-righteousness'. Thirdly, the overview is written for the purpose of understanding the biblical teaching on *economic* justice, and hence there is a focus not only on justice and righteousness but also on their application to economic life in particular. Fourthly, as the title suggests, the overview pays particular attention to the *unfolding*, through the whole of Scripture, of what is taught about economic justice. This makes it possible, for example, both to interpret the OT material in the light of the NT, and also to recognize that the NT builds on the foundations laid in the OT.[2] It also enables one to note various strands of teaching regarding justice and economic life within both Testaments, and to see how these strands hold together in the context of the unfolding of the canonical teaching.[3] Thus it is this canonical teaching which is normative[4]. Finally, the structure of the overview is provided by the events, as reported and understood by Scripture, which form the unfolding history of God's redemptive work. Before proceeding with the overview, a little more needs to be said about this framework of salvation-history.

A Salvation-historical Framework

In the same way that, in chapter 2, the gospel was central to the understanding of the righteousness of God, and thence to the locating of justice, so also here in chapter 3 this gospel of God's salvation is central. In the present chapter the gospel provides the key to the interpretation of God's action in history, and hence to the biblical understanding of justice. It is because Christian believers

---

[2]These foundations are laid particularly in the Pentateuch. Hence a large part of this chapter comprises an analysis of the Pentateuchal material, on which basis both the OT prophets and the NT authors proceed to unfold further the biblical notion of justice with regard to economic life.

[3]See also footnote 1 above.

[4]As Richard B. Hays argues - in his study of ethics in the NT in particular - the Scriptures present norms which govern the norms offered from all other sources. He writes that his study 'proceeds on the conviction that the canonical Scriptures constitute the *norma normans* for the church's life, whereas every other source of moral guidance...must be understood as *norma normata*. Thus, normative Christian ethics is fundamentally a *hermeneutical* enterprise: it must begin and end in the interpretation and application of Scripture for the life of the community of faith. Such a pronouncement will prove controversial in some circles, but it represents the classic confessional position of catholic Christianity, particularly as sharpened in its Reformation traditions' (*The Moral Vision of the New Testament*, Edinburgh: T&T Clark, 1996, p10). With regard to the role of the OT in NT ethics, Hays proceeds to argue, first, that the voice of the OT is and must be heard in the NT ('the full canon is the necessary context of intelligibility for the New Testament's treatment of any ethical topic'; p307); secondly, that the OT is the grounding for community, cross and new creation; and thirdly, that the NT is the lens for reading the OT (pp306-9).

have been brought to see the light of the knowledge of the glory of Jesus Christ that they are able, as already noted, both to interpret the OT in the light of the NT, and to recognize how the NT builds upon the OT.

The particular salvation-historical framework which underpins the overview offered in this chapter recognizes four key stages or events in God's dealings with humanity and humanity's response. These are: Creation; Fall; Redemption; and Eschatology (or Consummation).[5] These stages are not isolated from one another. Rather they are like acts in a play, whereby each act or event proceeds on the basis of what has gone before. Further, one of the benefits and features of this framework is that it easily enables each stage of salvation history to be understood in the light of the other three stages: not only is Eschatology, for example, to be viewed in the light of what has gone before, but the Fall is to be viewed in the light both of what went before (Creation) and of what follows.

It should be noted that, since the vast majority of the Bible is concerned with God's redemptive activity, and humanity's response - whether positive or negative - to the proclamation of God's salvation, therefore the salvation-historical framework adopted here seeks both to recognize the great significance of Creation, Fall and Eschatology (as well as Redemption), but also to acknowledge the focus of God's written word upon redemptive activity. Thus this chapter seeks to follow the lead of Scripture, and indeed be led by Scripture, in placing a powerful magnifying lens over God's *redemptive* work,[6] since this is where God's revelation is focused.

---

[5]This salvation-historical framework - sometimes denoted below as 'C-F-R-E' - is outlined further in, for example, Oliver O'Donovan, *Resurrection and Moral Order*, 2nd ed. (Leicester: Apollos, 1994), *passim*. As regards notation: in this and the following paragraph, each of these four terms is treated as proper nouns (commencing with upper case), in order to help clarify the shape of the basic framework. Thereafter the conventional presentation is followed, i.e. treating 'Fall' as a proper noun, but the other three as ordinary nouns.

[6]This (C-F-R-E) framework, although relatively simple, is well able to handle the complexities thrown up by Scripture. For example, the role in salvation-history of the people of God can be handled in the above framework by means of the recognition - worked out below in terms of justice - that a major aspect of redemption concerns the people of God. It is not the only aspect, however: for example, redemption also concerns individuals, and it also concerns humanity's relationship to the rest of the created order (e.g. Rom. 8:18-25). Rather than adding yet more complexity to the framework, it seems better to work within something that is relatively straightforward. Thus the above framework combines simplicity and complexity in a way that seems to reflect the Gospel itself: a Gospel which can be received even by little children, and yet which requires Paul to take 16 chapters of Romans for its exposition.

The Structure of Chapter 3

The utilization of this framework in the overview of the unfolding of economic justice helps to provide the following structure for this chapter. Part I considers in outline terms the significance, within Scripture, of creation and Fall for the understanding of righteousness and justice, and their application to economic life. The second, and longest, part - Part II - focuses on the events of redemptive history within the OT, from Noah onwards, with particular regard to justice and its economic aspects. One section of this part focuses on the Wisdom literature: for, although this literature does not, on the whole, address any particular events or stages within salvation history, it does provide, amongst other things, a vital commentary on those events, not least in terms of economic justice. Finally, Part III addresses the person and salvific work of Jesus Christ as taught primarily by the NT. To acknowledge such links between creation and Christology is very important. Moreover, since this Jesus is the one who fulfils all righteousness (Mt. 3:15), then at this point the present chapter reaches in many ways the culmination of all that the Bible has to say concerning righteousness and justice, including its application to economic life. And yet Jesus himself makes it plain that the full coming of the kingdom of God is 'not yet': hence the final section of Part III observes, briefly, that the biblical material on eschatology is a vital part of the overall framework for understanding justice and righteousness in economic life.

I. Economic Justice in the Light of Creation and Fall

Created Order and Moral Order

According to Genesis chapters 1 and 2, God created a world which was *good*; and which, after the creation of the first man and woman, was *very good*. Further, God is not only the good Creator, but is also the good Governor and Ruler of the world. One of the things emphasized in these chapters is God's rule over humanity. In 1:26-30 God mandates human beings - whom he has made in his image, after his likeness - to be fruitful and multiply, to fill the earth and subdue it, and to have dominion over every living thing. In 2:15 we read that the LORD God puts the man in the garden of Eden to till it and keep it. God also commands the man, saying that he may freely eat of any tree in the garden, except the tree of the knowledge of good and evil, 'for in the day you eat of it you shall die' (2:17). In the light of the rest of Scripture, this is not merely a word of prediction, but a word of *judgment* (cf. Rom. 5:16): if human beings go against God's good and perfect will, then God will ensure that they receive what they both deserve and choose. God holds human beings responsible regarding whether they do the will of God, or else disobey God and his will.

God's words and actions in these first two chapters of the Bible make it clear that the created order is a moral order. 'Goodness' is a matter not only of aesthetics but of moral right and wrong. And God is the one who both says what is good, and who rules.

Created Order and Economic Life: The Norm of Stewardship

These first two chapters of the Bible address, amongst other things, some basic issues of economic life.[7] Human beings are given, as noted already, both dominion over all other living creatures, and the responsibility of tilling and keeping the earth. In Christian accounts of economic life these aspects are commonly brought together under the heading of 'stewardship'. This perspective needs only brief outlining here, but it is a radically different perspective from that of most contemporary economic thought. As the Oxford economist Donald Hay argues, the idea of stewardship

> reminds us that our personal talents and abilities, and the natural resources with which we work, are God's provision for us. They are not our personal possessions but are entrusted to us. We will therefore have to give an account to God as to the use that we have made of them. We exercise our stewardship particularly in work, which involves an exercise of the will to direct our energies and talents.[8]

Elsewhere in Scripture it becomes clear that God holds human beings accountable, in their economic behaviour, according to their conformity to what is entailed in such stewardship. Thus there is, as will be seen more clearly in

---

[7]'Economic life' is taken here to refer, in general terms, to the control and use of material resources (including agricultural resources) by human beings, and to the human relationships which involve such material resources. Thus the definition of economics as the study of how *scarce* resources are allocated - a definition which takes scarcity as a key determinative feature of economic life - is not adopted here. Hence the theological understanding offered here for the nature of economic life disagrees at this point with the view that economics has come about only as a result of the Fall, since that view takes it as given that scarcity itself has come about only as a result of the Fall. (David J. Richardson offers one expression of that alternative view in his 'Frontiers in Economics and Christian Scholarship', *Christian Scholar's Review*, 17, 1988, pp381-400.)

[8]Donald Hay, *Economics Today: A Christian Critique* (Leicester: Apollos, 1989), p71. Alan Storkey offers a similar account of stewardship in his *Transforming Economics: A Christian Way to Employment* (London: SPCK, 1986) 'Steward' is, of course, the standard English rendering of the Greek οἰκονόμοσ, which is the linguistic root of the term 'economics'. The large disparity between this root understanding and the self-understanding of the modern discipline of 'economics' is commented upon further below. M. Douglas Meeks provides a fruitful theological exploration of the motif of 'economist' as applied to God - primarily, though not solely, in terms of economics - in his *God The Economist: The Doctrine of God and Political Economy* (Minneapolis: Fortress, 1989).

due course, a link between the economic behaviour of human beings and the reality of God's judgment.

Creation in the Context of God's Righteousness and Justice

Psalm 89 provides an illuminating commentary on the rest of the OT here, as the following brief exegesis seeks to show. For this Psalm links created order to righteousness and justice as the foundation of the Lord's throne, and to his faithfulness/*ĕmunah*/אמונה and steadfast love/*hesed*/חסד (the latter two nouns are paired in vv1,2,24,33,49: in the Heb., vv2,3,25,34,50). The major theological context of Psalm 89 is 2 Sam. 7:12-17, and the LORD's 'for ever' covenant promise regarding David - together with the consequent questions evidently posed by the empty throne of David (vv38-51), e.g. 'Lord, where is thy steadfast love/חֲסָדֶיךָ of old...?' (v49; Heb. v50[9]). With the eyes of the NT, it can be seen that 'servant' and 'anointed' (vv 49-50; Heb. vv50-51) look ahead to Jesus Christ, Messiah and Lord, in whom 'all the promises of God find their Yes' (2 Cor. 1:20).

After the opening verses (vv1-4) the Psalm continues by proclaiming the holy majesty of God (vv5-8) and the might of God (vv9-13), displayed in the universe he has founded and created (v11f). Underlying this might is God's righteousness/צדק and justice/משפט and the path this might is to take[10] is marked out by mercy/חסד (v14; Heb. v15). Thus we learn that God's righteousness and justice are the very foundation on which his Lordship of creation rests; and that God's rule is one characterized by steadfast love/חסד. God's people can appeal to his character so revealed as they long for his covenant promises to be fulfilled.

What is the meaning of 'righteousness and justice' here? The context strongly suggests that they relate to the very character and being of God - to his name (v16), his very holiness (e.g. v18) and his love and faithfulness (parallelled with righteousness and justice in v14). Similarly, Ps. 145:7 parallels God's 'abundant goodness' and his righteousness. Righteousness and justice are clearly dynamic (as opposed to abstract or static), for they underlie God's actual rule/throne. The use of 'righteousness' here fits well with part of the central meaning proposed in chapter 2, i.e. conformity to norm - and the 'norm' here is God's own character and being. Thus, it should be noted, the validity of the theological framework proposed in the previous chapter is further supported by the evidence of this Psalm.

With regard to the meaning of 'justice' in Psalm 89, its usage in verse 14 is clearly similar in meaning to righteousness (since it is a hendiadys): 'right

---

[9]The Hebrew is plural here.

[10]This phrase is drawn from Derek Kidner, *Psalms 73-150*, TOTC (Leicester: IVP, 1975), p322.

principles and right actions' expresses the sense.[11] Their close link in Psalm 89 with *hesed* and *èmunah* is significant[12]: it helps to show that righteousness and justice do not refer to some kind of merely distant and uninvolved impartiality. Rather, they teach that God is *both* utterly opposed to wickedness (which he judges, e.g. vv10, 22, 23, 32) *and* deeply committed to his covenant people (e.g. vv2-4, 20-29).[13] Justice is about doing right. This is one aspect of what is meant here by 'relational' righteousness and justice. (The other aspect is the actual relationship involved - where there is one: note that in v14 there is no explicit relationship involved, although the Lord is here declared to be, in broad terms, relating rightly and faithfully to his people and to the whole created order). Note finally that the primary sense of *mishpat* in Psalm 89 - as *doing right* (see above) - does *not* appear to be a juridical or judicial meaning[14]: this is in contrast to the apparent assumption of Brown, Driver and Briggs that 'judicial' justice is the central sense of *mishpat*.[15] All these points go some way in beginning to clarify the content of the biblical notion of justice.

Fall and Judgment

The Fall of humankind into sin - recorded in Genesis chapter 3 - is followed immediately by God's word of judgment: to the serpent, to the woman, and to the man.[16] According to Rom. 5:16: '...the judgment (κρίμα) following one trespass brought condemnation (κατκάρμα)...' This word of judgment is, therefore, not merely a verbal utterance: rather, it carries with it action. God's words are God's 'speech acts'.[17] In this case the action is the curse against the

---

[11]Alec Motyer expresses helpfully this basic idea, in the context of an exposition of Is. 1:21-26. He comments that justice and righteousness 'are equally rooted in divine holiness...righteousness embodies holiness in sound principles, and justice is the expression of righteousness in sound precepts' (Alec Motyer, *The Prophecy of Isaiah*, Leicester: IVP, 1993, p49).

[12]The Heb. translated by RSV in v14 as 'faithfulness' is actually *èmet*/תמא. But, like *èmunah*, *èmet* is often paired with *hesed*, e.g. Ps. 40:11 (Heb., v12); 57:3 (Heb., v4); and in God's self-revelation to Moses in Ex. 34:6. Thus God's love and faithfulness/truthfulness are closely linked as central features of God's character.

[13]The later verses of Psalm 89 play out the difficulties faced by Israel as they face the righteous judgment of God, and thus call into question God's covenant faithfulness. The perspective of the Bible as a whole indicates that only in Christ will a final resolution come.

[14]Cf. C. J. H. Wright, *Living as the People of God: The Relevance of Old Testament Ethics* (Leicester: IVP, 1983), p134.

[15]*The New Brown-Driver-Briggs-Gesenius Hebrew and English Lexicon* (Peabody, MA: Hendrickson, 1979), p1048f.

[16]This word of judgment is in turn closely followed by a word of mercy and grace, in Gn. 3: 21f: see below.

[17]Kevin Vanhoozer offers a theological application of the 'speech act' theory of

serpent (v14f), the childbirth pain of the woman and the man's ruling over her (v16), and the curse against the man (vv17-19), which includes damage to his relationship with the physical world. God is not only the Creator and Governor, he is also the Judge - as is seen further in relation to Cain (Gen. 4, especially vv10-15). The term 'judge' (שפט) is first used of God in Gen. 16:5, where Sarai, having seen that Abram is to have a child by her maid (Hagar), declares to him: 'May the LORD judge [יִשְׁפֹּט] between you and me'. In Gen. 18:25 Abraham declares that God is 'the Judge [שֹׁפֵט] of all the earth'.

The cognate connection between justice/*mishpat*/מִשְׁפָּט and judge/*shôphêt*/שֹׁפֵט is significant. The argument here is that 'right' or 'right action' is the prior and central meaning of this word root, and that the juridical aspect *derives from* this. Such an argument is the reverse of the claim that the juridical aspect is central, and that *mishpat* secondarily comes to gain the sense of 'fairness'.[18] The argument offered here is supported by the first two occurrences of *mishpat* in the book of Genesis,[19] both of which come in chapter 18. In the first of these, in v19, the LORD says of Abraham: '...I have chosen him, that he may charge his children and his household after him to keep the way of the LORD by doing righteousness/צְדָקָה and justice/מִשְׁפָּט; so that the LORD may bring to Abraham what he has promised him.' It is highly implausible that justice/*mishpat* here has a juridical meaning: Abraham was not a judge; and no formal, codified law had yet been given by Yahweh. The plain meaning is that *mishpat* is closely linked with righteousness/*sedaqah*. The hendiadys construction - as seen already in Ps. 89:14 - suggests that here 'righteousness and justice' is effectively one powerful idea expressed by two original words: hence we might well translate this phrase as 'right-principles-and-actions'. To do and to live like this - indeed, in other words, 'to keep the way of the LORD' (v19) - is Yahweh's desire and purpose for Abraham and his children and his household. And for all others too: this same parallel is drawn in Ps. 18:20-24 between keeping the ways of the LORD, observing his ordinances and statutes, and *righteousness*.[20]

The second occurrence of *mishpat* is in Gn.18:25. With regard to the possibility of righteous people living in the cities (Sodom and Gomorrah) which the LORD appears to be about to judge with destruction, v25 reports Abraham's conviction concerning Yahweh, the conviction that he will not slay

---

language in his 'The Semantics of Biblical Literature', in D. A. Carson and John D. Woodbridge (eds.), *Hermeneutics, Authority and Canon* (Carlisle: Paternoster, 1995/previously published: Leicester: Apollos, 1986), pp53-104. For the 'speech act' theory of language, see J.L.Austin, *How To Do Things With Words*, 2nd ed. (Cambridge, Mass: Harvard University Press, 1985).

[18]Cf., for example, C. J. H. Wright, *Living as the People of God*, p134.

[19]And by many other occurrences of *mishpat*: see below.

[20]Job 23:11f makes similar links: it parallels keeping God's way and *not* departing 'from the commandment of his lips'.

the righteous: 'Shall not the Judge of all the earth do right?' The Hebrew word translated here as 'right' is *mishpat*. Its meaning here cannot be merely a neutral, juridical one, otherwise the verse would be a tautology ('the judge will act judicially'). Rather, it must describe the moral quality of the action which Yahweh, the Judge, will take. And this action will be, as the RSV and many other English translations say, '*right*'. In punishing the wicked, God will *not* also indiscriminately slay the righteous. This would not be right. Thus, even in the context of God's action in judgment, as Judge, *mishpat* has here the meaning of 'right', or 'right action'. Hence the content of the biblical notion is clarified a little further.

Thus God is revealed, at this (chronologically) early point in the Scriptures, to be a God of righteousness and justice. God behaves in character. God will act in line with the knowledge he has already revealed of himself to Abraham. God defines what is right; he does what is right. So, even if there are as few as 10 righteous people in Sodom, God will spare that city. If there are none, however, then God's righteous judgment and punishment will proceed; and so it does (chapter 19).

The Fall of human beings into sin, and God's right judgment against them, did not, however, squeeze out God's mercy. Quite the opposite. Mixed in with God's active word of judgment in Genesis chapter 3 is his active word of mercy, made visible in his provision of garments for Adam and Eve. More even than this, however, God's character is such that the active word of judgment is accompanied with the promise of salvific action. In God's word to the serpent, he not only pronounces the curse of v14, but also promises that the woman's seed will bruise the heel of the serpent's seed.[21] Wenham argues plausibly that the serpent symbolizes sin, death, and the power of evil. He argues that the likely meaning of v15 is that 'the curse envisages a long struggle between good and evil, with mankind eventually triumphing'.[22] This seems the most plausible interpretation, especially given the allusions in the NT to this verse (especially Rom. 16:20, and also Heb. 2:14), in the context of the final defeat of Satan.

THE FALL INCLUDES GOD'S JUDGMENT UPON ECONOMIC LIFE

In context of the economic mandate given by God to humanity in Gen. 1-2, the impact of the Fall on economic life - enacted by God's word of judgment - is made plain by Gen. 3. This is a vital element of the Bible's account of God's justice and economic life. In general terms, as noted already, God's judgment brings about what is both deserved and chosen. If human beings - persons-in-community - rebel against God, then this will have consequences for all that

---

[21]This word of God regarding the woman's seed is, as Kaiser argues, God's 'first word of promise'. See Walter Kaiser, *Toward an Old Testament Theology* (Grand Rapids, MI: Zondervan, 1978), pp77-79.
[22]Gordon Wenham, *Genesis 1-15*, Word Biblical Commentary (Milton Keynes: Word, 1991), p80.

they are and all that they do. Thus it is entirely to be expected that God's judgment against sin and sinners affects, amongst other things, their economic life. Gen. 3:17-19, addressed to the man, pronounce that there will now be a real element of hardship, pain and toil[23] as human beings work with the physical world, and struggle through thorns and thistles as they seek to make a living. Since work is basic to economic activity, then the impact of the Fall upon economic activity is plain.

As already shown, however, humankind's Fall into sin is by no means, as far as God is concerned, the end of the story. Biblical glimpses of God's redemptive and eschatological action have already been seen. A particular point to note at the close of this section is that God's saving activity will be expected, both in view of God's sovereignty and Lordship over his world (e.g. Ps. 24:1), and in view of the holistic (though fallen) nature of the human beings he has created, to deal with the damage done by the Fall to economic life as much as any other aspect of life.[24] The mutual economic participation (κοινωνία) expressed by, and taught to, the early church (Acts 2:42-47; 4:32-37; 1 Cor. 11:17-34) is some initial evidence that God's saving action in Christ does and will transform all aspects of life, including the economic aspects.

II. Economic Justice in the Old Testament in the Light of Redemption

As noted in the Introduction to this chapter, redemption is the major theme of the whole Bible. The task of Part II is definitely not, therefore, to seek to retrace all that the Scriptures say concerning redemption. Rather it is, in the context of the unfolding of God's redemptive activity, to give a sense of the whole with regard to what is taught about righteousness and justice, especially as they relate to economic life.

Abraham

The terminology of covenant is very important in the context of God's dealing with Abraham (Gen. 15:18; 17:1-21).[25] The basis of the relationship is God's

---

[23] The sense of judgment upon *all* human beings is reinforced by noting that the phrases 'in pain' (spoken to the woman, v16) and 'in toil' (spoken to the man, v17) are identical in the Hebrew: בְּעִצָּבוֹן.

[24] Salvation does not, of course, exclude judgment, or negate it. The passage already cited from Rev. 12 shows, rather, that God's saving action *includes* his judgment against sin and evil. Further, chapter 2 has already referred to the way in which, on the cross of Jesus Christ, God's mercy and judgment meet perfectly. The ultimate question for human beings, in the light of God's salvation, is how they respond to the call of Jesus Christ for repentance and faith.

[25] In Gen.15:18 the text states that, on that day, 'the LORD made a covenant with Abraham'. Yet, given the powerful promise and relationship language of 12:2f and 15:6, it is clear that this covenant cannot be the beginning of a relationship between God and

gracious promise, which is a dominant theme from chapter 12 through to chapter 18.

FAITH AND RIGHTEOUSNESS

One significant verse linking Abraham and righteousness has already been commented upon (part I above), namely Gen. 18:19, which states that God chose Abraham 'that he may charge his children and his household after him to keep the way of the LORD by doing righteousness and justice; so that the LORD may bring to Abraham what he has promised him'. This doing of righteousness and justice, it was argued earlier, refers to one strong idea (rather than two separate things), namely 'right-principles-and-actions'.[26]

Part of the context for this statement, however, is that Abraham has already had righteousness 'reckoned to him', on account of his believing the LORD (Gen. 15:6). This earlier statement - 'one of the earth-shaking, epoch-creating statements in scripture'[27] - makes it very plain that righteousness concerns right relationship, most especially, as here, right relationship with God. God graciously calls Abraham into relationship with himself; God will sustain this relationship, on his part, by keeping his covenant promise (of many descendants, forming a great nation; of the promised land; and of ultimately worldwide blessing - cf. 12:2f and 17:1-6); and Abraham's response of faith is his part in this relationship. Abraham is right with God.

Thus the narrative concerning Abraham makes it clear both that righteousness is relational, and that - as the earlier chapters of Genesis have already begun to show - God's grace and the human response of faith are central and fundamental in right relationships between God and human beings. Again, therefore, the validity of the theological framework proposed in chapter 2 is endorsed by detailed study of the OT material. It follows that the type of framework developed here provides an important basis for understanding the nature of righteousness in general terms, and in particular for the interpretation of Scriptural material which addresses economic aspects of righteousness.

FAITH AND ECONOMIC BLESSING

Although the Abrahamic narratives do not seek to specify what righteousness

---

Abraham: the relationship already exists, on the basis of God's gracious promise. In a comparable way, between God's *predictive* statements about making/confirming his covenant with Abraham (17:2,7,19) comes God's statement that 'my covenant is with you' (17:4).

[26]And Abraham did keep the way of the LORD. In Gen. 26:5 the LORD, in renewing with Isaac his promise made to Abraham, says of the latter that he 'obeyed my voice and kept my charge, my commandments, my statutes, and my laws'. Abraham exhibited, as the outworking of his faith, genuine obedience and righteousness: that is, he demonstrated conformity to a norm, but a norm which was of course short of sinless perfection.

[27]John Goldingay, *After Eating the Apricot* (Carlisle: Solway, 1996), p72.

means in terms of economics, it should be noted that they do allot a significant place to economic life. This is seen most clearly with regard to God's promise to Abraham of 'the land' (Gen. 12:1). Land is of economic significance in any social or historical setting, but this is especially so in an agrarian setting such as Abraham's. The Abrahamic narratives go further than this, however, by linking together the economic and theological importance of 'the land'.[28]

The particular land referred to, of course - at least in the immediate context[29] - is 'the land that I will show you' (Gen. 12:1 - spoken to Abraham whilst he still lived in Haran), which turns out to be the land of Canaan (Gen. 12:5-7). This is the land which, when Abraham arrives there, the LORD promises Abraham that he will give to Abraham's descendants (12:7). The promise of the land is a central feature of the LORD's covenant with Abraham: it is one of the blessings promised by the LORD (Gen. 12:1-7), along with the promise that the LORD will make of him a great nation, that the LORD will bless him, and make his name great, so that he, Abraham, will be a blessing - a blessing which will extend to 'all the families of the earth' (12:1-3). All these promises, including that of the land, are restated and reemphasized in the following chapters of Genesis (13:14-17; 15:4-6; 15:16; 17:1-8). It should be noted here that in 15:16 God's promise is of a *return* of Abraham's descendants to the promised land, after a very lengthy period (spoken of in v13) of slavery and oppression 'in a land that is not theirs' (v13). The fulfilment of God's promise of economic (and other) blessing would not be a simple matter. But it would come.[30]

Thus God's covenant with Abraham (and his descendants) embraced economic life. Abraham's response to God's promise of economic and other blessings, was, as shown already, that he believed the LORD (15:6) - and it was this faith which the LORD reckoned to him as righteousness, and which had obedience as its correlate.

Finally, it should be noted that Gen. 18:19, discussed earlier, describes this obedience in terms of Abraham (and his descendants) 'doing justice and righteousness'. Thus a link is made between, on the one hand, just and righteous living and, on the other, blessing in terms of economic prosperity. This linkage is a significant strand of Scriptural teaching on economics and justice, and is developed further in Deuteronomy and in the Wisdom literature. How this strand relates to other strands - such as the prophetic rebukes of

---

[28]This is explored at length in, e.g., Walter Brueggemann, *The Land: Place as Gift, Promise and Challenge in Biblical Faith* (London: SPCK, 1978), and C. J. H. Wright, *God's People in God's Land: Family, Land and Property in the Old Testament* (Exeter: Paternoster, 1990).

[29]Hebrews chapter 11 explains that, in the wider context, 'the land' is 'the heavenly country' (especially vv8-16). This wider, eschatological, perspective is, as already mentioned, a key part of the redemptive-historical framework of the Scriptures.

[30]The significance of this long period of oppression for a biblically-rooted understanding of economic justice is discussed in section II.B on the Exodus, below.

wickedness - is assessed below.

Egypt, the Exodus and the Giving of the Law

The language of *redemption* is very strong in the account of God's rescue of the Israelites from their slavery and oppression in Egypt. Further, this rescue was the context for the giving of the Law through Moses at Mount Sinai, as Ex. 20:1 makes plain. Thus the Israelites' exodus clearly had a political and economic dimension. The full meaning of *redemption* - in the exodus context - is further explored below. First, however, the context of the exodus itself must be examined, with particular regard to the nature of justice and its economic aspects.[31]

THE ISRAELITES IN EGYPT

As God had prophesied to Abraham many years earlier (Gen. 15:13-16), his descendants did indeed come to suffer a very long period of oppression and slavery in a land which was not their own, i.e. Egypt.[32] This was some while after the death of Joseph and Jacob in Egypt (Ex. 1:6; Gen. 49:33).[33]

---

[31]This section does not offer any detailed account of the teaching of the Mosaic Law with regard to justice and economic life, because this is a major topic in its own right, and it is therefore dealt with in the following section. But the link between the exodus and the giving of the Law is vital to a proper understanding of the theological nature and significance of the Law.

[32]Verse 13 of Gen. 15 refers to 'four hundred years', and verse 16 states that the Israelites would return to the promised land in the fourth generation. Gordon Wenham suggests that, taken, together, these verses imply that 'four hundred years' is intended to be taken in terms of round numbers, with one generation equalling one hundred years (*Genesis 1-15*, WBC; Milton Keynes: Word, 1991, p332).

[33]Gen. 37-47 is largely taken up with the account of how, in God's providence (50:20), Joseph's presence and actions in Egypt were the means by which both Jacob (and family) and the nation of Egypt were saved from a severe, seven-year famine (47:25). And thus God's covenant promise to Abraham would be kept (50:24).

Joseph's actions - storing up grain from the seven surplus years, and selling it off during the famine, even in exchange for bonded labour (47:20-26) - are sometimes criticised, on the grounds of deliberately centralising power and gaining widespread political and economic control. On this view Joseph acted unjustly. M. Douglas Meeks puts this case in *God The Economist: The Doctrine of God and Political Economy*, Minneapolis: Fortress, 1989, pp78-80. He argues that the text itself contains at least suspicion regarding Joseph's actions. An alternative reading of the text is that Joseph's primary intention was to find a way in which people could have food to eat; and this he achieved - for which the people were grateful ('you have saved our lives', Gen. 47:25). See Gerhard von Rad, *Genesis*, OTL, rev.ed. (London: SCM, 1972), p410; and Wenham, *Genesis 1-15*, p449. On this reading, extreme need may have required extreme measures.

Something of the content of this social and economic oppression is described in Exodus chapter 1 - as is the multiplying of the Israelite population in the face of this Egyptian oppression, oppression which was intended to achieve precisely the opposite (vv9-10).[34] The oppression began with the Egyptians afflicting the Israelites with heavy burdens, and the requirement to build store-cities for Pharaoh (1:11). In the next phase (vv13-14), they made the Israelites 'serve with rigour', making their lives 'bitter with hard service'. A further turn of the screw came after Moses' attempt to persuade Pharaoh to allow the Israelites leave to go and worship God in the wilderness (5:1): Pharaoh's response was to require the Israelite slaves to gather their own straw, yet still make the same number of bricks, with physical beatings if they failed to do so (5:4-19).

It should be noted that a powerful range of vocabulary is used to describe all this treatment. Five Hebrew roots are employed. The Israelites ﬠ were afflicted/oppressed (ﬠנה: 1:11f), and suffered affliction (ﬠני: 3:7), affliction at the hands of taskmasters (the noun 'taskmasters' is from the verb נגש). They were 'oppressed with oppression' (3:9, lit. - the verb and the noun are both from the root לחץ). Elsewhere in the OT further words are used, and linked to the oppression in Egypt: the Israelites were not to oppress (ינה) a stranger, 'for you were strangers in the land of Egypt' (Ex. 22:21; cf. Lev. 19:33f); and they were not to oppress (עשק) a hired servant who was poor and needy (Dt. 24:14) - a command in a section of laws which concludes with the reminder (v18) that they had been slaves in Egypt. Thus all these five roots are used with reference to the oppression in Egypt, and the point here is simply to observe how the range of vocabulary emphasizes the importance of recalling what had happened there. The Israelites had, in their Egypt experience, a very real and tangible understanding of the content of oppression. When, therefore, they were exhorted not to engage in oppression, they knew what was meant. Prohibitions against oppression had clear, comprehensible and powerful meaning.

Returning to the events described in the book of Exodus, it is made plain in the text (e.g. 3:1-12) that God's response to the bondage of the Israelites - the heirs of his promises to Abraham - was to deliver them out of that bondage, to bring them out of the land of Egypt and into 'a good and broad land, a land flowing with milk and honey' (3:8): that is, the land of Canaan, the promised land. This promise of the land of Canaan was not, of course, a brand new promise. As seen already, God promised it to Abraham many years earlier; and Abraham, Isaac and Jacob had lived there alongside the original population. Thus the period in Egypt was in one sense an interruption to the main flow of God's purposes: the Israelites had never been intended to live there

---

[34]The verb 'multiply' in Ex. 1:7,12 is the same verb as in the creation mandate to humankind in Gen. 1:28 (and to birds and sea creatures in Gen. 1:22). A growing population was also one of God's blessings promised to Abraham (e.g. Gen. 15:5). These references suggest that God was showing himself to be both faithful and sovereign, even in circumstances which were, for the Israelites, clearly adverse.

permanently. Now God renews his promise regarding the land. In his sovereign over-ruling, therefore, God works even through the Egypt experience to bring good for his people and thus to all nations.

Precisely because of this divine sovereignty, it might be expected that Scripture would teach that God willed to use the Egypt experience to reveal something more of his character and purposes, to teach something more of his ways. This is indeed the case. One such lesson begins to become clear in Exodus chapter 6. Compared with God's promise of deliverance described in chapter 3 (see the previous paragraph above), his declaration to Moses in Ex. 6 contains two new elements which are significant here.[35] Not only will the LORD deliver the Israelites from bondage, but he will *redeem* them (6:6); and, further, he will redeem them 'with great acts of judgment' (6:6).[36] These two new elements are linked. To speak of 'judgments' implies action taken - 'doing right' - in response to, and against, some wrongdoing. And to 'redeem' suggests - at least in the wider canonical context - the need to ransom or save, at a price, from some adverse situation or eventuality:[37] this is indeed how 'redeem' is used elsewhere in Exodus (e.g. 13:13,15; 15:13; 21:30), and in Leviticus (ch.25, *passim.*).[38] Thus God announces that he will act both to save the Israelites, and to bring judgment against wrongdoing. Moreover, these two actions will occur at the same time, and are seen, indeed, as part of one overall act: redeeming the Israelites with great acts of judgment (6:6). The overall judgment act in question in Exodus chapters 6 to 13 is, as mentioned earlier, God's death judgment against all the firstborn in Egypt.[39] God's judgment against sin and wrongdoing in Egypt is thus a central feature of his redemption of the Israelites in that same context.[40]

---

[35]There are other new elements as well, but these are not to the point here.

[36]The phrase 'acts of judgment' is in the Hebrew one word, *mishpatim*, the plural of *mishpat*.

[37]In Ex. 21:30 and Ps. 49:7f. a redemption is explicitly linked to a price paid.

[38]The word in 6:6 and 15:13 is גאל, whereas that in 13:13,15 is פדה. However, the two words share a similar semantic range, as shown by their interchangeable use in Lev. 27:27.

[39]The focus upon the firstborn makes it clear that this judgment was less than final: it cannot be that only the firstborn were guilty of sin. Hence this judgment must be understood as in some sense a foreshadowing of, and also a warning regarding, God's final, eschatological judgment.

[40]Within the narrative account of the exodus from Egypt (Ex.6-13), the *redemption* of the Israelites is equivalent to their deliverance (see below): there is, as Vos argues, no particular thought at this point in the text of a price being involved (Geerhardus Vos, *Biblical Theology: Old and New Testaments*, Edinburgh: BOT, 1975, p.114). However, the very substantial emphasis elsewhere in Scripture on the price involved in redemption (again see below) implies that a biblically canonical (systematic) understanding of the redemption from Egypt must - given the use of redemptive language in Exodus - include this aspect of price, in one way or another.

It will be argued now that a full biblical understanding of the exodus from Egypt requires a threefold conception of this deliverance; in other words, God's deliverance, or redemption, was operating at three different levels, or, equivalently, there were three aspects to the deliverance.[41] First, it was a deliverance of the Israelites from their politico-economic oppression in Egypt. This is plain from the text, not least from the way in which God states on two occasions that he knows their condition, and has determined to bring them out from it (Ex. 3:7f; 6:5f). The implication cannot be missed that God's character is such that he is opposed to such oppression of his people, and he will act in judgment against it. Hence, as suggested earlier, God uses this episode to reveal something important about himself and his ways. Oppression of his people, not least in economic life, is not tolerable to God.

Secondly, there is a sense in which God delivered the Israelites from the consequences of *their own* sin. The fact that blood was required for God to pass over the firstborn of the Israelites (12:13) is a clear pointer to the reality of their own sin. Although these narrative chapters of Exodus do not teach an explicit theology of sacrifice and the importance therein of blood,[42] the text is explicit that, were it not for the blood, God's wrath would fall on the Israelites (12:12f, 27): it was only because of the blood that they were spared (12:27). Since God's judgment is just (e.g. Gen. 18:25), it follows that there had to be a just cause for God's judgment to stand over the Israelites. They must have been guilty of sin. Two factors reinforce this deduction. The first is that there is no reason from the text to believe that the Israelites in Egypt were sinlessly perfect; and the witness of Scripture as a whole is, of course, that all have sinned. The second factor is that, elsewhere in the OT, the fact of the sin of the Israelites in Egypt is explicitly stated.[43] In Jos. 24:14 Joshua commands the Israelites to 'put away the gods which your fathers served...in Egypt'. And in Ezekiel chapter 23 it is stated three times that the Israelites had practised harlotry in Egypt (vv8,19, 21).[44] The need for the Israelites to be delivered from the consequences of their own sin - an act of sheer grace on God's part - must therefore be held alongside the importance of their deliverance from oppression.

Thirdly, God's deliverance of the Israelites from Egypt is seen, in the wider Scriptural context, as a *foreshadowing* and a *picture* of God's deliverance from the bondage of sin in *all* its aspects and consequences - and thus foreshadowing

---

[41]No particular significance is intended in the order with which these three aspects are presented here.

[42]Such teaching comes shortly after, especially in Leviticus. For an account of the biblical understanding of blood, see A. M. Stibbs, *The Meaning of the Word 'Blood' in Scripture* (London: Tyndale Press, c1948).

[43]Vos, *Biblical Theology*, presents this powerfully (pp112f.).

[44]Whatever is precisely meant by this 'harlotry', it has to be some form of disobedience against God.

that greater deliverance, won by Jesus Christ's substitutionary death.[45] Ever since the exodus, 'redemption has attached to itself this imagery of enslavement to an alien power'.[46] Hence Jesus refers to the slavery of sin, and to his unique salvific power to make free from sin, for ever, those who believe in him, continuing in his word (Jn. 8:31-36). Romans 8:20-21 explains that the whole of creation is in *bondage* to decay, but will one day be set *free* and obtain the glorious *liberty* of the children of God; and the apostle goes on to explain that Christian believers await 'the redemption of our bodies' (v23). It should be noted, finally, that for the Israelites' redemption to function effectively in this way as a foreshadowing picture, it is at least plausible to say that it had to be a real redemption in its own right (i.e. not *only* a picture or metaphor); and the first two aspects explain that this was indeed the case.[47]

Thus the redemption from Egypt must be understood in this threefold sense: deliverance of the Israelites from politico-economic oppression; deliverance from the consequences of their own sin; and a foreshadowing and a picture of God's unmerited act of deliverance, through the person and work of the Lord Jesus Christ, of all believers, and of the whole of creation, from sin and its effects. These three aspects go together.

That framework of understanding should be kept in mind as this section moves to its final topic, the link between the exodus and the giving of the Law at Sinai. The text of the book of Exodus makes it clear that God's purpose was not only to deliver the Israelites *from* their bondage, but to bring them *to* something new. This new thing was, in the first instance, a meeting of the whole people with the LORD, at the mountain of Sinai. Thus it was that the whole company set out from Egypt, crossed the Red Sea as the LORD acted to part those waters - with the pursuing Egyptians then drowned as the waters returned - and came in due course to Sinai (Ex. 19:1-2).[48]

---

[45]Vos is again very clear on this. He does not explicitly draw out the first of the three above aspects of deliverance - that from politico-economic oppression - but seems to merge that aspect with the third, i.e. with the exodus as a picture, or type, of deliverance from the whole 'objective' aspect of sin. (In Vos' framework, the second of the three aspects in the analysis offered here is termed sin's 'subjective' aspect.)

[46]Vos, *Biblical Theology*, p110. Thus redemption can refer, elsewhere in the OT, to being released from captivity (e.g. Is. 51:11), and to the strong redeemer acting in favour of a dispossessed poor person and against their oppressor (Prov. 23:10-11).

[47]Thus Dillard and Longman say of the exodus that 'this great act of salvation becomes in essence the paradigm for future deliverances' (Raymond B. Dillard and Tremper Longman III, *An Introduction to the Old Testament*, Leicester: Apollos, 1995, p66).

[48]The actual numerical size of the Israelite population that left Egypt is disputed. For contrasting views, see: John Durham, *Exodus*, Word Biblical Commentary (Waco, TX: Word, 1987), p171f.; J. W. Wenham, 'Large Numbers in the Old Testament', *Tyndale Bulletin*, 18, 1967, 19-53; R. K. Harrison, *Numbers*, Wycliffe Exegetical Commentary; Chicago: Moody, 1990, p47; Gordon J. Wenham, *Numbers*, TOTC (Leicester: IVP, 1981), p64.

This meeting with God, however - although referred to initially as a 'sacrifice to the LORD' or a 'feast' to him (Ex. 3:18; 5:1,3) - turned out to be of substantially more significance than was initially indicated.[49] For here at Sinai God made a covenant with the people of Israel. This covenant (19:5) did not *replace* God's earlier promises to Abraham, Isaac and Jacob - verses 1 to 8 of Exodus 6 have already stressed the continuity between those promises and God's action now for the people - but was more a (partial) fulfilment of them. The Mosaic or Sinaitic covenant follows the same pattern as God's earlier promises: it starts with God's unmerited grace, with human obedience coming only in response (19:4-6). There are two significant new features, however. First, this covenant is explicitly with the *people* of Israel, 'the house of Jacob', rather than solely with individuals such as Abraham (and his descendants being included only indirectly). Thus the Israelites' *identity* as the people of God is established in a new way. Secondly, the covenant responsibilities upon the people of Israel include, specifically, obedience to God's voice (v5); and the immediately ensuing narrative makes it clear (partly by means of the dramatic accompanying sights and sounds) that what was said by God's voice comprised 'all these words' (20:1): that is, the Law - given through Moses - commencing in Exodus chapter 20. The giving of the Mosaic Law, therefore, is of great significance.

If, moreover, in response to God's grace, the people obey God's voice and keep His covenant, then God promises them this: 'you shall be my own possession among all peoples; for all the earth is mine, and you shall be to me a kingdom of priests and a holy nation' (19:5f). It is clear, then, that God's deliverance of his people has a corporate dimension: they are not saved solely as individuals, but in order to be a nation, a holy nation. This immediately carries the implication that the behaviour of the people together, and towards one another, will be of central significance. And this is confirmed by the major emphasis in the Law upon relationships and behaviour within the Israelite community. Such relationships and behaviour must conform to the standards and norms set by God. This is, as suggested earlier, precisely the content of *righteousness* and *justice*. So, although the *language* of righteousness and justice is not present in Ex. 19-20, these notions do form a central theological theme here[50] - again endorsing the validity of the theological framework being developed in these two chapters.

Righteousness and justice, moreover, will undoubtedly have implications for the economic life of a community setting out, like Israel, with this newly

---

[49]Given the focus of this chapter on righteousness and justice and their economic aspects, the treatment here of the Sinaitic covenant will be brief, concentrating on those aspects rather than attempting a thorough exegesis.

[50]And the vocabulary of righteousness/*s-d-q* and justice/*mishpat* is certainly present in Ex. 21-23: e.g. 23:6 ('justice'/*mishpat*); 23:7 ('righteous'/*saddiq*); 23:8 ('those who are in the right'/*saddiqîm*).

established identity and purpose. Indeed, the preface to the 'Ten Commandments'[51] (20:2) begins with the recognition that sin and politico-economic bondage is what the Israelites have just come out of. God says: 'I am the LORD your God, who brought you out of the land of Egypt, out of the house of bondage'. It would therefore be inconceivable that God would tolerate economic oppression within this newly established nation, which was meant to be a holy nation. The Law confirms this many times over. Moreover, the first occurrence of the word 'holy' in Exodus is to describe as 'holy' the ground surrounding the burning bush (3:5): that is, the ground which is the precise location for the immediately following declaration of this demonstrably holy God that he has seen the affliction of his people and is about to free them from it.[52] Action to *remove* oppression of his people is part of God's holy character, and therefore the existence of oppression could never be acceptable within a holy nation, within God's 'own possession' (19:5). Economic righteousness and justice will be central in the life of God's holy people.

The Mosaic Law, Righteousness, Justice and Economic Life

Given the commitment of this chapter to follow a structure given by the salvation history of God's redemptive acts (see the Introduction), it might seem strange to focus upon the content of Yahweh's law or instruction, given through Moses (the 'Mosaic Law'). There was, indeed, a sense in which, by bringing the Israelites out of Egypt, God had already redeemed them (Ex.15:13). On the other hand, the wider biblical context demonstrates that redemption was not yet complete. As noted in the previous sub-section, God's purpose in delivering the Israelites turns out to be in order that they would be a holy nation, his own possession. If it were to be the case that in practice they did not obey God's voice, then, as is shown elsewhere in the OT, God would punish them for their disobedience; and God's faithfulness to his covenant promise would mean that he would then, in his grace, take further salvific and redemptive action. Thus the Mosaic Law - and Israel's obedience (or else disobedience) to it - is in that sense an important part of salvation history.[53]

---

[51]The quotation marks are intended as a reminder that many more than ten commandments were given: 'the ten' may well provide the framework for all the rest, but Israel was to obey them all, not the ten only.

[52]This in no way detracts from the often emphasised point that the basic idea of 'holy' is 'separateness', 'otherness'. Precisely because God is unlike sinful humanity, he is utterly opposed to oppression of his people. The Scriptures considered thus far do not address God's attitude towards oppression *outside* the context of his own people; hence this chapter has resisted any attempt to infer conclusions about that. Later chapters will address this question.

[53]Although the subject of *redemptive* action is normally God (so human beings cannot and do not redeem themselves), the Scriptural usage of *salvific* vocabulary does sometimes place human beings as the subject. For example, Paul exhorts the Philippians,

The particular focus of this analysis of the LORD's law/instruction is to seek to discern what it says about righteousness and justice, especially their economic aspects. Thus it is assumed that the Mosaic Law contributes significantly to an understanding of the biblical notions of righteousness and justice. This further assumes that, although the Mosaic Law has a more negative, pedagogic function - revealing to sinners their own unrighteousness, and their need for the grace of Jesus Christ (Gal. 3:19-25) - it also has a more positive function, that of helping to instruct people in the ways of God.

To this must be added an important rider. Jesus taught that he had not come to abolish the Law but to fulfil it (Mt. 5:17-20). In that fulfilment, however, Jesus does not simply restate the Mosaic Law (see Mt. 5:21-48).[54] Rather, he explicates the full meaning of the Law: the meaning to which the OT was always intended to point, but which was not fully brought out within the OT itself. Thus Jesus sums up the Law as: 'You shall love the Lord your God with all your heart, and with all your soul, and with all your mind.' And: 'You shall love your neighbour as yourself. On these two commandments depend all the Law and the prophets' (Mt. 22:40). Christians are not bound by the Law as Law: their obligation and allegiance is to the word of Christ. As Moo puts it: 'What emerges from Jesus' teaching is a shift of focus from the [Mosaic] law to Jesus himself as the criterion for what it means to be obedient to God'.[55] The Mosaic Law has a part to play, when interpreted in the light of the rest of Scripture, in helping Christians to understand the ways of God and the will of Christ; but as the Law it has no direct hold upon them. Christ has fulfilled it in his own person, and therefore its demands as the Law upon the Christian believer have been met, and hence they are no longer demands as the Law upon believers. Christians are *not* in the same place as the OT Israelites with regard to the Law.[56]

Turning now to the Mosaic Law itself - particularly regarding righteousness and justice and their economic aspects - the first point to observe is that the use

---

in the context of God already being at work in them, to *work out* their own salvation (Phil. 2:12f); they were already 'saints in Christ Jesus' (Phil. 1:1), but their salvation was to be worked out.

[54]The view of the Mosaic Law adopted here is developed and defended further in Part III of this chapter.

[55]Douglas Moo, 'The Law of Christ as the Fulfilment of the Law of Moses', in Wayne Strickland (ed.), *Five Views on Law and Gospel* [previously titled *The Law, The Gospel and the Modern Christian*] (Grand Rapids, MI: Zondervan, 1996), p357.

[56]Arising from this last point is one methodological lesson concerning how believers should be informed by the Mosaic Law. That Law expressed God's will for the nation of Israel at that time, but it was not the final revelation of His will for all time. Thus the Law must be understood as a particular codification of God's will for OT Israel. Hence the Law *expresses* amongst other things, 'justice and mercy and faithfulness' (Mt. 23:23; NASB), and it is for understanding of these 'weightier matters' (*ibid.*) that the Mosaic Law should be mined, interpreting it in the light of the rest of Scripture.

of the *s-d-q* (צדק) words in the Law fits well with the central meaning of *s-d-q* as put forward in the previous chapter, and as explained with regard to the Scriptural material so far addressed in the current chapter. Righteousness as conformity to the norms set and commanded by God - the clear meaning with reference to Abraham and his descendants (Gen. 18:19) - is at least part of the meaning of 'righteousness' in Dt. 6:25, where Moses, proclaiming the word of the LORD, says:

> And it will be righteousness for us, if we are careful to do all this commandment before the LORD our God, as he has commanded us.

Righteousness is centrally concerned, therefore, with conforming to the norms - here, the commandment - given by God.[57]

The second main aspect of biblical righteousness - its relational meaning - is also clear in this verse, and in Dt. 4:8, where Moses asks with regard to Israel:

> And what great nation is there, that has statutes and ordinances so righteous/צַדִּיקִם as all this law which I set before you this day?

The giving of the Law, as shown already in the previous section's discussion of the exodus, is in the context of God's covenant relationship with Israel. The initiative for this relationship was from God. The means of entering into that relationship was *not* righteousness - in terms of keeping the Law - but rather was the free, unmerited grace of God.[58] And it was 'before the LORD our God' that Israel was instructed to keep the commandment of this God, a phrase which again emphasises the relational meaning of righteousness: for righteousness is set within the context of their covenant relationship with God.

One task under the heading of the Mosaic Law is to test further the proposal made in the first part of this chapter, namely that the central meaning of *mishpat*/justice in the OT is appropriate treatment of human beings, according to the norms commanded by God for a given relationship. A second task here is to address the content of these norms: that is, to ask what Yahweh's Law/instruction actually means by justice. The starting point will be to list and then examine all the occurrences of *mishpat*[59] within the Law sections of Exodus, Leviticus and Deuteronomy, although in general excluding those occasions where *mishpat* clearly refers to 'ordinances'.[60]

---

[57]The singular 'commandment' (in the Hebrew of Dt. 6:25) helps to signify that the Law was a whole, and that it was the whole Law that was to be obeyed.

[58]Indeed, Dt. 9:4-6 make it plain that God was *not* bringing Israel into the promised land because of their righteousness, for in fact they were a *stubborn* people.

[59]These verses are numbered for convenience in the ensuing analysis.

[60]The plural form of *mishpat* - *mishpatîm* - occurs frequently in the Law, generally meaning 'ordinances' (as RSV). These occurrences demonstrate that the laws and 'ordinances' are all concerned with justice in the general sense - the appropriate

(1)   Exodus 23:6: You shall not pervert the justice/*mishpat* due to your poor in his suit.

(2)   Leviticus 19:15: You shall do no injustice in judgment/*mishpat*; you shall not be partial to the poor or defer to the great, but in righteousness shall you judge your neighbour.

(3)   Leviticus 19:35: You shall do no wrong in judgment/*mishpat*, in measures of length or weight or quantity.

(4)   Leviticus 19:37: And you shall observe all my statutes and all my ordinances/*mishpatim*, and do them: I am the LORD.

(5)   Leviticus 24:22: You shall have one law/*mishpat* for the sojourner and for the native; for I am the LORD your God.

(6)   Deuteronomy 1:17: You shall not be partial in judgment/*mishpat*; you shall hear the small and the great alike; you shall not be afraid of the face of man, for the judgment/*mishpat* is God's; and the case that is too hard for you, you shall bring to me, and I will hear it.

(7)   Deuteronomy 4:8: And what great nation is there, that has statutes and ordinances/*mishpatim* so righteous/*saddiqim* as all this law which I set before you this day?

(8)   Deuteronomy 7:12: And because you hearken to these ordinances/*mishpatim*, and keep and do them, the LORD your God will keep with you the covenant and the steadfast love which he swore to your fathers to keep;

(9)   Deuteronomy 10:18: He [the LORD your God] executes justice/*mishpat* for the fatherless and the widow, and loves the sojourner, giving him food and clothing.

(10)   Deuteronomy 16:18 :You shall appoint judges and officers in all your towns which the LORD your God gives you, according to your tribes; and they shall judge the people with righteous judgment/*mishpat-sedeq*.[61]

(11)   Deuteronomy 16:19: You shall not pervert justice/*mishpat*; you shall not show partiality; and you shall not take a bribe, for a bribe blinds the eyes of the wise and subverts the cause of the righteous.

---

treatment of human beings in various contexts. But the 'ordinances' occurrences in themselves do not add to our understanding of the actual content of 'justice'. Hence those occurrences are generally excluded from the list in the text.

[61] Judgments/*mishpat* of righteousness/*sedeq*.

(12)   Deuteronomy 16:20: Justice/*sedeq*, and only justice/*sedeq*, you shall follow, that you may live and inherit the land which the LORD your God gives you.[62]

(13)   Deuteronomy 17:9: and coming to the Levitical priests, and to the judge who is in office in those days, you shall consult them, and they shall declare to you the decision/*mishpat*.

(14)   Deuteronomy 18:3: And this shall be the priests' due/*mishpat* from the people, from those offering a sacrifice, whether it be ox or sheep: they shall give to the priest the shoulder and the two cheeks and the stomach.

(15)   Deuteronomy 21:17: but he shall acknowledge the first-born, the son of the disliked, by giving him a double portion of all that he has, for he is the first issue of his strength; the right/*mishpat* of the first-born is his.

(16)   Deuteronomy 24:17: You shall not pervert the justice/*mishpat* due to the sojourner or to the fatherless, or take a widow's garment in pledge;...

(17)   Deuteronomy 25:1: If there is a dispute between men, and they come into court/*mishpat*, and the judges decide between them, acquitting the innocent and condemning the guilty,...

(18)   Deuteronomy 27:19: 'Cursed be he who perverts the justice/*mishpat* due to the sojourner, the fatherless, and the widow.' And all the people shall say, 'Amen'.

(19)   Deuteronomy 32:4: The Rock, his work is perfect; for all his ways are justice/*mishpat*. A God of faithfulness and without iniquity, just/*saddiq* and right/*yashar* is he.

It will now be argued that, with regard to the understanding of justice in economic life, at least four main themes or principles emerge from these Scriptures, taken in their context.[63]

---

[62]Strictly speaking, Dt. 16:20 should be excluded from the current list, since *mishpat* is not present. However, *sedeq* occurs twice and, given the substantial overlap between the s-d-q and sh-p-t words (see chapter 2), and their concentrated use within Dt. 16:18-20 (verses numbered (10) to (12) here), this is an important reference for the purposes of the current list. Hence its inclusion.

[63]The focus for the following discussion, then, is the meaning of *mishpat* (taking the above verses in their context); where appropriate, however, the discussion will embrace other verses from the Law which (as will be argued) are relevant to the meaning of justice in economic life.

JUSTICE MEANS APPROPRIATE TREATMENT, ACCORDING TO THE NORMS COMMANDED BY GOD

The central meaning of *mishpat* in these verses is that of appropriate treatment of people ('doing right to people'), according to God's norms, with the *juridical* usage of *mishpat* as a sub-category of this - rather than *vice versa*.[64] This can be seen partly from the three occurrences of the plural (*mishpatim*) included in the list - Lev. 19:37; Dt. 4:8; 7:12 - each of which (as with *mishpatim* generally in the Law[65]) is a general reference to all the commandments and statutes, rather than to specifically juridical matters. Throughout the Mosaic Law the *mishpatim* are typically addressed to all the people, not only judges. The same point can be seen also from those references which do specifically involve juridical aspects. Verse (1), for example - which is part of a short paragraph (Ex. 23:6-8) dealing with matters facing a court or judge - refers to the 'justice due to your poor' (lit. the '*mishpat* of your poor') in his suit. What, though, is this 'justice of your poor'? In the context (making court-type decisions on the basis of the norms set by God) it can refer only to what the law itself lays down as what is just and right with regard to the poor. This will include laws which refer to the poor specifically (such as Ex. 22:25-27, on zero-interest lending and the use of pledges; and Ex. 23:10f, on leaving fallow year produce for the poor); and also laws given more generally, but which obviously apply to the poor if they are a relevant party (such as Ex. 23:12f on the seventh day as a rest day). The same reasoning applies to, for example, Lev. 19:15; 24:22; Dt. 1:17; 16:18-19.

The argument here, then, is that the law defines what is just - what is good and appropriate treatment of people. Decisions in court - juridical decisions - are *derived from* that basis. Hence justice in the Mosaic Law is fundamentally about good and appropriate treatment of people, according to the norms commanded by God in each particular case.[66]

---

[64]'Juridical' here means, broadly, 'pertaining to decisions by a judge'.

[65]E.g. Ex. 21:1; 24:3; Lev. 18:5; Dt. 4:14.

[66]How this biblical notion of justice compares and contrasts with other conceptions is a matter for later chapters. It is worth observing briefly, however, that the notion of justice underlying the Mosaic Law is *not* based on any 'rights' which are inherent to the person, but is based rather on norms *given and commanded by God*. Further, since God is the world's good and loving Creator, the norms he sets match perfectly with what best enables human flourishing in his created order. Thus the norms commanded by God are not arbitrary but appropriate. This is the ontological reality.

That reality must be distinguished from the epistemological question of how (and how much) human beings come to understand with regard to God's will. The OT Israelites had knowledge of the Mosaic Law (part of God's revelation). Outside of special revelation (in the Scriptures and in Jesus Christ), as noted in chapter 2, a much more limited amount of understanding is available to humanity as a result of God's general revelation.

GOD'S JUSTICE INVOLVES JUSTICE TO THE NEEDY

The second main point arising from these verses concerns justice with regard to the poor, the needy and the weak within the community.[67] What is the foundation for the substantial emphasis given, in the verses listed (e.g. Ex. 23:6; Lev. 19:15; Dt. 10:18; 24:17; 27:19), concerning justice and the needy? What is the basis for the justice due to the needy? It can hardly be said that the thrust of these verses is upon 'impartiality', upon treating the needy in precisely the same way as everyone else in the community.[68] For the phrase 'justice due' is used three times with specific reference to one or more groups of needy people, but is not used with reference to the people as a whole. Moreover, as already noted (Ex. 22:25-27; 23:10-11), certain specific behaviour is commanded of the people regarding their treatment of the poor: behaviour which is not commanded regarding their treatment of one another more generally. There is undoubtedly a particular concern for the vulnerable and needy; and the explanation for this concern may well lie in the understanding that the sinfulness of humanity is such that, in all communities and societies, the needy tend to be treated badly and oppressively by the more powerful and better-off people. Certainly the OT Law is blatant and specific in its combatting of that tendency. It does not follow, however, that this is the *foundation* for the Mosaic Law's emphasis on justice and the needy.

Pursuing further this matter of foundation, it is important to notice that the Mosaic Law does refer to the importance of not showing partiality (see Lev. 19:15; 24:22; Dt. 1:17; 16:19).[69] These four references are each in the context of a court or judge making some kind of case decision. In such a context the Law strongly emphasises that partiality (literally, 'noticing the face') must not be shown, either to the poor or to the rich. What does this mean? To refuse partiality to the needy cannot possibly mean refusal to allow the needy the particular help specified (as discussed above) in the Mosaic Law. Therefore the meaning must be that, where there is some kind of dispute between parties, either or both of which is needy, then the resolution of the dispute is to be totally in line with the particular relevant law(s). The relevant law might be one

---

[67]The term 'needy' will sometimes be used in the next few paragraphs as shorthand for these various groups of poor, vulnerable or marginalised people. This shorthand usage should not disguise the significance of the differences in the ways in which different groups were to be treated (as discussed further on in this section). For example, there appears to be a clear distinction in the Mosaic Law between treatment of relatively more 'able bodied' people and treatment of relatively more 'dependent' people. (John D. Mason demonstrates this in 'Assistance Programmes in the Bible', *Transformation* 4(2), April/June 1987, 1-14.) Further attention to this distinction will be given below.

[68]Cf. E. Calvin Beisner, 'Justice and Poverty: Two Views Contrasted', in Schlossberg, Herbert et al (eds.), *Christianity and Economics in the Post-Cold War Era: The Oxford Declaration and Beyond* (Grand Rapids, MI: Eerdmans, 1994), pp57-80.

[69]These references, however, as already shown, do not permit the conclusion that impartiality is the core of the Law's notion of justice.

that stipulates some specific behaviour regarding the poor (e.g. the ban on interest); or, in another case, it might be a law that has no such specificity (such as the law on injuries which result from a quarrel: Ex. 21:18f). But the key point is that the standard for justice is the Mosaic Law. Justice in these cases means treating people in the way that conforms to the Law, to the norms commanded by God for any given relationship. Thus the Law does not appeal, with regard to treatment of the needy, to any 'innate' sense of what is 'just', or 'socially just'. Rather, it refers people to its own standards and norms as the definition and basis of the 'justice of the needy'.

The *foundation* of the Law's emphasis on justice and the needy can now be seen more fully, by combining two things: a recognition of the Law's combatting of the likely maltreatment of the needy; and a recognition that, in all situations, justice means good treatment, treatment according to God's laws - which include specific statements of the 'justice due' to various needy people. It follows from this combination that the ultimate reason why the needy are protected under the Mosaic Law is that this is God's will and pattern. Similarly the reason why the needy are not to be given preferential treatment in criminal cases is, ultimately, that such 'partiality' is not God's will and pattern. God's way is the just way; and the just way is God's way. The foundation of the Law's emphasis upon justice and the needy is, therefore, that God's will is that his just way should be followed, particularly in cases where human nature would tend to push in the opposite direction (whether towards maltreatment and oppression, or towards some inappropriate kind of partiality).

That understanding means that other candidates for the ultimate basis of justice regarding the poor must fall aside. Thus the ultimate foundation of the Law - in terms of justice and the needy - is *not* a concern to ensure they are provided for (although the Mosaic Law's justice includes that concern); nor is it some abstract principle of 'social justice', external to the Law, from which the Law's stipulations are derived; nor is it a desire to ensure that they participate in the community; and nor is the foundation to do with some abstract principle of juridical equality, equality under the law. There can be only one ultimate foundation, only one ultimate 'given': and that is God's own justice, as revealed in the laws he has given for different relationships, conformity to which is the justice he commanded Israel to practise. Moreover, God's norms are appropriate, not arbitrary,[70] both because they arise from his own perfect being and character of righteousness and justice, and because they are the norms which best enable human flourishing.

The main point here is that the Law's justice includes the particular justice due to the needy, but it can never be solely about justice for the needy. This conclusion is corroborated by Dt. 18:3 and 21:17, which specify a 'justice due' not to the needy, but to certain other specified parties, namely the priests (Dt.

---

[70] See footnote 66 above.

18:3) and the firstborn son (Dt. 21:17).[71] Justice means conformity to God's laws and norms, as given for each particular relationship.

JUSTICE IS NOT ONLY ALLOCATIONAL, BUT ALSO CONCERNS THE QUALITY OF RELATIONSHIPS

The third main point to emerge from these verses is that justice in the Mosaic Law is not solely about the allocation of resources - such as food, seed and land - but is also centrally concerned, in the context of how resources are used and shared, with *relationships*. The stipulation of the 'justice due' to the needy, and to others, demonstrates that justice does involve how resources are allocated across members of the community.[72] But this is not the only important thing. For a frequent feature of the OT laws pertaining to the socio-economic treatment of others in the Israelite community is that the treatment commanded is enjoined partly on the basis of how the LORD has treated the Israelite community, and of how the Israelites were treated when they were in Egypt. This teaching on treatment of one another illustrates the emphasis here on the quality of relationships. For example, Dt. 24:17 (from the above list), is only the first part of a sentence. The whole sentence (Dt. 24:17-18) reads:

> You shall not pervert the justice/*mishpat* due to the sojourner or to the fatherless, or take a widow's garment in pledge; but you shall remember that you were a slave in Egypt and the LORD your God redeemed you from there; therefore I command you to do this.

That reference appeals to the Israelites' treatment by Yahweh. Ex. 23:9 appeals to their (entirely opposite) treatment by the Egyptians:

> You shall not oppress a stranger; you know the heart of a stranger, for you were strangers in the land of Egypt.

Further, the laws which give detail on the treatment of the needy - the laws which (as argued above) underlie the phraseology of 'the justice due' to the needy - are evidently concerned with more than allocation. Thus in the law requiring loans, and their cancellation in the seventh year, the one with something to lend is taught to lend to '*his* neighbour, *his* brother' (Dt. 15:2). And, as seen already in verse (1), the concern is for justice to '*your* poor' in his suit (Ex. 23:6). The use of these personal pronouns, and the language of neighbour and brother, is clearly intended to strengthen - rather than distance - the relationships within the community.

Moreover, the basis and pattern for relationships was to be justice, mercy

---

[71]These verses use the identical Hebrew construction as in those which specify the 'justice due' to the needy, i.e. the '*mishpat* of' (*mishpat* in the construct form) such-and-such.

[72]The details of this allocation are considered under the next main point.

and faithfulness - the same justice, mercy and faithfulness shown to the Israelites by the LORD. It has been shown already that righteousness and justice were central for the life of the people of Israel. At the heart of this righteousness was to be love: love for God, and for neighbour. This is brought out very clearly in Dt. 10:12-22. Yahweh states that he requires the Israelites to fear him, to walk in his ways, to love him, to serve him with all their heart and with all their soul, and to keep his commandments and statutes (v12f). The LORD himself has given the example to follow:

> For the LORD your God is God of gods and Lord of lords, the great, the mighty, and the terrible God, who is not partial and takes no bribe. He executes justice for the fatherless and the widow, and loves the sojourner, giving him food and clothing.

And the immediately following words are these (v19):

> Love the sojourner therefore; for you were sojourners in the land of Egypt.

Justice and love are bound together. Love for God and for neighbour - even the sojourner - are bound together. This is at the heart of what is meant by this section's emphasis on the place of relationships within the Law.

It is not being argued here that love and justice are synonymous, nor that they should be. What is being claimed, however, is that - in terms of biblical usage - justice and love are much closer to one another, and are more closely bound together, than they are in much modern thought. This claim can accommodate a critique of what may be termed 'the traditional Christian analysis of neighbour-love'.[73] According to that analysis, neighbour-love is considered to be 'self-sacrificing equal regard which is indifferent to the value of its object'.[74] A more biblical characterization of neighbour-love would be

---

[73]Linda Woodhead, 'Love and Justice', *Studies in Christian Ethics*, 5(1), 1992, p47.

[74]*Ibid.*, p46. This understanding of neighbour-love seems to be deficient in various ways (see Woodhead, *ibid.*). For example, the idea of *indifference to* the value of love's 'object' - whilst perhaps intended to allow a stress on the God-given, rather than humanly-created, value of each person - appears to lack an adequate emphasis on the *unique* significance of each person: created and loved by God as unique. Similarly, the notion of 'regard' speaks of a 'cool, emotionally detached attitude' (*ibid.*, p47), whereas biblical neighbour-love seems to involve the whole person: mind, will and emotion. This is revealed *par excellence* in the person of Jesus himself, for example on the occasion when, on seeing that the people gathering to him were weary and scattered, as sheep without a shepherd, 'he was moved with compassion for them' (Mt. 9:36; NKJ). Thus the Law's appeal to Israelites to 'love the sojourner, therefore; for you were sojourners in the land of Egypt' is to be understood as an appeal not only to a mental comparison between themselves and present-day sojourners, but also to an emotional engagement with the sojourner: 'you know what it feels like, to be a sojourner and to be loved; so love the sojourner in the same way'.

along these lines: 'an active desire for the well-being of the neighbour, and for communion with him or her, based on a recognition of the neighbour's unique worth'.[75] This analysis brings out, for example, the involvement of the whole person in neighbour-love ('active desire'), and the importance of communion and reciprocity (as shown between the persons of the Trinity, which is in turn the model for love within God's people - see, e.g., Jn. 17). The close link between justice and this kind of love is that both justice and love are about the quality of relationships.

Although some conceptions of justice limit it to legal claims and fairness, the biblical conception - as argued in this and the previous chapter - goes well beyond this. Justice is about appropriate treatment of people, according to the norms commanded by God, in the setting of a relationship. Justice, mercy and faithfulness go together. Again, this does not mean that justice and love, or justice and mercy, are synonymous. Love involves an active desire for the well-being of the neighbour, and it involves close communion with that neighbour. Thus love goes further than justice: in particular, it goes deeper and further than any norms would require or suggest. Nevertheless, love and justice, in a biblical understanding, are much closer than is generally conceived.

Returning to the OT's relational framework for justice, it should be noted, finally, that this framework sets out responsibilities for all parties: responsibilities and obligations are reciprocal. Whilst there is heavy emphasis in the Law on the responsibilities of the better-off to treat the needy justly, in accordance with the norms given by God, there are also significant responsibilities, implicitly at least, for the needy themselves. This can be seen especially with regard to the way in which welfare provision was to take place. The principal forms of provision for the more able-bodied people amongst 'the needy' were the legal right to gather the fallow-year harvest (Ex. 23:10f), and the provision of a compassionate loan: in the first instance, an unsecured loan (Dt. 15:1-11);[76] with the possibility also of a secured loan, if the person was still in need (Ex. 21:1-11; 22:26; Dt. 24:10-13).[77] For more dependent people amongst the needy, the provisions included not only a fund of third-year tithes collected specifically for them (Dt. 14:28f; 26:12f), but also the legal right to glean and harvest corners of the fields - a right granted to, specifically, the widows, orphans and strangers (Lev. 19:10; 23:22; Dt. 24:19-21).[78] The key

---

[75]*Ibid.*, p56. The uniqueness of the neighbour's worth derives from him/her having been created by God, in God's image.

[76]Those verses make it plain that the loan was compassionate: in certain cases it would probably amount to a gift; and no interest was to be charged to a fellow Israelite.

[77]The security might take the form of bond-servitude - very different from the dehumanising slavery associated in more recent times with Western countries. Or it might be in the form of specific pledges (Dt. 24:10-13; Ex. 22:26).

[78]This legal right was granted also to those poor called *ani* (Lev. 19:10; 23:22): it can be argued that, in these verses at least, the *ani* are deliberately distinguished from the *ebyon*, who appear to be more able-bodied, since the provision for them includes

point here is that, for all of the needy people, and especially the more able-bodied, the forms of provision specified above generally involve the needy themselves in significant expenditure of effort in order to get hold of the resources made available. To harvest a crop obviously involves considerable effort; to repay a compassionate loan requires sufficient labour, in some context or other, to generate resources in excess of 'living costs'; and gleaning evidently involves considerable labour (illustrated by the case of Ruth in Boaz's field: Ruth 2:9,16).[79]

Thus there were significant responsibilities laid upon the shoulders of the needy, as well as the clearly stated responsibilities, already discussed, laid upon the better-off. This framework of reciprocal responsibilities appears significantly different from many primitive economic settings, in which welfare focused on inter-personal *gift*-giving.[80] A plausible explanation for Israel's distinctiveness in this regard is that, in God's wisdom, his instructions to them recognised that, for the able-bodied, a system of compassionate loans would help to avoid the rival dangers of, on the one hand, stigmatization and, on the other hand, excessive dependency. Similarly, for the more dependent people to be able to play some part in providing for themselves, where they were able so to do, may well have been intended in order to discourage such people from the fallen human tendency towards shirking.[81] Whatever the merits of these explanations, however, it seems clear that the OT Law did establish specific reciprocal responsibilities - and this feature, therefore, is an important aspect of justice in its application to economic life.

---

harvesting the natural growth (Ex. 23:10f). Mason, *op.cit.*, offers a detailed account of all these provsions, and argues the case for the same type of distinction made here, i.e. between able-bodied and dependent groups of needy people. Norbert Lohfink argues for a similar distinction, within the book of Deuteronomy: those without landed property (the Levites, the sojourner/alien, the orphans and the widows) were to be provided for in such a way that they were *not* to be of a lower status than everyone else; for those, however, who had, or might be able to have, landed property, but who were at any given time materially poor, the various provisions (e.g. compassionate loan and bond-servitude) were structured with the aim of those people being able to climb out of poverty. See Lohfink's 1995 Lattey Lecture, published as a booklet, *The Laws of Deuteronomy: A Utopian Project For a World Without any Poor?* (Cambridge: Von Hugel Institute, 1996).

[79]To gain access the fund of third-year tithes would not, however, involve much effort. This provision was specifically for the sojourner, the fatherless and the widow - people who would probably have no land of their own, and thus the most vulnerable people.

[80]Mason, 'Assistance Programmes in the Bible', p4. See also R. Posner, 'A Theory of Primitive Society, with Special Reference to Law', *Journal of Law and Economics* 23, April 1980, 1-53, pp10ff.

[81]See Mason, 'Assistance Programmes in the Bible', pp4-7.

JUSTICE IN THE ALLOCATION OF RESOURCES MEANS THAT
EVERYONE PARTICIPATES IN GOD'S BLESSING

The fourth main point to emerge from this examination of justice/*mishpat*
concerns the nature of the allocation of resources, as prescribed by the Mosaic
Law. In the list of verses presented earlier, the references to the 'justice due' to
various needy groups raise the matter of whether the Law teaches that there is
some kind of 'just share' for each person and household. It has already been
shown that a central feature of justice in the Law is a concern with
relationships. Nevertheless this does not rule out the possibility that justice also
refers to the allocation, or distribution, of resources. The previous sub-section
implied that this might be so. Moreover, once it is realised that, as shown
already, the Law sets out specific provisions regarding various groups, that the
Law in general codifies righteousness and justice for the Israelites, and that
(again as already shown) the phrase 'justice due' is used with clear reference to
specific details of what is to be provided (as well as how), then it is established
beyond doubt that the actual allocation of resources was part of justice.

This in turn raises the question of what sort of allocation the Law
proclaimed to be just.[82] It is argued here that the theological context of the
Mosaic Law - explained earlier - is of vital importance. God had redeemed the
people of Israel from bondage in Egypt, and was bringing them into Canaan,
the land of blessing, as promised to Abraham. The Israelites' responsibility
under the covenant the LORD made with them was that they should obey the
whole commandment he was giving them: if they so obeyed him, then his
blessings would continue.[83] Since God had saved them in order that they would
be a holy *nation*, and since he was bringing all of them into the land of promise,
it is inconceivable, in the context of the covenant promise and covenant
obedience, that any of the people should *not* participate in God's blessing. Put
more positively, the theological principle of the promise to the people of Israel
was that *all* the people would enjoy God's blessing.

This is made clear in the references in Deuteronomy to three (potentially)
vulnerable groups, who had no landed property: the sojourner, the fatherless
and the widows. It is explicitly stated that the Israelites are to ensure that these
groups of people participate in God's blessing. Thus the Israelites are told to

---

[82]This territory is, of course, highly explosive. Multitudes of words have been written
and spoken, sometimes in considerable anger, regarding whether biblical justice favours
some kind of equality in income and/or wealth, or whether it is concerned with only a
minimal provision for the most needy, or whether it is in line with one of the many
positions that can be found between those two. This discussion does not seek to appraise
such viewpoints - this is done in a later chapter - but to understand what is taught, in
context, by the Mosaic Law.
[83]One of several explicit statements within Deuteronomy of all this is Dt. 11.

include these groups in various feasts which celebrate God's blessing (Dt. 16:11,14). It is therefore a fundamental principle of Israel's religious and economic life that everyone enjoys God's blessing.

The same three groups are referred to explicitly in the instructions for the third year tithe.[84] This tithe, it should be noted, carries with it the motive clause 'that the LORD your God may bless you in all the work of your hands that you do' - a clause which again emphasises the theological principle of participation for all in God's blessing, because (to offer a paraphrase) 'as you bless others, so the LORD will bless you'. The instructions for the third year tithe also contain a very important statement which helps to give more detail to our understanding of the kind of allocation seen as just. Are the vulnerable to be given only some minimal provision? Consider Dt. 14:28f again:

> At the end of every three years you shall bring forth all the tithe of your produce in the same year, and lay it up within your towns; and the Levite, because he has no portion or inheritance with you, and the sojourner, the fatherless, and the widow, who are within your towns, shall come and eat and be filled; that the LORD your God may bless you in all the work of your hands that you do.

The key phrase here is 'shall come and eat and be filled'. The verb 'fill' (שׂבע) is used frequently in the OT, and is the same word as the one used to denote the blessing of 'eat and be filled' that is for *all* the people (e.g. Lev. 25:19; Dt. 8:10). Moreover, to eat and *not* be 'full' is God's warning of the outcome if the people walk contrary to God (Lev. 26:26). Thus the vulnerable people are to participate in God's blessing on the same basis as everyone else. Everyone is to take part, and everyone is to share in and enjoy God's blessing.[85]

The emphasis here is not on some kind of numerical 'equality' but on *everyone*. No-one is to be left out; everyone is to be filled. Indeed, the very reference to the existence of these vulnerable groups, and to the other groups of 'poor and needy', assumes the 'inbuilt' tendency for differences to emerge, over time, in the material well-being of different households and individuals, whatever the causes. The emphasis of the Law is not upon permanently wiping out these differences, but on ensuring that everyone participates in God's blessing. The reality of this participation, moreover, will be that the

---

[84]It seems likely that the 'third year' was specific to a given field, so that in *every* calendar year food was coming in for these (potentially) vulnerable groups to eat. See Mason, 'Assistance Programmes in the Bible', p6.

[85]Note that the focus here is on participation in *God's blessing*, rather than, as has become a feature of some recent Christian treatments, participation 'in the life of the community' (e.g. National Conference of Catholic Bishops, *Economic Justice For All: Pastoral Letter on Catholic Social Teaching and the U.S. Economy*, Washington, D.C.: United States Catholic Conference, 1986). The latter phrase, rather remarkably, is at least in danger of excluding God from what are meant to be *theological* accounts of justice and economic life.

significance of those differences will tend to diminish in people's minds. Widows, for example, will not cease to depend on the justice and mercy of others; but everyone will be so focused on sharing in God's bountiful blessing that the vulnerability involved in being a widow is overcome by the reality of God's love demonstrated in the love shown by neighbours and family. Similarly, the provisions in the Law for the relatively more able-bodied 'poor and needy' do not mean an immediate elimination of poverty, but they do work towards that; and, more importantly in the present context, they also ensure that the poor people, as all others in the community, participate in God's rich blessing. Thus in the instructions for the compassionate loan (Dt. 15:1-11) the better-off Israelite is commanded by the LORD to be generous in lending and (if the seventh year is near) in giving:

> You shall open wide your hand to your brother, to the needy and to the poor, in the land.

The fourth aspect of justice in Israel's economic life, then, is that justice involved such a sharing in the allocation of resources that everyone, regardless, participated in God's bountiful blessing.

At this point it is appropriate to restate the four aspects of economic justice that have been discerned from the Law. First, justice means appropriate treatment, according to the norms commanded and set by the Creator God for each particular case. Secondly, God's justice involves justice to the needy. Thirdly, justice is not only allocational, but also concerns the quality of relationships. Fourthly - as just shown - justice in the allocation of resources means that everyone participates in God's blessing. The first and third of these aspects are highly consistent with the theological framework proposed in the previous chapter, and thus serve to endorse the validity of that framework. The second and fourth aspects serve to extend that framework, especially in terms of justice in economic life. As the overview of Scriptural material now moves to other parts of the OT, and into the NT, the compatibility of that developing framework with the Scriptural teaching will continue to be assessed.

Kingship, Justice and Economic Life

The considerable importance attached to the responsibilities and behaviour of the kings, with regard to economic justice, is clear from the Scriptural material examined briefly below.[86] Nevertheless, the place of kingship in God's work of salvation and redemption can be understood fully only in the light of the person of Jesus Christ. Without his coming, the history of Israel's kings recorded in the OT would appear to have very little to do with redemption.[87] However, given

---

[86]There is space here only to refer briefly to a small selection of the relevant material.

[87]Aspects of the Fall are, not surprisingly, strongly evident in all this material.

the life, death, resurrection, ascension and crowning of Jesus Christ, 'the King of kings and Lord of lords' (e.g. Rev. 19:11-16), then the performance of Israel's evidently imperfect kings can be understood as, at one level, preparing the ground for this great and perfect King. Thus it is the wider redemptive context that enables the kingship narratives to be understood as consistent with the OT material already discussed in this chapter - rather than as some kind of rival perspective.[88]

One of the central things that King Solomon requests of God - God having apparently invited Solomon (1 Ki. 3:5) to choose what to ask for - is that he may have 'discernment to understand justice' (v11; NASB). 'Justice' here is *mishpat* (מִשְׁפָּט). The meaning of this request can be seen better by considering it in the light of the surrounding verses (vv9-12; NASB). Solomon prays:

> 'So give Thy servant an understanding heart to judge [שָׁפַט] Thy people to discern between good and evil. For who is able to judge this great people of Thine?' And it was pleasing in the sight of the Lord that Solomon had asked this thing. And God said to him, 'Because you have asked this thing and have not asked for yourself long life, nor have asked riches for yourself, nor have you asked for the life of your enemies, but have asked for yourself discernment to understand justice, behold, I have done according to your words. Behold, I have given you a wise and discerning heart, so that there has been no one like you before you, nor shall one like you arise after you...'

The meaning of *mishpat* here, in the context, is clearly linked closely to Solomon, as king, doing good rather than evil, and to the discerning of good and evil. Solomon requests wisdom to do right, and thus to govern the people rightly. This fits well with the general understanding of justice/*mishpat* developed in the previous chapter: doing right, in conformity to God's norms,

---

Redemption always presupposes sin.

[88]It is the omission of such a redemptive context that seems to explain why Brueggemann, for example, views the Mosaic-covenant perspective and the kingly-wisdom perspective as *alternative* histories of Israel. (See, e.g., Walter A. Brueggemann, 'The Epistemological Crisis of Israel's Two Histories (Jer. 9:22-23)' in John G. Gammie *et al* (eds.), *Israelite Wisdom: Theological and Literary Essays in Honour of Samuel Terrien*, Missoula, MT: Scholars Press, 1978). Brueggemann's approach leads him to claim the following regarding the prophet Jeremiah (regarding, in particular, Jer. 9:22-23: MT): 'Jeremiah asserts that if Judah will have something of legitimate pride, she must *terminate the royal history* which leads to death and embrace the history of the covenant' (emphasis added). This is despite Jeremiah's explicit embracing of a 'royal' perspective in Jer. 22:15f and 33:14-17. Brueggemann's type of approach at least casts doubt on the integrity and coherence of the OT regarding, amongst other things, economic justice. Given a redemptive context, however, the quest for a king - even a king who would bring economic justice (Ps. 72) - can be understood as embraced by God in his salvific purposes: and thus the 'two histories' become aspects of one richer history.

and typically in a relational setting.

The fact that God accepts Solomon's request is made evident immediately in the account (vv16-27) of Solomon's wise treatment in the case of the two women and the infant son. The response of the people is clear (v28):

> When all Israel heard of the judgment [*mishpat*] which the king had handed down, they feared the king; for they saw that the wisdom of God was in him to administer justice [*mishpat*].

A similar verdict is recorded by the visiting Queen of Sheba (10:9):

> Blessed be the LORD your God who delighted in you to set you on the throne of Israel; because the LORD loved Israel forever, therefore he made you king, to do justice and righteousness.

The verb translated here as 'do' is *asah*/עשה - the same verb as that translated as 'administer' in the verse previously cited (3:28). Thus the narrative as a whole states, with considerable emphasis, that Solomon, at least in these early days, was one who did, administered and maintained justice-righteousness.

Psalm 72 explicitly gives to Israel's king a major role in the establishment and maintenance of justice and righteousness.[89] In addition, it recognises that the justice-righteousness involved is *God's*. And it clearly envisages an economic dimension: justice and righteousness involve prosperity and the poor. These three aspects are notably evident in the opening section of the Psalm (vv1-4). First, in combination with the narrative material already discussed, this Psalm makes it plain that, as the OT witness unfolds, specific responsibilities as regards justice-righteousness are placed upon the king that were not placed upon Abraham. Moreover, not even Moses was given this particular role of 'defending the cause of the poor of the people', or of bearing in himself God's own justice.[90] This does not mean that there is no longer any role for local elders with regard to justice: there is no suggestion in the text that those 'decentralised' responsibilities, first enunciated in Ex. 18 and Dt. 1:9-18, are now removed. Nevertheless a particular responsibility is now placed on the king, the national leader.

Secondly, the prayer that the king may have God's justice involves a clear allusion to *God's* action in bringing the Israelites out of Egypt, and in crushing that particular oppressor. Thus the king here is not being asked to do a novel thing, but rather to imitate (at least to some extent) God's justice as he has already demonstrated it. In the Egyptian context, God himself did not expect

---

[89]Note that Psalm 72 is attributed in the MT to Solomon.
[90]Those specific responsibilities were *not* given to Moses in Ex. 18 and Dt. 1: instead, they were delegated to local elders. Moses, of course, never led the people in a settled land, and thus it may not be surprising that he was never given these particular responsibilities. Nevertheless the point here is that the king *is* given them.

the achievement of justice without his leading role; in the same way, in the context of living in the promised land, God does not expect the attainment and maintenance of justice without the leading role of the delegated human authority, namely the king.[91]

Thirdly, the king's role is linked with prosperity and (as already seen) with the poor; and both of these features clearly involve economic life. The word in verse 3 translated by the RSV as 'prosperity' is *shalom*, and the context of the mountains and hills bearing *shalom* for the people supports the suggestion that the meaning of *shalom* here is, at least in part, material:[92] hence the appropriateness of its translation here as 'prosperity' or 'welfare'. But it is also clear that justice and righteousness are necessary conditions for such material well-being. The bearing of prosperity by the hills is 'in righteousness'; and the expectation of such welfare in verse 3 is sandwiched between verses 2 and 4 which both speak strongly of justice for the poor. The call in verse 4 for the king to defend the cause of the poor [*ani*] of the people, to give deliverance to the needy [*ebyon*], and to crush the oppressor clearly involves economic life.[93] Thus Ps. 72 does not simply reaffirm the connection (made explicit in Deuteronomy, and discussed earlier) between, on the one hand, covenantal obedience and righteousness in all dimensions of life (including economic), and, on the other hand, material blessing. Rather it expands on that connection by allotting to the king a particular role in bringing about economic justice for the poor. None of this is at odds with the content of economic justice as found in the Law; indeed this Psalm *assumes* such content, for it retains the obedience-blessing connection just mentioned,[94] including the aspects of that connection which involve justice and the poor, in economic terms. Nevertheless there is here a further unfolding (compared with the revelation given in the Law) in the understanding of justice and economic life, namely the emphasis upon the particular responsibilities of the king to bring about economic justice for the poor and needy. Other parts of the Wisdom literature share this emphasis.[95]

Clearly the Mosaic Law was to be the standard according to which the king was to decide what was, in any given case, just. In this respect the king simply shared the role which the judges had (Ex. 18; Dt. 1): which included ensuring justice for the poor, ensuring they received what was due, according to the

---

[91]This justice is that which he, the Lord, continues to demonstrate: as recognised by, e.g., Ps. 146:7.

[92]As opposed to a meaning which is totally divorced from material aspects, such as a meaning in terms of harmonious relationships *abstracted from* material well-being.

[93]Thus the terminology of 'poor' here must include economic aspects. None of this implies, though, that the meaning is limited to economic life.

[94]Similarly, Solomon's own wealth, which came from Yahweh, was accompanied by the call to obedience to his commandments (1 Ki. 3: 13f).

[95]Thus the same theme is clear in, e.g., Ps. 82:2-4 and Prov. 31:5-9; see also Ps. 45:6f.

Law. And it seems clear that the king was not to do this single-handedly (that was Moses' mistake, Ex. 18): instead, he would have a network of officials and princes. Nevertheless the focusing upon the king of the task of 'doing justice', especially justice for the poor and needy, is an additional emphasis within the OT. The Mosaic Law still had to be interpreted and applied - for which wisdom was required (1 Ki. 3). But the king was now to be the champion of justice and of upholding the Law. That, at least, was the ideal.[96]

In contrast to that ideal, the rebellion of various kings against Yahweh, and their failure to meet the ideal, receives strong rebuke from the prophets, not least Jeremiah. Jeremiah makes strong connections between forsaking God, worshipping false gods, and socio-economic injustice. The first two of these tend to come first (e.g. Jer. 1:16; 2:13). But this heart-rebellion, and choice of non-gods, means that moral restraints are abandoned as regards socio-economic behaviour: hence, e.g., 6:13-15. Jer. 7:5-7 ties together these two aspects ('vertical' and 'horizontal') in the same paragraph; and so do the following verses (7:8-10). In addition v10, referring (amongst other things) to stealing, and to oppression of the alien, the fatherless and the widow (see vv6-9), even speaks of 'all these *abominations*'.

In chapters 21 and 22, Jeremiah shows the particular responsibilities of kings as regards justice; and he compares the good with the bad. The responsibilities of the king are twofold, as summarised in 22:3: in his own dealings he is to 'do justice and righteousness'; and he is, as king, to 'deliver from the hand of the oppressor him who has been robbed' (which is very similar to, though briefer than, the statements in Ps. 72:1-4). The king is to do right; and he is to put things right - all in conformity with God's norms, as appropriate in each particular setting or case. Thus the king is pictured again as the champion of justice and righteousness.[97]

The king's responsibility to do justice does not seem to require him specifically to feed and provide for all the poor and needy. His role, rather, is to defend their cause, to deliver them from oppressors, to 'judge thy poor with justice' (as Psalm 72 prays). This may be summarised as *upholding justice*, by *upholding the Law*. Faithful obedience to the Law by the people would ensure (amongst other things) that the poor and needy were 'satisfied' (see the above analysis of the Law), and that they were appropriately treated.[98] Upholding the

---

[96]Thus there is a sense in which 'Solomon' is presented as a kind of ideal-type of king, an ideal which Solomon himself, and his successors, failed to meet. Solomon's rebellion against God is recorded in 1 Ki. 11: it is clear that the heart of the problem was Solomon's forsaking of God himself (e.g. vv4,9).

[97]One king who blatantly rebelled in this regard is Jehoiakim (one of the kings mentioned in Jeremiah's prologue, 1:3). 2 Ki. 23:35 refers to how he exacted (נשא – cf. p62 above re. Ex. 3:7) wealth from the people, in order to help pay a tax to Pharaoh Neco. This is but one example of exaction/oppression: it is clear from, e.g., Jeremiah, that socio-economic oppression was widespread, not isolated.

[98]Cf. Absalom acting as a king to whom the people had a right of appeal (2 Sa. 15:1-4).

Law would mean that, where this was not the case, those acting unjustly were punished for their wrongdoing, *and* that the poor and needy were henceforth rightly treated. The role of the king was to do these two things. In addition, it is conceivable that, in certain situations, the only way to ensure that the poor received their due might be for the king to collect food and provide it directly to the poor and needy. This was not, then, a specific stipulation: but in certain circumstances it might conceivably be the wise course of action, the best way of applying the Law and its values.

Economic Justice and the Wisdom Literature: Redeemed People Living for Yahweh

Despite the OT's recognition of the need for that righteous Branch, and its acknowledgment of the fact that redemption was as yet incomplete, another strand of the OT deals explicitly with issues concerning what it means for redeemed people - given what was yet to come - to live for Yahweh in the here and now. The Wisdom literature addresses contemporary living by combining the perspectives of creation, Fall and redemption: and the starting point for such wisdom is the fear of the LORD (e.g. Prov. 1:7; 9:10), the fear of the God who 'has sent redemption to his people' (Ps. 111:9f). Therefore the life of wisdom is inextricably linked with the theology of providence, with the recognition (given the perspectives of creation, Fall and redemption) of God's providential and sovereign concern for his world and its inhabitants.[99] And thus it is axiomatic that 'the fear of the LORD is the beginning of wisdom' (Prov.1:7; 9:10; cf. 2:5f).[100]

In the NT, further light is shone on this Wisdom literature with the revelation that Jesus Christ is 'the power of God and the wisdom of God' (Col. 1:24), 'whom God made our wisdom, our righteousness and sanctification and redemption' (Col. 1:30). Thus the Wisdom literature, not least as it addresses justice and economic life, is to be read not only as part of the OT, but also with

---

[99]The close relationship between providence and redemption is stated by Paul Helm as follows: 'it is impossible to separate the events of providence from those of God's redemption, since redemption occurs in history in accordance with the plan of God...[W]hile providence includes common grace, it also embraces the events of God's special grace in redemptive history' (Paul Helm, *The Providence of God*, Leicester: IVP, 1993, p119).

[100]Such an understanding of the Wisdom literature does not seem credible to some of those who utilise the tools of critical scholarship, e.g. R. N. Whybray in his *Wealth and Poverty in the Book of Proverbs*, JSOTSS, 99 (Sheffield: JSOT Press, 1990), for whom the overtly theological references in Proverbs are only 'an interpolation glossing the advice to acquire wisdom above all else' (p104). The understanding offered in the text is perfectly compatible, however, with the canonical understanding of the Wisdom literature advocated by, for example, Brevard S. Childs, *Introduction to the Old Testament as Scripture* (London: SCM, 1979); see especially pp557-8.

NT and Christological eyes.

Given all of that wider context, the interest here is partly in how the understanding of justice in economic life unfolds in the Wisdom literature, and partly in the question of whether the Wisdom literature is harmonious with other parts of Scripture.[101] The approach here will be to focus on selected material in the book of Proverbs, material which illustrates the perspectives found more generally in Proverbs, in those Psalms which can be classified as part of the Wisdom literature, in Job, and in Ecclesiastes.

One clear additional emphasis in the book of Proverbs - compared with the Mosaic Law - is upon the choice, at a very practical level, between righteousness and wickedness in economic life: or, in other terms, between wisdom and folly. Given the importance of a theology of providence, this emphasis is not surprising. In Proverbs the path of economic evil and folly is presented as a very real possibility; and the case against it is not so much (as in the OT Law) that it will destroy the covenant relationship with God, but that it is simply the way of evil and folly, and that the consequences will, sooner or later, be bad. And this is contrasted with the wise way, the way of fearing the LORD - the consequence of which is goodness and human flourishing.[102] One example of the bad consequences of wickedness, in economic terms, is 20:17:

> Bread gained by deceit is sweet to a man, but afterward his mouth will be full of gravel.

Similarly 21:6:

> The getting of treasures by a lying tongue is a fleeting vapor and a snare of death.

Many proverbs *contrast* wickedness and righteousness, as regards economic life, not least in terms of consequences:

> The wage of the righteous leads to life, the gain of the wicked to sin (10:16).

> Treasures gained by wickedness do not profit, but righteousness delivers from death (10:2).

---

[101]Cases such as the following might suggest, in particular, a more favourable attitude to the rich - and less favourable to the poor - than that seen in, e.g., the Exodus and the prophets: 'A slack hand causes poverty, but the hand of the diligent makes rich'; 'The blessing of the LORD makes rich, and he adds no sorrow with it' (Prov. 10:4,22). According to R. N. Whybray, therefore: 'despite the widely differing points of view expressed in the different parts of Proverbs, the book nowhere gives any hint of a changing situation or of a pressing need for change. What we see here is a self-portrait of a society on the whole uncritical of the *status quo*' (*Wealth and Poverty in the Book of Proverbs*, JSOTSS 99, Sheffield: JSOT Press, 1990, p10).

[102] As has been emphasized already, there is a matching between God's will and that which enables human flourishing. This is the moral order that God has created.

One man gives freely, yet grows all the richer; another withholds what he should give, and only suffers want (11:24).

He who sows injustice will reap calamity, and the rod of his fury will fail. He who has a bountiful eye will be blessed, for he shares his bread with the poor (22:8-9).

Amongst the proverbs which apply wisdom and righteousness to specific aspects of economic life is 11:26:

The people curse him who holds back grain, but a blessing is on the head of him who sells it.

To force up the price artificially, therefore (the aim of withholding stock[103]), results in a *curse*, whereas to make goods available for sale leads to *blessing*. There is no doubt here as to which way is wise.

In these and many other references, the notions of justice and righteousness in Proverbs are totally consistent with those examined already from other parts of the OT. Thus the Mosaic Law is specifically upheld at various points (e.g. 11:1; 23:10), with 'balances and scales of justice/*mishpat*'[104] strongly commended (16:11). Part of being righteous is that one 'knows the rights of the poor' (29:7), an understanding central to the righteousness-justice taught in the Law (as shown earlier in this chapter). Further, justice and righteousness in Proverbs have the same emphasis on the quality of relationships as found elsewhere in the OT - they go well beyond any narrow piety. This relational dimension includes: giving to those in need, rather than holding back (21:26); being the opposite of the godless, who would destroy their neighbours (11:9); and having regard even for the life of one's beast (12:10). The strong emphasis on the quality of relationships is also implied in the statement of 29:2:

When the righteous are in authority, the people rejoice; but when the wicked rule, the people groan.

Thus righteousness and justice involve right relationships and appropriate treatment of people, even by those in authority - which is why those people rejoice.

The Wisdom perspective, and its particular teaching in relation to economic life, also include a strong commitment in relation to the poor. As noted already, a righteous person knows the rights of the poor (29:7). In addition, Proverbs encourages kings to judge the poor with equity (29:14);[105] it states that Yahweh 'tears down the house of the proud, but maintains the widow's boundaries' (15:25); and it notes ways in which the wicked seek to accrue wealth through

---

[103]Derek Kidner, *Proverbs*, TOTC (Leicester: IVP, 1964), p94.

[104]I.e. scales that weigh accurately and thus do not cheat purchasers (cf. Lev. 19:36).

[105]A clear parallel to God's judging of 'the peoples' with equity (Ps. 98:9).

oppression and other forms of immorality (e.g. 15:17; 17:23). Further, the invocations to be kind to the poor and to give generously (e.g. 14:21,31),[106] and not to oppress the poor (22:16; 28:3) - if understood in the context of the OT Law (which, as shown earlier, is radical in its programme for combatting poverty) - are radical. Hence Ceresko argues that the proverbial injunctions could represent an attempt 'to reinforce and promote the traditional networks of mutual aid toward those suffering misfortune among the families and clans of Israel, as enjoined by the covenant laws and customs'.[107] The argument of the present chapter is that, bearing in mind all the discussion above, this is not merely a possible interpretation, but by far the most valid. This is reinforced by the recognition of the writer of Ecclesiastes that oppression of the poor is very real but is also (by implication) thoroughly displeasing to God (Eccl. 3:16; 5:8).[108] It is further reinforced in the book of Job, by Job's account of his passionate efforts to defend the poor and remove oppression (Job 29:7-17).[109]

Taken as a whole, then, the Wisdom literature extends the understanding of economic justice already found in the OT, by applying it in specific contexts, and by drawing out the life-and-death contrast between, on the one hand, wisdom and righteousness, and, on the other, folly and wickedness. In broader terms, the Wisdom literature, whilst sharing the perspectives of creation, Fall and redemption, as already found in the OT, is particularly insightful, not least as regards economic justice, because of its emphasis on God's providence and sovereign over-ruling in day-to-day economic life.

The Old Testament Prophets on Economic Justice: The Depths of Sin and the Depths of Redeeming Grace

Continuing under the general heading of economic justice in the light of

---

[106]A commitment originating with Yahweh himself, according to Ps. 112:9 (a Psalm generally classified within the Wisdom literature: see Leslie C. Allen, *Psalms 101-150*, Word Biblical Commentary, Waco, TX: Word, 1983; p95).

[107]Anthony R. Ceresko, *Introduction to the Old Testament: A Liberation Perspective* (London: Geoffrey Chapman/Maryknoll, NY: Orbis, 1992), p284. The consequences of taking the OT as Scripture are again very different from those of frequently questioning its validity on the grounds of critical scholarship: herein seems to lie the most plausible explanation for Whybray's claim, regarding poverty and the book of Proverbs, that 'nowhere is any possibility of eliminating it envisaged' (R. N. Whybray, *Wealth and Poverty in the Book of Proverbs*, JSOTSS 99, Sheffield: JSOT Press, 1990, p113).

[108]Note that each of these references explicitly sees justice and righteousness as the precise opposite of actual practice (whether oppression of the poor, or plain wickedness). Thus the writer can scarcely be commending such malice. However, since his goal is not prophetic denunciation but to call his readers to shun vanity, he is not concerned in the text to call for action to combat poverty.

[109]Efforts which are explicitly described in terms of righteousness and justice (29:14).

redemption,[110] this final section of Part II considers the teaching of the OT prophets. Matters of socio-economic justice and injustice are prominent in the prophetic material, and there are many details which merit analysis, but the relatively brief treatment here is confined to three issues: economic justice and the nation's rebellion against God; God's response of judgment and grace; and economic justice and righteousness in the prophets compared with the rest of the OT.[111]

ECONOMIC JUSTICE AND THE NATION'S REBELLION AGAINST GOD

The earlier section on kingship has already made brief reference - in the context of the injustices of successive kings of Israel - to economic wrongs on the part of the people of Israel.[112] The focus here is on the people of Israel, and also on economic injustice in the surrounding nations. Thus the emphasis is on people and nation rather than on the king.

Justice and righteousness in economic life is an important theme in, amongst others, Isaiah, Jeremiah, Ezekiel, Hosea, Amos and Zechariah.[113] Whilst some of these references are to the behaviour of individuals as individuals (e.g. Ezk. 18:5-24), the majority are addressed to the people or nation as a whole (e.g. Is. 58:1-14; Am. 2:6); or, on occasion, to particular communities within the nation (e.g. Am. 4:1-3). The consistent message, in this regard, to the people of Judah and Israel is to rebuke them for their economic injustice, and then to call them to repentance and to the re-establishment of justice and righteousness in economic life. Two of the key emphases here are on *social* and *communal* behaviour and responsibility, and on the treatment of economic behaviour - at the corporate level - in Godward, theological terms, i.e. as a matter of sin and repentance.[114] These emphases are particularly significant in the consideration of the *content* of economic justice in the Scriptures.

Underlying the emphasis on social/communal (not simply individual) behaviour - not least in economic terms - is a clear understanding that a nation or community is a real entity in its own right.[115] And this does not seem to be

---

[110]Which is the theme of Part II as a whole.

[111]Although the treatment here of these three issues is somewhat brief, it is intended to give a sense of the whole with regard to the prophetic material. Thus the twofold claim here is that the teaching of the OT prophets on these issues is plain, and that the text provides a balanced summary of that teaching.

[112]Whether the southern kingdom, or the northern, or Israel before the political divide.

[113]See, for example: Is. 1:17,21,27; 10:1f; 28:6,17; 42:1-4 (see below for the socio-economic dimension of the use of *mishpat* here); 51:4; 59:8-15; 61:8; Jer. 5:28; 7:1-10; 17:11; 21:11; Ezk. 18:5ff; 22:29; 33:12-16; 45:8-11; Hos. 12:1-9; Am. 2:6-8; 4:1-3; 5:10-15; Zec. 7:8-10. (See also the following footnote.)

[114]These two themes emerge very clearly from, for example, the texts listed in the previous footnote.

[115]This is the case for pagan nations as well as for Israel/Judah: see, e.g., Am. 1:1 - 2:5. There is no claim here that the prophets were totally novel in this understanding of

only a metaphysical reality, with no linkage to actual behaviour. Rather, the understanding is of behaviour patterns and value-commitments which become *embedded* in social and communal practice. An example of this is seen in Is. 10:1-2:

> Woe to those who decree iniquitous decrees, and the writers who keep writing oppression, to turn aside the needy from justice and to rob the poor of my people of their right, that widows may be their spoil, and that they may make the fatherless their prey!

The prophet speaks here of a case where oppression has, in a travesty of justice, become legally permitted: 'decreed' and 'written'. These iniquitous laws evidently did not write themselves: rather, they arose from the behaviour and values of certain people.[116] But the effect of them becoming decreed and written is that their force is thereby passed on to others, over time. Current injustice is reinforced - unless radical counteracting steps are taken.

The second emphasis is equally important, namely that the economic behaviour of people in community and society is directly to do with the relationship between that community or society and God. Sin is always rebellion against God (cf. Gen. 3), and this is true for communities as well as individuals. One of the powerful ways in which this is taught by the prophets is by emphasizing the close link between idolatry and injustice. These are not two totally unrelated types of sin, which merely happen to co-exist, at various times, within Israel. Rather, they both express Israel's heart, the choice of rebellion against Yahweh. And, more than this, they are directly related to one another. In the same way that the Law taught that faithfulness to Yahweh and the doing of justice go together,[117] the prophets teach that unfaithfulness to Yahweh and the doing of injustice go together. Yahweh is the only God who makes personal commitment to him and mutual commitment to one another inseparable. Therefore, when some false idol is adopted in place of, or even alongside, Yahweh, socio-economic justice is necessarily turned to oppression. The latter is no accident, no chance outcome: rather, it is part and parcel of the same underlying rebellion against God and his way. Thus it is that the prophet Isaiah can, in one parapraph, condemn the people of Israel for decreeing iniquitous laws (10:1-4) and, in the next, condemn her idolatry as he proclaims judgment against 'Jerusalem and her idols' (10:11).

---

corporate behaviour and responsibility: the earlier treatment of the Mosaic Law made it plain that Israel was addressed as a nation, not simply as a collection of individuals. Nevertheless the degree of emphasis in the prophets on the corporate dimension, especially regarding economic life, is also clear; hence the presentation offered in this sub-section.

[116]A similar example is Am. 5:12, which refers to the legally sanctioned oppression of the needy ('turning aside the needy in the gate').

[117]See the first part of this chapter.

In the same way, economic injustice is necessarily found alongside what has become a mere facade of faithfulness to God in what might be termed 'religious life'. This is plain from Amos' warning to the northern kingdom (Am. 5:4-7). It would do no good were they to have further 'religious' festivals or pilgrimages; such would not make up for their perverting of justice and righteousness. Rather they had to seek Yahweh and live. What did that mean? Verses 14 and 15 of chapter 5 explain:

> Seek good, and not evil, that you may live; and so the LORD, the God of hosts, will be with you, as you have said. Hate evil, and love good, and establish justice in the gate; it may be that the LORD, the God of hosts, will be gracious to the remnant of Joseph.

To establish justice in the gate is not *identical* with seeking the LORD: but the two are inseparable.

GOD'S RESPONSE OF JUDGMENT AND GRACE[118]

The previous pages have observed something of the depths of Israel's sin, as recorded by the prophets, especially as a people and in terms of economic life. Yet it is clear that the rationale for God's word through the prophets was not to catalogue the sins of the people. For the theological context of the prophetic material is always God's covenant with his people; and God's covenantal faithfulness - despite their unfaithfulness - means that, throughout the prophets, a central theme is God's redemptive mercy and grace. This is the rationale.

God's response to Israel's sin is not *solely* grace, of course. The prophets present to the covenant people a choice: repentance, or judgment. God's grace does not remove their responsibility. But, in his patience, he warns them again and again of the day of judgment to come, in order that they might turn to him and live.[119] Further, in his sovereign grace, God promises that the day is coming when he himself will make his people new (Jer. 31:33; Ezk. 36:26). Again this does not remove their responsibility (cf. 1 Pet. 1:15), nor the severity of the warnings of judgment (cf., e.g., Mt. 7:21-27); but it does point to the magnitude of God's immeasurable mercy.

The emphasis that is especially relevant here, however, is that God's redemptive grace, in the particular context of the people's corporate wrongdoing in economic life, entails a radical returning to justice and righteousness. This is a very powerful theme throughout the prophetic material. Thus in Isaiah chapter 58, the prophet proclaims that Israel's religious piety and

---

[118]This short sub-section does not directly expand the understanding of the *content* of economic justice in the Bible: but it does address a theme which is important for a balanced overall understanding of justice and economic life.

[119]For the nation of Israel, that day - at least in its first sense - did come: hence the exiles to Assyria and to Babylon. But judgment in its second sense - final judgment for all of the human race - is still delayed: again because of God's mercy and patience (Rom. 2:4).

fasting counts for nothing before God, because of their practice of socio-economic oppression (vv1-5). In verse 2, he speaks of their apparent daily seeking of the LORD, '*as if* they were a nation that did righteousness' - which in practice they do not do. Yet the surrounding chapters contain many promises of God's redemptive, salvific action in and for his people.[120] What this redemption entails for the people's behaviour is made plain in 58:6-9a:

> "Is not this the fast that I choose: to loose the bonds of wickedness, to undo the thongs of the yoke, to let the oppressed go free, and to break every yoke? Is it not to share your bread with the hungry, and bring the homeless poor into your house; when you see the naked, to cover him, and not to hide yourself from your own flesh? Then shall your light break forth like the dawn, and your healing shall spring up speedily; your righteousness shall go before you, the glory of the LORD shall be your rear guard. Then you shall call, and the LORD will answer; you shall cry, and he will say, Here I am."

Here is their responsibility; here is the way of true righteousness (v8) and true glory.

The same theme of repentance, of a decision to turn back to God and to justice and righteousness - not least in economic life - is found in, for example, Jer. 21:11 - 22:4; Mic. 6:1-8; and Zec. 7:8-10. And the warning which repeatedly comes alongside that theme is, where no such radical repentance occurs, of severe judgment.

ECONOMIC JUSTICE: THE PROPHETS COMPARED WITH THE REST OF THE OLD TESTAMENT

The argument here is that the teaching of the prophets on economic justice is entirely harmonious with that in the rest of the OT. This does not mean that they simply restate what was said, for example, in the Law - for they do not (as is shown below). However, it does mean that different emphases within the OT do not undermine one another but, rather, reinforce one another.

The section of prophetic material which is nearest to a restatement of the Mosaic Law is in Ezekiel chapter 18, where the prophet lists a series of actions (vv6-9) which describe what it is to be righteous, and to do what is lawful and right (v5) - actions which are each drawn directly from the Law, and several of which involve economic behaviour[121]. The context, however, makes it plain that Ezekiel is not calling upon the Israelites in precisely the same way that Moses did when the Law was first given. For part of the thrust of chapter 18 is that there were evidently many amongst God's people who were *not* righteous (e.g. vv24f). It is not enough for such people simply to start obeying the Law. This word of the LORD closes as follows (18:30-32):

---

[120]E.g. 56:1b; 57:14-18; 59:20.
[121]See verses 7 & 8.

"Therefore I will judge you, O house of Israel, every one according to his ways, says the Lord GOD. Repent and turn from all your transgressions, lest iniquity be your ruin. Cast away from you all the transgressions which you have committed against me, and get yourselves a new heart and a new spirit! Why will you die, O house of Israel? For I have no pleasure in the death of any one, says the Lord GOD; so turn, and live."

The phrase which is novel here is this: '...get yourselves a new heart and a new spirit!' But from where can they get such a new heart and spirit? If it was solely in the hands of these people, then this is not good news at all: they are the problem! However, later in the book Ezekiel returns to precisely these things, a new heart and a new spirit, and proclaims that God himself will bring them into being (36:26f). Thus Ezekiel is not simply restating the Mosaic Law, but is proclaiming the addition, by God, of the missing ingredient.

In so doing, Ezekiel demonstrates that the purpose of the Law, ultimately, is that it be written on the heart: he upholds the Law totally, but also proclaims the need for, and the reality of, a new heart.[122] Jeremiah made this link between Law and a new heart explicit; for in 31:33 he proclaims this word from the LORD:

But this is the covenant which I will make with the house of Israel after those days, says the LORD: I will put my law within them, and I will write it upon their hearts; and I will be their God, and they shall be my people.

In a similar way Amos also proclaims the importance of internalizing the Law. This can be seen from his assault on the economic injustice rife in his day. As well as more general admonitions regarding such injustice (e.g. 2:7; 8:4), Amos addresses some specific cases of oppression, notably in 2:6 and 8:6:

Thus says the LORD: "For three transgressions of Israel, and for four, I will not revoke the punishment; because they sell the righteous for silver, and the needy for a pair of shoes - they that trample the head of the poor into the dust of the earth, and turn aside the way of the afflicted; a man and his father go in to the same maiden, so that my holy name is profaned..." (2:6f)

Hear this, you who trample upon the needy, and bring the poor of the land to an end, saying, "When will the new moon be over, that we may sell grain? And the sabbath, that we may offer wheat for sale, that we may make the ephah small and the shekel great, and deal deceitfully with false balances, that we may buy the poor for silver and the needy for a pair of sandals, and sell the refuse of the wheat?" (8:4-6)

In the phrases about buying and selling the poor and righteous for silver, and

---

[122]This 'internalizing' of the Law has implications for the content of economic justice, as will be shown below.

the needy for sandals or shoes, Amos seems to be referring not to slavery as such (which the Law permitted) but rather to slave-*trading*, to the selling and buying of slaves between owners.[123] Such trading contravenes the specifics of the Law: in particular, Israelites were not to be sold as slaves (Lev. 25:42); and slaves were to be freed after 6 years, and thus *not* sold on to some other 'owner' (Ex. 21:1-6; also Dt. 15:1-18). It follows that the reference to the price of such 'deals' ('the silver' for some; 'a pair of sandals' for others) is a powerful further rebuke: in other words, 'you trade *people* for *cash*' - or even for a mere pair of sandals.

The background in the Mosaic Law indicates that Amos' rebuke is drawn from the Law, as well as from conscience. He compares the behaviour of Israel against the standard set by the Law. It follows that Amos' understanding of what 'oppression' consists of is based, not only on moral intuition, but on the Law revealed by God. To treat the needy in the opposite way to that required by the Law is to oppress them.[124]

The importance of the Law to Amos is further confirmed by his frequent explicit references to iniquities, transgressions and sins - terms which would, to an Israelite, automatically be heard as references to breaking the Law, in one or more respects. Thus the chief wrong of Samaria's southern neighbour, Judah, was that they rejected the law of the Lord, and did not keep his statutes (2:4). Similar references to Israel/Samaria include 3:2,10,14; 4:4; and 5:12 - which directly associates 'transgressions' and 'sins' with afflicting the righteous, taking a bribe (explicitly ruled out by Dt. 16:19 and Ex. 23:8), and turning aside the needy in the gate (explicitly ruled out by Ex. 23:6).

Thus Amos draws very close links between righteousness-justice, the Law, and their implications for economic life. The Law has played a major part in his identification of what was wrong, of how Israel had turned 'justice to wormwood' and had 'cast down righteousness to the earth'. It follows that the true repentance that Amos was calling for - 'let justice roll down like waters, and righteousness like an ever-flowing stream' (5:24) - must also involve a

---

[123]The alternative interpretations are either that the phrase 'for a pair of sandals' (Am. 8:6) is a reference to illicit selling onto slavery; or that Amos is referring to people being forced into debt slavery, i.e. slavery because they cannot pay debts, even (in these cases) trivial debts. These interpretations are presented by F. I. Andersen and D. N. Freedman, *Amos*, The Anchor Bible, 24A (New York: Doubleday, 1989), pp312f. However, the first of these fails to make sense of the phrase 'for silver' (2:6; 8:6); and the second makes sense only of 2:6, and not of the parallel in 8:6 where 'buy' rather than 'sell' is used. Thus the most plausible interpretation is that the poor/righteous are being both bought and sold as slaves, i.e. traded as slaves.

[124]The same is true for Ezekiel - see 18:5ff, where oppression and specific requirements of the Law are dealt with directly alongside one another - and indeed throughout the prophets. The teaching of the Law (see section II.C above) was that God's justice involves justice to the needy. Oppression of the needy, therefore, is precisely the opposite, i.e. withholding or removing that which is due.

central role for the Law. This is not a matter merely of strict adherence to the Law,[125] but of internalizing the Law, being continually taught by it, so that in both its detail and its principles it is followed ever more closely, as a central part of what it means to love God with all one's heart, soul and strength (Dt. 6:4-6).

As this last section covering the OT (under the general heading of redemption) draws to a close, it is appropriate to note the consistency and harmony which has been found in the OT - whether in the Mosaic Law, the Wisdom literature, the Psalms or the prophets - regarding the content of justice and righteousness, and, in particular, in the economic aspects of justice and righteousness. This harmony has been especially noticeable given the approach of this chapter in examining the *unfolding* of the teaching on economic justice, in the context of the unfolding of God's words and action in redemption and salvation. Four main aspects of economic justice have been discerned from the Law (section II.C above), and these are reiterated, and expanded upon, throughout the OT, namely:

1.   Justice means appropriate treatment, according to the norms commanded by God for each particular case - norms built into the moral order of creation.
2.   God's justice involves justice to the needy.
3.   Justice is not only allocational, but also concerns the quality of relationships.
4.   Justice in the allocation of resources means that everyone participates in God's blessing.

III. Economic Justice in the Light of the Person and Work of Jesus Christ, the Redeemer[126]

The first two parts of this chapter have noted, at various points, how the OT looks forward to, and expresses humanity's desperate need for, a Redeemer. The good news proclaimed with boldness and joy throughout the NT is that the Lord Jesus Christ is this Redeemer, that he has come, and that he has secured

---

[125]See D. A. Hubbard, *Joel and Amos*, TOTC, (Leicester: IVP, 1989), p168, commenting on 5:7.

[126]As is the case throughout this chapter, the aim of this section is to focus on the content of economic justice, as it is unfolded through the Bible, and thus to obtain a clear sense of the whole, as regards justice and righteousness in their application to economic life. Hence this section does not seek to provide a thoroughgoing analysis of, say, Christology in the NT, or of redemption in the NT, but, rather, restricts itself to the question at hand. Consequently - and also because some of the relevant NT material has already been addressed in chapter 2 - this part of the chapter is relatively short. This does not mean, of course, that it is any less significant.

redemption.[127] Thus the apostle Paul declares that Jesus is the Father's beloved Son, 'in whom we have redemption, the forgiveness of sins' (Col. 1:14). The question at hand in this final part of the chapter is to examine how the understanding of the content of economic justice unfolds further in the light of the person and work of Jesus Christ. It should be noted immediately that the NT, in its material regarding justice in the light of redemption and salvation, is clear that it builds upon, rather than replaces or displaces, the OT material. This has already been demonstrated at length in chapter 2.[128] In particular, the NT usage of δικαιοσύνη embraces both the 'righteousness' and the 'justice' emphases which are so profound and frequent in the OT. Thus the consistent understanding throughout the Scriptures is that justice means practical righteousness in human relationships, conforming in general to the norm of appropriate treatment of people, and in particular to the norms commanded by God for any given relationship.

Focusing especially on the content of economic justice, an important question that must now be addressed is the role today of the Mosaic Law. Three other matters of vital importance to be dealt with here - rather more briefly - are the economic dimension of relationships within the Christian community, the meaning in the Scriptures of economic 'oppression' (especially in a wider Christological context), and the significance of eschatology - the consummation of the kingdom of God.[129]

The Role of the Law in a Christological Conception of Economic Justice

The instructions in the Law, given by God, through Moses, to the OT people of Israel, contain a substantial amount of material concerning economic life, as seen earlier in this chapter. Nevertheless, there is considerable controversy regarding the application or relevance of the Mosaic Law in the lives of Christian believers, not least in terms of economic matters.[130] In order to make

---

[127]See, e.g., Lk. 1:68; 2:38; 1 Cor. 1:30; Gal. 3:13; Rom. 3:24; Eph. 1:7; Tit. 2:14; Heb. 9:12-15; Rev. 14:1-5. It must be noted that the first coming of the Redeemer anticipates the second coming which is as yet still awaited: this future hope is, as noted earlier, an essential component of the salvation-historical framework within which economic justice is to be understood.

[128]See sections I and II of chapter 2.

[129]The issues regarding these latter three matters, in the present context, are far less complex that those regarding the role of the Mosaic Law. Hence they are treated far more briefly here.

[130]For example, the theonomist and 'Christian Reconstruction' schools of thought argue both that the Law essentially applies in all its original detail (except in ceremonial aspects), and that its application to economic life requires a largely laissez-faire and free market economy (e.g. Greg Bahnsen, *Theonomy in Christian Ethics*, Nutley, NJ: Craig Press, 1977; Gary North, *Leviticus: An Economic Commentary*, Tyler, TX: Institute for Christian Economics, 1994). On the other hand, Donald Hay argues both that the OT

progress in understanding the content of economic justice, it is necessary first to examine the more general question of the Law's relevance today.[131]

There are five key elements to the approach proposed here regarding this question.[132] First, as Moo puts it: 'It is the law *as fulfilled by Jesus* that must be done, not the law in its original form'.[133] This refers to Jesus' own teaching in Mt. 5:17-48. The logic of this interpretation rests partly on exegeting vv17-20 in the light of the six cases which follow. These cases show that the essence of how Jesus 'fulfills' the law is not in his explanation or extension of it, but rather that he proclaims the standards of kingdom righteousness that were anticipated in the law.[134]

Secondly, the attention of the NT, as regards Law as much else, is Christ-centred. 'What emerges from Jesus' teaching is a shift of focus from the law to Jesus himself as the criterion for what it means to be obedient to God'.[135] This is a conclusion drawn from the Synoptics more broadly (especially Mt. 19:3-12; Mk. 7:1-23; Mt. 28:19f). This conclusion is a very important Christological point.[136]

Thirdly, the apostle Paul teaches that love is the fulfilling of the law (Rom. 13:8-10; Gal. 5:14). The text cannot mean that he who loves his neighbour has in actual fact obeyed the law in all its detail. Rather, he has fulfilled it in the sense that he has done that to which the law always pointed forward. The parallel with Jesus fulfilling the OT, and his teaching fulfilling the OT law (the second argument above), is very important.

Fourthly, Paul teaches that Christians are not under the law (Rom. 6:14,15; 1

Law, along with the rest of Scripture, provides a set of *principles* for economic life - rather than a detailed codebook - and that these principles entail a radical critique of laissez-faire economic thought and practice (*Economics Today: A Christian Critique*, Apollos: Leicester, 1989). This chapter does not address issues to do with laissez-faire economics, but it does focus, in the current part, on the issues regarding the Mosaic Law.

[131]The present discussion is limited to the Law's relevance to Christian believers; the further, and important, matter of how the Mosaic law relates to *non-Christians* today is addressed (indirectly, at least) later in the book.

[132]The view proposed here is similar to that propounded by Douglas Moo, 'The Law of Christ as the Fulfilment of the Law of Moses: A Modified Lutheran View', his chapter in Wayne Strickland (ed.), *Five Views on Law and Gospel* (Grand Rapids: Zondervan, 1996) = *The Law, The Gospel and the Modern Christian* (Grand Rapids, MI: Zondervan, 1993).

[133]Moo, *ibid.*, p353.

[134]Cf. Moo, 'The Law of Christ', p352. For similar arguments, see D. A. Carson, *Matthew*, The Expositor's Bible Commentary, Vol. 8 (Grand Rapids, MI: Zondervan, 1984), and Vern S. Poythress, *The Shadow of Christ in the Law of Moses* (Phillipsburg, NJ: P&R Publishing, 1991).

[135]Moo, 'The Law of Christ', p357.

[136]These first two arguments run closely together; but it is helpful to distinguish them.

Cor. 9:2 [four occurrences]; Gal. 3:23; 4:4, 5, 21; 5:18). Thus 'the Christian lives in a new regime, no longer dominated by the law with its sin-producing and condemning power, but by Christ and the Spirit'.[137] So Christian believers are not - unlike the OT Israelites - bound by the Law as Law. Christians are certainly to regard the Law as holy, just and good - for such it is.[138] They are to rejoice - as does Psalm 19, for example - in the law of God, in this perfect expression of God's will for His people in the OT. But they are also to remember that they do not live according to a written code, but by the Spirit who writes the law and word of God in their minds and hearts.[139]

Fifthly, Christian believers *have* fulfilled the Law. How? By their incorporation into Christ, and hence their possession of all the benefits achieved by his life on earth, and especially his death on the cross. Romans 8:4 (in context, of course) is a key verse here. Note that Paul speaks of the demand of the Law in the singular: το δικαίωμα τοῦ νόμου (not the unwarranted plural 'righteous requirements' - imposed by the NIV). And the passive form of the verb πληρόω points away from *any* activity here on the part of human beings.[140] Hence 'believers who are "in Christ" and led by the Spirit fully meet the demand of God's law *by having it met for them in Christ*'.[141]

Clearly the theme of fulfilment runs very strongly through these five arguments. (The fact that the Greek uses the πλη- root in several of the relevant verses is striking, but by itself is of course not conclusive.) This helps to make a powerful theological case. Here we have Christology, salvation history, OT and NT, the Gospel, and even a little pneumatology. A complete picture will require two other elements: creation, and eschatology; and these are dealt with elsewhere in this chapter.

A possible problem with the type of framework sketched out above is that it might seem inconsistent. This is suggested by both Bahnsen and Kaiser,[142] for example, with regard to Moo's argument, which is similar to the one offered above. The criticism here revolves around Moo's claims that, on the one hand, the Mosaic law does not directly apply to Christians, and, on the other hand, that what he calls 'the essential "moral" *content* of the law'[143] *is* applicable to believers. A second charge - irrespective of whether Moo's argument here is ultimately inconsistent - is that such an approach is so dialectical that it is simply unclear (Bahnsen, e.g. pp384, 390), and (logically related) that it is so unclear that the only resultant moral teaching will be confusing, and hence

---

[137] Moo, 'The Law of Christ', p366.

[138] Cf. Rom. 7:12.

[139] 2 Cor. 3:6; cf. Heb. 8:8-12.

[140] Moo, 'The Law of Christ', p371.

[141] Moo, *ibid.*, p372 (emphasis added). This interpretation of Rom. 8:4 is defended further below.

[142] In Strickland, *Five Views on Law and Gospel*.

[143] Moo, 'The Law of Christ', p376 (Moo's emphasis and notation).

immoral behaviour will inevitably follow (Kaiser, *op.cit.*, p400). The problem may be that Moo has not adequately defined what he means by 'the essential "moral" *content* of the law'. In order to achieve that, it is necessary, *but not sufficient*, to build a Christological framework. As Bahnsen points out (p390f), his own theonomic approach is also explicitly Christological.

One important issue here concerns 'methodology' in the relationship between OT law and NT usage. Two rival rules are often offered in this regard. One says: 'all OT laws are revoked unless specifically affirmed in the NT'. (This approach tends to rely, in practice, on a tripartite separation of OT laws into moral, civil and ceremonial laws, with the further rule that only the moral law still applies in the NT era. This approach clearly struggles with a verse like Lev. 20:15, which appears to combine moral and civil aspects.[144]) The alternative - that of theonomy - says: 'all OT laws are affirmed, unless specifically revoked in the NT'. The emphasis of Scripture, however, is upon fulfilment - which is a richer notion than either revoking or affirming. It is suggested here that, under the heading of the general principle of fulfilment, a number of methodological pointers for interpreting OT law can be identified.

One pointer is that OT laws should be studied in the context of the overall created order. Sexual behaviour is addressed in many places throughout Scripture, but it is important to recognise the context of the created order that God had made, and the location, starting from Gen. 1-2, of sexual intercourse solely within lifelong heterosexual monogamous marriage. Further, it would appear that the NT assumes and affirms this framework when it addresses questions of sexual morality. In particular, Paul teaches the Corinthians to 'flee from sexual immorality' (1 Cor. 6:18). How are his readers to know what counts as sexual immorality? Paul refers back (in verse 16) to Gen. 2:24, and shows that sexual intercourse between a man and a female prostitute means becoming one with her in body. This is immoral: the body is not intended for immorality, but for the Lord, the Lord Jesus (v13). The saved believer is by no means to disregard the created order. Rather, salvation is to restore believers to created glory - and, more, to take them forward to an even greater, new-creation, glory, one which is perfectly in line with the original.

A second pointer is to compare different OT laws with one another. For example, there are clear lessons that can be learned from the details of the punishments sanctioned under OT law. From these laws, Christians can seek to discern principles concerning God, his character, and his will for humankind. Thus the relative severity of punishments for different offences should give some guidance concerning the relative seriousness of those offences. Since the governing authorities still have, even in the NT era, the responsibility to reward good and punish evil (e.g. Rom. 13:1-7), then the principles that can be

---

[144]The approach of tripartite separation seems to lack sufficient Scriptural warrant to have the authority to state, without further argument, that half of one verse is affirmed whilst the other half is revoked.

discerned from the OT, in the light of the NT, will be of much value.[145]

It follows from this that Christians must seek moral *principles*, in the light of the way in which the Lord Jesus Christ and the NT fulfil the OT law; and also that where these principles require application in everyday life, then Christians are effectively 'free' to decide how to apply them: that is, 'free' (and therefore responsible) in the sense that God has not chosen to give detailed and specific commands for each and every situation.[146]

The central claim here is that clear moral *content*, which *does* apply today, can be discerned in the OT Law, once that Law is studied in the context of the whole of Scripture, and especially in the light of the fulfilment of that Law as taught and displayed by the Lord Jesus Christ, both in his life and death and in the authoritative writings of the apostles. The three general principles advocated here involve: creation (studying particular laws in the context of the overall created order); comparison with other OT laws; and Christology. The resultant methodology is likely to be more complex, but arguably more true to Scripture, than either of the two simple hermeneutical rules normally offered ('revoked unless affirmed' and 'affirmed unless revoked').[147]

By contrast with the above methodology, the standard approach of making a tripartite separation of OT laws (into 'moral', 'civil' and 'ceremonial') would struggle with verses like Lev. 20:15: this is because such a verse seems to combine a 'moral' and a 'civil' law, and therefore the hermeneutic of 'keep the "moral", drop the rest' is strained beyond breaking point in such a case.

The conclusion of the theonomists, by contrast, is eminently self-consistent. The argument offered here, however, is that theonomy has not grappled sufficiently with the central NT hermeneutical principle, that of fulfilment. By studying creation, other OT laws, and by doing all this Christologically, what appears a more thoroughly Scriptural way forward has been advoacted.

Returning now to the main theme - justice and economic life - the application of the type of method advocated above has significant implications for the content of economic justice. This must be seen, however, in the light of the person and work of Jesus Christ himself. In particular, the four gospel accounts of the NT each bear witness to the utterly righteous life of the Lord Jesus Christ. Thus, for example, Peter falls to his knees as he, a sinful man,

---

[145]This general argument is in clear contrast to that of the theonomists, who argue that the punishments meted out under the OT law still stand today, in detail (unless clearly revoked). For example, Bahnsen argues that God's law still stands, and therefore those criminals who have committed offences for which the due (OT) penalty is death '*are* to be executed during the New Testament era' (*Theonomy*, p446).

[146]In the OT, by contrast, the detailed way in which the laws were formulated and expressed did express, to a far greater extent, what was required in each and every situation - even if that required a certain amount of logical deduction on the part of Moses and his team of judges (Ex. 18:13ff; Deut. 1:13-17).

[147]How the methodology offered here might be applied to other OT laws is an important matter for further research, but is well beyond the scope of this book.

recognises the holiness and righteousness of Jesus (Lk. 5:8). And this was evident to all observers, not only to Jesus' close followers: thus it was that one of the robbers crucified alongside Jesus confessed that 'this man has done nothing wrong' (Lk. 23:41).

Jesus' fulfilment of 'all righteousness' (Mt. 3:15) - his perfect obedience to the Father's will (Jn. 4:34) and his totally right relationship with the Father - included his dealings in regard to oppression. Not only did he never do any wrong to any person; he also brought deliverance to those who were oppressed. This positive action for the oppressed was also spoken of in the OT as a crucial aspect of righteousness. Psalm 72 anticipates such righteousness of 'the king'. Job argued that he had displayed something of this righteousness (Job 29:7-17)[148]. Jesus' action for the oppressed is stated in his programmatic statement at the start of his ministry, recorded in Lk. 4:17-21, where he reads from the prophet Isaiah, especially 61:1-2 ('The Spirit of the Lord is upon me...to set at liberty those who are oppressed...'), and then announces: 'Today this scripture has been fulfilled in your hearing'.[149] The succeeding chapters of Luke's gospel account unfold something of Jesus' actions in fulfilment of Is. 61:1-2, including his liberation of those oppressed in various ways.

This has significant implications for where Christian believers stand, in general terms, in regard to the OT material on justice and oppression.[150] For all those who are in Christ, God sent his own Son in the likeness of sinful flesh, and condemned sin in the flesh, in order that the just requirement of the law might be fulfilled in them (Rom. 8:1-4), fulfilled in its entirety, including in relation to non-oppression. As has been argued earlier, the demands which the Mosaic Law placed upon OT Israelites are *not* placed upon Christian believers, upon those who are in Christ. Christians have a new ontological status and reality; they have been declared righteous. They have also been made regenerate: 'If anyone is in Christ - new creation!' (2 Cor. 5:17).[151] This does

---

[148]See especially v14 ('I put on righteousness...') in the context of v12 ('...I delivered the poor who cried') and v17 ('I broke the fangs of the unrighteous, and made him drop his prey from his teeth'.)

[149]The verses cited from Isaiah - 61:1-2; 58:6 - are in the context of oppression amongst Israel (ch. 58), and of the prophesied coming of the Messiah who will be covered with the robe of righteousness (61:10).

[150]The nature and meaning of economic oppression - as compared to the place of NT believers with regard to the OT material on oppression – is discussed below.

[151]A literal rendering of the Greek. English translations generally insert at this point a phrase such as 'he is': e.g. 'If anyone is in Christ he is a new creation' (RSV). In the Greek, however, no such phrase is present here. The point being emphasized here is that this new creation is *not* a matter only of potential, potential that is not realized until the believer's life, actions, thoughts and words begin to change. Rather, there is already 'new creation': 'the old has gone; the new has come' (2 Cor. 5:17). Thus the believer is *now* 'new creation' - that newness, that regeneration, is an ontological reality – by the grace of God and through the work of the Spirit of God.

not mean that Christians are therefore unable to sin, nor that the sinful nature is no longer a present reality. It does mean, however, that the 'old self' has been crucified with Christ (Rom. 6:6) - an ontological reality - 'so that [with the purpose that] the sinful body might be destroyed, and we might no longer be enslaved to sin' (Rom. 6:6; cf. Gal. 2:20). Therefore, for everyone who is in Christ: 'new creation; the old has passed away, behold, the new has come' (2 Cor. 5:17; RSV).

Further, it may be argued, the new righteousness and the new life that Christian believers possess and begin to display are in fact the righteousness and life of the Lord Jesus Christ himself. Paul writes to the Corinthians that God has made Christ Jesus 'our righteousness' (1 Cor. 1:30). He speaks to the Colossians about the future appearing of 'Christ who is our life' (Col. 3:4). And he tells the Galatians that 'it is no longer I [=old self] who live, but Christ who lives in me' (Gal. 2:20). This does not mean that believers cease to be persons, and instead somehow become absorbed into the person of Christ. That would deny the uniqueness of each person as created by God, and also the distinction between Creator and creature. Rather, the point is that it is the very righteousness and the very life of the Lord Jesus Christ himself, the image of the invisible God (Col. 1:15), imparted to and indwelling believers by the presence of the Holy Spirit, that makes their 'new creation' a reality.

It follows from the previous two paragraphs that Christian living is a matter of Christian believers living out this new Christological reality; of believers being and becoming what they already are in Christ.[152] Here there is a vital role for the Holy Spirit (Rom. 8:11):

> If the Spirit of him who raised Jesus from the dead dwells in you, he who raised Christ Jesus from the dead will give life to your mortal bodies also through his Spirit which dwells in you.

The Spirit who indwells all believers gives, or brings about, this life: this being and becoming what they already are. Thus it is possible for Paul to contrast Spirit-life with being under the law (Gal. 5:18).

The Christological basis of the ethical Christian life is illustrated by Paul's teaching in 2 Cor. 8-9, with regard to the collection for 'the relief of the saints' (8:4). Paul's appeal to the Corinthians is not based on law. Rather, he appeals first (8:7) to the example set by the churches of Macedonia, whose liberal, almost reckless, generosity sprang from their experience of God's grace through Christ (8:1). For 'first they gave themselves to the Lord and then to us' (8:5): thus it was out of their relationship with the Lord Jesus that their overflowing love arose. Secondly, Paul appeals to the example of grace of the Lord Jesus Christ himself (8:9), 'that though he was rich, yet for your sake he became poor, so that by his poverty you might become rich'. This is not an

---

[152]This was discussed at some length in chapter 2.

appeal to follow some written code, but rather to overflow with thanksgiving in the same love - and thereby to be demonstrably Gospel people. Thus Paul says to the Corinthians, in the context of the testing of their service: 'you will glorify God by your obedience in acknowledging the gospel of Christ, and by the generosity of your contribution...' (9:13). This is the reality of what it means to belong to Christ, in practice, and for Christ to indwell them.

Economic Relationships Within the Christian Community

It must also be emphasized that this Christological reality is - as in 2 Cor. 8-9, and in general throughout the NT - set in the context of relationships within the Christian community. Moreover, the economic dimension of these relationships is vital. As Wright says regarding 2 Cor. 8-9:

> ...in commending the Corinthians for their eagerness to share in the financial *koinonia* collection (2 Cor. 8:4; 9:13), Paul describes it as proof of their *obedience to the gospel*, implying that such concrete economic evidence of fellowship was of the essence of a genuine Christian profession.[153]

Thus a further feature of the content of economic justice, as unfolded in the NT, is that there is a heightened emphasis on righteousness being worked out in relationships between Christians, not least in economic terms. For Paul explicitly uses the language of righteousness-justice (δικαιοσύνη) in his exhortation of the Corinthians. In 2 Cor. 9:9 he cites Psalm 112, a psalm which describes the blessedness of the one who fears Yahweh, who greatly delights in his commandments, and whose righteousness endures for ever.[154] Paul argues as follows in vv6-10 of chapter 9:

> The point is this: he who sows sparingly will also reap sparingly, and he who sows bountifully will also reap bountifully. Each one must do as he has made up his mind, not reluctantly or under compulsion, for God loves a cheerful giver. And God is able to provide you with every blessing in abundance, so that you may always have enough of everything and may provide in abundance for every good work. As it is written, "He scatters abroad, he gives to the poor; his righteousness (δικαιοσύνη) endures for ever." He who supplies seed to the sower and bread for food will supply and multiply your resources and increase the harvest of your righteousness (δικαιοσύνη).

Righteousness and justice are about relationships: they refer to being in a right relationship, and to treating people appropriately. And Paul's emphasis here is

---

[153]Christopher J. H. Wright, *Living as the People of God: The Relevance of Old Testament Ethics* (Leicester: IVP, 1983), p98. Cf. also Hays, *The Moral Vision*, 464-8.

[154]Psalm 111 - a parallel to Psalm 112 in various ways - uses of Yahweh the phrase 'his righteousness endures for ever' (Ps. 111:3). In Ps. 112:3,9, however, it is used of a human being who walks in the ways of Yahweh.

on God's desire and will for generosity as part of this righteousness and justice, especially generosity and sharing between Christian believers. A similar stress on generous sharing comes, e.g., in 1 Tim. 6:17-19. The practice of this sharing in the very earliest days, recorded in Acts chapters 2 and 4, is well known. And this kind of message was widely accepted and applied by the early Christians. As Gonzales says, having surveyed all the leading Christian writers of the first few centuries A.D.:

> all agree on the fundamental criterion that wealth is to be shared. This principle...is both the basis of economic life and the reason those who have more than they need must share it with the needy... [T]he purpose of wealth is to meet human need. Therefore, those who accumulate wealth as if it were an end in itself or who accumulate it in order to live in comfort and ostentation are misusing wealth.[155]

The Meaning of Economic 'Oppression'

A further issue concerning the way that Jesus Christ fulfils the OT concerns the OT's teaching in regard to economic justice and oppression. The argument given earlier in this chapter is that Christian believers should look to the Mosaic Law for moral *content*, but that they are absolutely not bound by that Law, whether in detail or in any 'principles' which might be found in it. What is its content? Fundamentally, the OT material on justice and oppression reflects the mercy and justice of God. And it gives *examples* of what is merciful and just, and of what is not. The Mosaic Law was given as an example; but it has no hold, as Law, upon Christians. Thus Paul's appeal in Gal. 6:7-10 to 'do good' is not by means of legalistic demand, but as the living of Spirit-filled life.

As for the content of justice, especially with regard to oppression, it is implicit in the earlier parts of this chapter that the OT does not define justice solely with regard to oppression: justice in the Bible is a very rich notion, and it is not simply the opposite of oppression. Nevertheless, it is evidently the case that justice is, amongst other things, utterly opposed to oppression.[156] It follows that careful study of the OT material concerning the content of oppression, in the light of the NT, is likely to yield significant understanding concerning the content of justice, not least in terms of economic life.

The substantial amount of OT material on oppression is strongly linked to Israel's own experience of oppression by the Egyptians.[157] That experience, that

---

[155]Justo L. Gonzales, *Faith and Wealth: A History of Early Christian Ideas on the Origin, Significance and Use of Money* (San Francisco: Harper & Row, 1990), pp228-9.
[156]As simply one example, Ezk. 18:5ff make it clear that one aspect of justice and righteousness is the total absence of oppressive behaviour and practices.
[157]The total number of occurrences of words translated as, for example, 'oppress' or 'exploit' runs to over 170. This is apart, of course, from all those references where no actual word for 'oppress' is present, but where the material does refer to oppression.

oppression, was (as noted earlier, in section II.B) the benchmark definition of what the Israelites were *not* to practise. This is clearly stated in, for example, Ex. 22:21. This strong link to the Egyptian oppression can also be seen in the language employed by the OT. The five different Hebrew roots which carry some connotation of oppression are variously translated into English as 'oppress', 'exploit', 'wrong', 'crush', 'ill-treat', 'extort', and 'afflict'.[158] Each of these roots is used, at least once, with reference to what the Jews experienced at the hands of the Egyptians.[159] The key point here is that the people of Israel had been through a very real example of oppression. Oppression was no abstract notion. They knew what it was. They had a very definite understanding of the content of oppression. And they were not to practise any such oppression. In the OT the content of oppression is also clearly linked to various aspects of economic experience, including (amongst others): wages (Lv.19:13); prices (Lv. 25:14-17); property (Ezk. 46:18); and robbery[160] (Lv.19:13). Thus the OT gives concrete examples, in terms of *economic* life, of what oppression is.

As suggested earlier, it is by way of *example* that this material from the OT - both the experience of Israel in Egypt, and the specifics of the Law - should be studied and meditated upon. The role of the OT material today is not to provide a tightly prescriptive blueprint for economic justice, but rather to exemplify (in a different cultural context) something of the nature and content of economic justice. In this way it can serve to instruct Christians, under the guidance of the Holy Spirit, about what it means today to act justly rather than unjustly. All this is consistent with the notion of justice as appropriate treatment of people, in accordance with the norms commanded by God for each particular case. But it is essential to understand norms in the sense already indicated: not rigid rules, but moral principles - built into the created order - informed and directed by Scripture under the guidance and empowering of the Holy Spirit, and following the pattern and example of Jesus Christ himself.

---

[158]These five roots are: נגש; לחץ; ינה; עשק; עניענה.

[159]See (taking the roots in the order given in the previous footnote) Gen. 15:13/Ex. 3:7; Dt. 24:14-18; Lv. 19:33; Ex. 22:20; Ex. 3:7.

[160]Calvin argues that the eighth commandment has a wide range of application - not merely to taking property that is not one's own, but also to all sorts of unjust gain at the expense of others. See his *Commentary on the Four Last Books of Moses Arranged in the Form of a Harmony Vols I-IV*, tr. C. W. Bingham (Edinburgh: Calvin Translation Society, 1852-55), Vol.III, p111.

Eschatology[161]

The final theme to be treated in this analysis of economic justice in the Scriptures - all within a salvation-historical framework - is eschatology. Salvation history is ultimately directed towards the consummation of the glorious kingdom of God in the age to come: towards that day when every knee shall bow, 'in heaven and on earth and under the earth, and every tongue confess that Jesus Christ is Lord, to the glory of God the Father' (Phil. 2:10-11). The consistent conviction throughout the NT is that the day is coming - the day anticipated in some measure in the OT - when Christ will come again to the earth, and when he will deliver 'the kingdom to God the Father after destroying every rule and every authority and power' (1 Cor. 15:24).[162] This eschatological transformation of the created order will remove, totally and for ever, all the effects of the Fall; and thus God's redemptive work in Christ will come to its fulfilment and culmination.

Justice and righteousness - including the economic dimensions thereof - are central to this coming of Christ, and the end of the present age, in two senses. First, the eschaton will bring full and final judgment upon evil and injustice (e.g. Mt. 25:31-46; 2 Pet. 3:7; Rev. 19:2). The judge of all the earth will indeed do right (Gen. 18:25). The OT is very clear that judgment will come upon economic wrongdoing and evil (e.g. Amos 5:10-18; Ezk. 28:15-23), and the judgment prophesied in the book of Revelation against Babylon drives this message home yet more firmly. Secondly, the eschaton will also bring in a new order which transforms the present fallen created order into something that is perfect, just and righteous. Thus the second epistle of Peter, immediately after explaining the destructive judgment God will bring, continues with this encouragement: 'But according to his promise we wait for new heavens and a new earth in which righteousness [δικαιοσύνη] dwells' (2 Pet. 3:13).

Together these two aspects fulfil the anticipation found, for example, in Psalms 96 and 98, where people and indeed the whole of creation are exhorted to sing to Yahweh a new song, because of his salvation, victory, vindication, marvellous works, and his steadfast love and faithfulness to the house of Israel (Ps. 96:1-9; Ps. 98:1-6). Both of these psalms conclude with a further

---

[161]As indicated previously, eschatology is treated only briefly here. Whilst a detailed examination of the Scriptural material on eschatology might (or might not) have a minor impact on the conception of economic justice developed in this and the previous chapter, it is taken here that the major thrust of that material with regard to a biblical understanding of economic justice is the givenness of both the end (and judgment) of this age and the arrival of the age to come. A complex and lengthy treatment of eschatology is thus not necessary in an account which aims to give a sense of the whole, with regard to the Scriptures and economic justice.

[162]A sample of other NT references to the (second) coming of Christ and the final judgment is: Mt. 25:31ff; Acts 17:31; Rom. 2:5; 1 Th. 3:13; 1 Pet. 1:7; 2 Pet. 3:10; Rev. 22:20.

exhortation, to 'sing for joy before the LORD'. And the reason is this (Ps. 96:13):

> for he comes to judge [לִשְׁפֹט] the earth. He will judge [יִשְׁפֹּט] the world with righteousness [*sedeq*], and the peoples with his truth.[163]

The certainty of this judgment, and of this transformation of the created order, is guaranteed by the resurrection and ascension of Jesus Christ (e.g. Acts 17:31; Rev. 1:17f). And, as shown already, this will include the economic dimension of the created order. Thus, as O'Donovan emphasizes, what is coming is *transformation*:

> The eschatological transformation of the world is neither the mere repetition of the created world nor its negation. It is its fulfilment, its *telos* or end. It is the historical *telos* of the origin, that which creation is intended *for*, and that which it points and strives *towards*... The resurrection of Christ, upon which Christian ethics is founded, vindicates the created order in this double sense: it redeems it and transforms it.[164]

Not only, however, will perfect economic justice be part of this eschatological transformation. In addition, that coming judgment and transformation have a central place in the importance of economic justice now, in the present age. Eschatology is essential to ethics, including ethics in economic life, in two broad senses. First, Christian believers are to seek economic justice now, and thereby to *bear witness to* the coming transformation. Secondly, the coming judgment stands over all the economic *in*justice of the present age.[165]

Conclusion

The overall goal of this and the previous chapter was to offer a theological account of economic justice and, in particular, to develop a conception of economic justice that is rooted firmly in the Scriptures. Part of the methodology adopted for these two chapters has been to put forward and examine the hypothesis that a vital key to interpreting the biblical material on economic justice concerns the righteousness and justice of God. Chapter 2 concluded with strong provisional support for this hypothesis. The survey of Scriptural material in the present chapter, proceeding on the initial understanding provided by the above-mentioned theological framework, has yielded substantial further insights, and has again demonstrated strong consistency with the conception of

---

[163]Psalm 98, similarly, has 'and the peoples with equity' (v9).

[164]Oliver O'Donovan, *Resurrection and Moral Order*, 2nd ed. (Leicester: Apollos, 1994), pp55-56.

[165]These two aspects are taken up later, especially in chapter 6.

the righteousness of God, and of righteousness and justice more generally, presented earlier. Therefore, it is a confident and firm conclusion that the righteousness of God is indeed a valid and reliable foundation for a theological framework for economic justice.

Chapter 3 has sought to give a sense of the whole, with regard to the biblical material on economic justice, within the context of God's salvific work unfolded in creation, Fall, redemption and, ultimately, eschatology. It has been shown that a biblical conception of economic justice, extending the theological framework developed in chapter 2, must include the following four elements. First, justice means appropriate treatment, according to the norms commanded by God for each particular case - norms built into the moral order of creation. Secondly, God's justice, in terms of economic life, involves justice to the needy. Thirdly, economic justice is not only allocational, but also concerns the quality of relationships. Fourthly, justice in the allocation of resources means that everyone participates in God's blessing. These aspects of economic justice emerged particularly from the examination of the Law, but it has been shown that the rest of the OT reinforces and amplifies them. Further, it has also been shown that the NT builds on and fulfils - rather than negating - the OT. Each of those aspects has been developed, in various ways, in the NT. It must be emphasized, however, that this 'NT fulfilment' is Christological: thus it is Jesus Christ, in his person, teaching and ministry - most especially in his death and resurrection - who fulfils the OT. Those four aspects of economic justice, therefore, are fully indicative of a biblical conception only to the extent that their fulfilment in and through Jesus Christ has been comprehended and explored.

Finally, the meaning of a biblical conception of justice for the *contemporary* economic world will be more fully understood only when engagement takes place between, on the one hand, alternative ideas and practices in the contemporary world, and, on the other hand, a biblical conception. This is the task of the following chapters.

CHAPTER 4

An Appraisal of Some Other Treatments of Justice, with Particular Reference to Justice in Economic Life

Introduction

This chapter appraises, in the light of the biblical conception of justice developed in the previous two chapters, some alternative treatments of justice, both secular and Christian. Rather than attempting to survey all the various secular treatments that have been offered, three particular and influential contributions are treated here: utilitarianism, as propounded by John Stuart Mill, and developed by others; the contract approach of John Rawls, in his theory of justice; and the libertarianism of Robert Nozick in his entitlement conception of justice. The reason for selecting these three - and no others - is that, between them, they provide powerful evidence of the strength and breadth of secular thought in this field, and thus they are a sufficient indication, for the purposes of this book, of the ideas with which a biblically-rooted conception of justice must engage. Utilitarianism, for example, is of great significance in the field of justice, both in historical and contemporary terms. The Rawlsian perspective, similarly, makes a major contribution, and Nozick's libertarian approach - whilst not developed in the same detail as that of Rawls - reflects another highly influential strand of thought.

The main aim of the appraisal offered here is to perceive and acknowledge the challenges posed by the treatments considered, especially the secular ones, for a biblically-rooted understanding. The purpose here is to recognize the kinds of contemporary challenges and questions with which such an understanding must grapple if it is to engage seriously with other conceptions of justice. Hence this process will serve to clarify where the biblically-rooted understanding developed thus far requires further sharpening. It might conceivably be the case, of course, that existing Christian treatments of justice (such as Roman Catholic social teaching, the work of Reinhold Niebuhr, and liberation theology - the Christian treatments considered here) have already responded adequately to the challenges posed by secular conceptions. It will be argued here, however, that this is not the case.

The final introductory point to note is that, within the bounds of the main aim of this chapter - that of acknowledging the challenges posed for a biblical conception of justice by the various treatments considered - it is also appropriate to provide here some critical evaluation of those treatments. This will be offered both on their own terms, and in the light of the biblical understanding developed in chapters 2 and 3.

Utilitarianism and Justice

Three questions are addressed in this section: first, what utilitarianism says regarding justice; secondly, what its weaknesses are in this regard; and thirdly, what questions and challenges it poses for a Christian understanding of justice. These questions are examined in turn.

Utilitarianism on Justice

Whilst utilitarianism is not an entirely uniform or rigid body of ideas, it is appropriate to refer to a general school of thought by the name of utilitarianism, a school which shares a common core of utilitarian concepts and values. At its heart is its offer of 'a single rational criterion for appraising actions, practices and institutions: the maximisation of utility'.[1] It should be noted that utilitarianism is thus seen to be a thoroughly teleological approach to questions of morality (in which the *good* is always prior to the *right*): it entirely rejects any deontological understanding whereby certain actions would be regarded as right (or wrong) in and of themselves.

In order to assess utilitarianism's approach to justice, John Stuart Mill's account will be taken as the starting point.[2] According to Mill, '...the notion which we have found to be of the essence of justice...[is] that of a right residing in an individual'.[3] For this conception he makes a strong claim (p55):

> While I dispute the pretensions of any theory which sets up an imaginary standard of justice not grounded on utility, I account the justice which is grounded on

---

[1]Geoffrey Scarre, *Utilitarianism* (London: Routledge, 1996), p25. It should be noted that the utilitarianism offered by Scarre's lucid and wide-ranging book is taken in this chapter as broadly representative of mainstream modern utilitarianism. Much other modern utilitarian literature exists - as testified by Scarre - but it seems unnecessary to cite multiple sources for arguments that have been ably presented in one place.

[2]Mill's treatment is not the first, historically, but it is the most influential of all the utilitarian accounts of justice.

[3]John Stuart Mill, *Utilitarianism* (1861); (reprinted, with an introduction by A. D. Lindsay, in John Stuart Mill, *Utilitarianism, Liberty and Representative Government*, London: Dent [Everyman's Library], 1910), p55. [Page references are to this 1910 edition.]

utility to be the chief part, and incomparably the most sacred and binding part, of all morality.

Mill seeks to deny an alternative conception, namely that justice has a totally different, and independent, origin from utility or happiness; that it is 'a standard *per se*' (p51). Such a view is clearly incompatible with his utilitarianism, in which 'Utility or Happiness is *the* criterion of right and wrong' (p38; emphasis added).

How can Mill affirm a high status for justice, whilst simultaneously denying it any absolute or independent origin? He attempts to do so by locating all human understandings of justice *within* utilitarian morality. He proceeds as follows. First, he argues - from observation of everyday understandings of 'justice' - that the sentiment of justice has two essential ingredients: first, 'the desire to punish a person who has done harm'; and secondly, 'the knowledge or belief that there is some definite individual or individuals to whom harm has been done' (p47). Next, he asks whether our *natural* feeling of retaliation or vengeance is itself moral. His answer is: No. 'For the natural feeling would make us resent indiscriminately whatever any one does that is disagreeable to us; *but when moralised by the social feeling*, it only acts in the directions conformable to the general good' (p48; emphasis added). Thus our sentiment of retaliation or vengeance 'has nothing moral in it; what is moral is, the exclusive subordination of it to the social sympathies, so as to wait on and obey their call' (p48).

In Mill's system, then, the absolute moral standard is social utility, general happiness. Thus he argues that any claim that a particular action is just, or unjust, can in fact only be finally evaluated by reference to the over-riding criterion of social utility. In support of this argument, he says that in any case where the question at issue is the matter of what justice requires, the appeal to 'justice' cannot provide an answer.

Typically, he claims, 'justice' will have at least two sides to it, which cannot be brought into harmony. One example he gives (pp53f) is the question of whether, in a co-operative industrial association, talent and skill should receive superior remuneration. On the one hand, justice might suggest a negative answer: talented and skilled individuals already have other advantages, and justice ought to reward the disadvantaged. On the other hand, it may be argued that society *owes* the more efficient labourer a greater return for his services; and also that 'if he is only to receive as much as others, he can only be justly required to produce as much, and to give a smaller amount of time and exertion, proportioned to his superior efficiency' (p54). One disputant 'looks to what it is just that the individual should receive, the other to what it is just that the community should give. Each, from his own point of view, is unanswerable; and any choice between them, on grounds of justice, must be perfectly arbitrary. Social utility alone can decide the preference' (p54).[4]

Thus Mill claims that the lack of general agreement about the specific meaning of justice demonstrates that it cannot in itself be an absolute standard. Instead it is the principle of social utility which gives rise to the notion of justice. And the priority of social utility - general happiness - is axiomatic in utilitarianism.

It should be noted at this point that the standard utilitarian justification for regarding the priority of social utility as axiomatic is along the lines that such a principle is intrinsically reasonable. If it is possible to achieve a greater level of overall happiness than the present level, then it is *un*reasonable not to bring about that greater level of happiness. The philosophical framework here is a naturalistic one,[5] in which the apparently common human desire to bring about greater, rather than lesser, utility and happiness is taken as given and therefore as the basis for moral reasoning. Hence the Good is taken to be the greatest possible human happiness and utility. As Scarre points out (*op.cit.*, pp99-101), the justification of this framework assumes that individuals see things from an aggregative ('objective') perspective - that of the universe - rather than their own individual perspective.[6] They desire the greatest good in an overall sense, not necessarily the maximisation of their own individual utility. This justification has a practical difficulty, however (as Scarre demonstrates), if individuals do *not* actually desire the maximum objective utility: for any given individual might on occasions be required, according to utilitarian reasoning, to sacrifice their own personal utility for the sake of a greater overall utility.[7]

Despite this difficulty, utilitarianism claims that it does provide an appealing and coherent approach to moral reasoning, not least with regard to justice. In Mill's chapter in his *Utilitarianism*, 'On the Connection Between Justice and Utility', he deals with the matter of why he should refer to 'justice' at all, since

---

[4]The fact that Mill does not proceed at this point to debate how social utility would decide this particular matter is irrelevant. Social utility *is* able to decide (in principle at least), simply by virtue of the fact that all the relevant gains to happiness (or utility) can, at least in principle, and on certain assumptions, be computed, and thus a decision made on the basis of maximisation of utility. There is no shortage of articles in the economics journals, for example, offering treatments of a very wide range of cases on the basis of maximisation or optimisation along such lines.

[5]Scarre, *Utilitarianism*, pp97-100.

[6]Mill did not appear (in *Utilitarianism*) to recognise this aggregative/individual distinction, and so his 'proof' of the validity of the principle of maximising social utility failed. 'Mill attempted the hopeless task of justifying an *impartial* concern for human welfare on the basis of the partial concern of each individual agent for *his own* welfare' (Scarre, *Utilitarianism*, p99). Henry Sidgwick *did* recognise the distinction (Scarre, *ibid.*), but the justification for his argument still faces the serious practical difficulty mentioned in the text.

[7]Scarre devotes two whole chapters (VII and VIII) to the attempt to solve this difficulty.

the just action, in any given situation, cannot be anything other than that action which maximises utility. If, then, 'justice' has no meaning independent from utility, how can he attribute any significance to it? Mill's response helps to make clear both what he means by justice, and what sort of place justice plays in his moral framework.

He argues that 'the idea of justice supposes two things; a rule of conduct, and a sentiment which sanctions the rule. The first must be supposed common to all mankind, and intended for their good. The other (the sentiment) is a desire that punishment may be suffered by those who infringe the rule.'[8] It is clear from this that justice is subsumed under the general good: it is not, for Mill, an entity or value independent from the general good of mankind.

Within this utilitarian understanding of justice there are rights. 'When we call anything a person's right, we mean that he has a valid claim on society to protect him in the possession of it, either by the force of law, or by that of education and opinion.'[9] Mill proceeds to explain how what *is* such a right may be distinguished from what is *not* such a right (p50):

> ...a person is said to have a right to what he can earn in fair professional competition; because society ought not to allow any other person to hinder him from endeavouring to earn in that manner as much as he can. But he has *not* a right to three hundred a-year, though he may happen to be earning it; because society is not called on to provide that he shall earn *that sum*.[10] On the contrary, if he owns ten thousand pounds three per cent. stock, he *has* a right to three hundred a-year;[11] because society has come under an obligation to provide him with an income of that amount.

Thus Mill's understanding is that, in a qualified sense, each individual has *rights*, within the overall goal of maximising general happiness. 'To have a right...is, I conceive, to have something which society ought to defend me in the possession of. If the objector goes on to ask, why it ought? *I can give no other reason than general utility*' (p50; emphasis added). By this he means that it is the interests of *all* that the rights of each are protected and secured. 'The interest involved is that of security, to *every one's* feelings the most vital of all interests' (p50; emphasis added).[12] There is here some - at least implicit -

---

[8]*Utilitarianism*, p49.

[9]*Ibid.*

[10]These emphases added.

[11]Emphasis in the original.

[12]It might be objected that Mill is here making an unjustified and unwarranted assumption, namely that the disutility suffered by a particular individual from society's failing to protect their interests, plus the general disutility suffered by all due to the consequent lessening of the feeling of security, is necessarily greater than the utility gained from anyone who *benefits* in the particular case (such as a destitute person who

notion of a social contract, whereby all members of a society acknowledge that their interests as individuals are bound up, to some extent, with the interests of everyone else in the society, and whereby all the members agree to participate in that society on those terms.[13]

Mill's purpose in using the language of rights and justice is not, then, to suggest some moral standard independent of that given by utilitarianism. Rather, he sees justice and rights as referring to cases where the general utility or happiness is most at risk, and where the largest utility gains (or losses) are at stake. This is the basis for Mill's distinction between what is just and what is merely expedient.[14] To do the morally right thing is always, in a sense, no more than doing what is expedient in terms of utility. But justice concerns cases where there is a greater 'intensity of sentiment', an intensity of sentiment 'which places the Just, in human estimation, above the simply Expedient' (p57). Thus 'justice is a name for certain moral requirements, which, regarded collectively, stand higher in the scale of social utility, and are therefore of more paramount obligation, than any others' (p59).

The principle of upholding justice, however, is not the ultimate principle, according to Mill. That ultimate principle, clearly, is social utility itself. Thus the last phrase quoted is followed immediately by the qualification that '...particular cases may occur in which some other social duty is so important, as to overrule any one of the general maxims of justice'.[15] As an example, Mill claims that 'to save a life, it may not only be allowable, but a duty, to steal, or take by force, the necessary food or medicine, or to kidnap, and compel to officiate, the only qualified medical practioner' (p59). And - consistent with his framework in which the ultimate principle is social utility - he denies that such measures are *unjust*. 'In such cases...we usually say, not that justice must give way to some other moral principle, but that what is just in ordinary cases is, by reason of that other principle, not just in the particular case'.[16] As he puts it a little earlier: 'All persons are deemed to have a *right* to equality of treatment, except when some recognised social expediency requires the reverse (p59; emphasis added). Scanlon notes the strength of the utilitarian case here:

steals a large sum of money from a wealthy person). The answer is that, while Mill indeed makes this (simplifying) assumption here, his framework *does* permit a right to be infringed *if* it can be shown that such an infringement *is* in the general interest. (See below.)

[13]To recognise such a social contract, however, poses serious practical difficulties for any utilitarian analysis, because of the interdependencies involved. See Scarre, *Utilitarianism*, Chs.6-8. Further comment is made on this point in the discussion below of rule- and act-utilitarianism.

[14]*Utilitarianism*, pp55-57. See also Scarre, *Utilitarianism*, pp102-5.

[15]Mill, *Utilitarianism*, p59.

[16]*Ibid.* Given that justice is determined by social utility, it would be inconsistent for Mill to term something 'unjust' if it were nevertheless beneficial in terms of general utility.

In attacking utilitarianism one is inclined to appeal to individual rights, which mere considerations of social justice cannot justify us in overriding. But rights themselves need to be justified somehow, and how other than by appeal to the human interests their recognition promotes and protects? This seems to be the incontrovertible insight of the classical utilitarians.[17]

This utilitarian approach to justice, therefore, regards the notions of justice and rights as useful tools - even useful rules to follow - but tools which must be set aside if the overall good of social utility requires it.[18] This does imply a severely qualified understanding of justice. The application of this approach to, for example, the matter of the distribution of income and wealth in a society is that the final arbiter is always social utility.[19] A utilitarian has no final appeal to any principle of 'social justice'. In principle, the 'rights' of the poorest in society may not be relevant if a particular action or change will produce sufficiently large gains in utility elsewhere in society: perhaps amongst the rich. Equally, however, the 'rights' of the wealthy - such as their 'right' to the agreed return on interest-bearing financial assets - may not be relevant if, through the setting aside of this 'right', sufficiently large gains in utility come about elsewhere: for example, amongst the poor.

On a point of practical detail, it is evident nowadays that the application of utilitarianism faces severe difficulties. Even if inter-personal comparisons of utility can be made - which the welfare economics literature demonstrates to be, at best, highly problematic[20] - the utilitarian principle requires that those inter-personal comparisons are actually made, and that the social outcomes are determined solely on that basis. This will be achieved, without any government action, in perfectly free and competitive markets - which are rarely found in reality - but not in any other economic situation. The notion of a Pareto optimum is only of limited help here. A Pareto optimal situation in an economy is where no individual can experience an increase in their own utility without at least one other individual experiencing a reduction in their utility. It should be noted that, under perfectly free and competitive markets, a Pareto optimum will be achieved; and, further, there is no requirement for inter-personal

---

[17]T. M. Scanlon, 'Rights, Goals and Fairness' in Samuel Scheffler (ed.), *Consequentialism and Its Critics* (Oxford: OUP, 1988), p74.

[18]The language of 'justice' and 'rights' is effectively a kind of shorthand for cases where particularly large changes in utility may occur. In order for what would normally be termed an 'injustice' (=large loss of utility) to occur to be required, there must be an even larger corresponding increase in social utility.

[19]In the utilitarian tradition it is disputed whether this should be *average* utility or *total* utility. If the size of the country's population is constant, these two are equivalent. If this condition does not hold, however, then a choice has to be made.

[20]See, e.g., Kenneth Arrow, *Social Choice and Individual Welfare* (New York: Wiley, 1963).

comparisons of utility in this case. However, there may be a large number of socio-economic situations which satisfy the Pareto criterion. Hence it does not follow that, in any particular Pareto optimum, social utility is maximised (in the sense required for the application of utilitariansim); all that can be said is that no-one can be made better off without at least one other person being made worse off. In addition, as already noted, perfectly free and competitive markets are rarely found in reality. If markets will not do the trick, the task of social utility maximisation is left to governments, and/or to democracy. It is not obvious that the concern of either is to maximise social utility: one common interpretation of modern democracies, for example, is of competing interest groups, competing on the basis of being the most powerful and influential. This understanding is a very long way from anything that would point with any confidence to the maximisation of social utility.

ACT-UTILITARIANISM AND RULE-UTILITARIANISM

Returning to the main theme, Mill's essay opens the door to the now long-running debate, within utilitarianism, between the relative merits of acts and rules. The particular interest here is the relationship of this debate to the notion of justice. Mill does not formally distinguish act- and rule-utilitarianism. But his emphasis on the centrality of justice, and his use of it as a maxim, suggests that it does, in his view, function as a rule, to be applied in the majority of cases - although, as just described, it is not to be applied absolutely. More generally, it can be seen that, within rule-utilitarianism, there can be scope for some kind of emphasis upon justice.

By contrast, act-utilitarianism - at least where defined and applied rigorously - has no meaningful place for 'justice'. This is illustrated by Smart's discussion, as a utilitarian, of a (hypothetical) case whereby 'the sheriff of a small town can prevent serious riots (in which hundreds of people will be killed) only by 'framing' and executing (as a scapegoat) an innocent man'.[21] Smart acknowledges that this story can be strengthened to the point that 'we would just have to admit that if utilitarianism is correct, then the sheriff must frame the innocent man'. And, although Smart finds such an act of injustice unpalatable, he accepts it; in this sort of case, he says, one ought to be unjust. He adds the rider that 'any injustice causes misery and so can be justified only as the lesser of two evils' (p71).

Smart's discussion of this case occurs in his section entitled 'Utilitarianism and justice'. In previous sections he has argued strongly in favour of act-utilitarianism and against rule-utilitarianism. As Williams points out, Smart is

---

[21] J. J. C. Smart, 'An Outline of a System of Utilitarian Ethics' in Smart, J. J. C. and Bernard Williams, *Utilitarianism: For and Against* (Cambridge: CUP, 1973), pp69f.

thoroughgoing in his espousal of the former, and highly critical of the latter.[22] From all this it follows that, at least for Smart's version of act-utilitarianism, the notion of justice is entirely redundant. Indeed, although Smart uses the terms 'justice' and 'injustice' in the above discussion, they cannot have any operational role in his act-utilitarian methodology. As he states it (p42):

> the rational way to decide what to do is to perform that one of those alternative actions open to us (including the null-action, the action of doing nothing) which is likely to maximise the probable happiness or well-being of humanity as a whole, or more accurately, of all sentient beings.

In this methodology, unlike Mill's, justice has no meaningful place. For the same kind of reason it is extremely difficult, if not impossible, for an act-utilitarian to accept that it is ever morally important or desirable to keep promises, or to keep to many other useful kinds of rules and conventions.[23] 'The underlying problem is that act-utilitarian styles of justification do not take seriously the real dynamics of a practice like promising... Promising functions as a useful practice only if people desist from thinking about the advantage to be gained or lost by keeping particular promises, and agree to abide by the rules which are constitutive of the practice.'[24] Scarre reaches the following conclusion: 'Most of the time we should reason as act-utilitarians; but we should accept the *utilitarian* value of such products of human "artifice" as the rule-governed practice of promising.'[25]

Weaknesses of Utilitarianism regarding Justice

A number of weaknesses are highlighted here. First, one objection to Mill's approach concerns the fact that his notion of justice is dependent upon, rather than independent of, utility. This might seem to give to justice a lesser status and significance than that held by many people in their moral traditions and practice regarding justice. These latter sentiments appear to give an absolute place to justice, whereas Mill clearly does not allow that.

---

[22]Bernard Williams, *Morality: An Introduction to Ethics* (Harmondsworth: Penguin, 1973), p109.
[23]Scarre, *Utilitarianism*, p130.
[24]*Ibid.*, p131.
[25]*Ibid.*, p132, emphasis added. The problem for any variant of rule-utilitarianism here is that, since no inherent moral value attaches to promising - Scarre is admirably consistent to observe that its value is only a utilitarian one - then there can be no meaningful place for *trust* between persons. All we have to hold us together are contracts, specified and justified in utilitarian terms. Even for moral reasoning based, like that of Mill and most utilitarians, on observation, this is a serious problem, since many people in practice *do* seem to think that trust is, in and of itself, morally important.

How do utilitarians respond? They do not mind having no absolute place for justice. Mill is, as shown already, explicit about denying 'justice' the status of a standard *per se*. More fundamentally, Mill argues that, however strong our sentiments regarding justice, to adopt it as an absolute criterion simply does not work. This is not only because different people clearly have differing, and mutually inconsistent, conceptions of 'justice'. It is also because no notion of justice, on his argument, can bear the weight of being an ultimate standard. As he seeks to show in his example of saving a life (cited above), justice is (he thinks) ultimately determined in accordance with expediency. Therefore, social utility is the final arbiter.

This will not do, however. The observation that different people define justice differently does not refute the existence of actual absolute justice. And the example of saving a life shows only that the principle of justice might not be the only moral principle that is relevant in certain situations. It may be, then, that to discern what is the good, the best thing to do, requires us to take account of two or more moral principles. But that would not mean that justice is no longer absolute, only that justice by itself is not always sufficient for moral decision-making.

Secondly, a more profound criticism is that social utility itself is unable to bear the weight placed upon it by Mill; i.e. to bear the weight of being a foundation for justice. He argues that one's own desire for justice, in terms of retaliation or vengeance, is not in itself a moral thing. That feeling becomes 'moralised' only when understood in the context of the *social* good. There is a fallacy of composition here.[26] If my concern for my own 'unjust' treatment has no moral content, then it is not clear on what basis someone else's concern for my 'unjust' treatment *does* have moral content. Either my well-being matters, or it does not matter. If it matters only if it matters to someone else, then it is not my well-being that actually matters, but the fact that someone else is expressing care for 'another'. Thus Mill's assertion that general happiness is the absolute moral standard is mere assertion: he has effectively plucked it out of the air, and simply announced its axiomatic status. This is thoroughly inadequate - all the more so, in view of Mill's stated commitment to a *rational* morality.[27]

---

[26] This error on Mill's part is widely recognised (Scarre, *Utilitarianism*, pp96-7). Whether modern utilitarians have a valid alternative, however, is less clear. See below.

[27] Scarre attempts (in Chapter VIII) to get around this general difficulty by defining the goal of utilitarianism in terms of 'making things go well': thus he intends to safeguard the utility of the individual as well as of all individuals, since it can hardly be in the *wellbeing* of all if the wellbeing of one is totally disregarded. He claims that such an outcome necessarily *diminishes* society. This, however, will not do. His argument works only if all in society accept the premise that such an outcome diminishes society, i.e. if all share Scarre's vision of the Good. But if they do not have that vision in their utility function, then Scarre's desire will go unmet.

Thirdly, *rule*-utilitarianism is fundamentally flawed, for it is incoherent: it fails to provide any of the rigorous rules which it claims to offer. When Mill argues (as cited earlier) that 'all cases of justice are also cases of expediency', it is already becoming clear that rule-utilitarianism can, ultimately, be nothing other than a re-packaging of expediency (i.e. of what is expedient in terms of social utility). This is confirmed when Mill claims that some particular measure that is normally considered just can in a certain instance not be just. Note that he does *not* argue that justice is only one principle amongst others, and that they must be weighed together. No, he claims that justice is expediency, and therefore what *is* just in normal cases can on occasion be *not just*. It seems impossible for rule-utilitarianism to avoid collapsing into act-utilitarianism.

Fourthly, the inadequacy of *act*-utilitarianism in relation to justice is, simply, its total exclusion of any meaningful notion of justice from its methodology. This means it is unable to handle even those ethical questions which to many people are relatively straightforward (e.g. whether it is always unjust to torture babies). Unless one is prepared to accept a view of the world in which there is no such thing as justice, then this inability even in relation to more straightforward ethical questions requires the severest critique. As Williams says, in contrasting [act-] utilitarianism with other ethical frameworks:[28]

> utilitarianism...does make do with fewer ancillary principles and moral notions, but then...the lightness of its burden in this respect to a great extent merely shows how little of the world's moral luggage it is prepared to pick up. A system of social decision which is indifferent to issues of justice or equity certainly has less to worry about than one that is not indifferent to those considerations. But that type of commitment is not enticing.

Utilitarianism's Challenges to a Christian Understanding of Justice

Whatever its weaknesses, utilitarianism does present some serious challenges, two of which are highlighted here. First, at the most general level, and in common with consequentialism - of which utilitarianism is a particular form - it asks Christians to explain how allegedly 'moral' acts which do *not* promote the best overall outcome, in utilitarian terms, in a given set of circumstances, can possibly be defended. As Scheffler puts it: 'Anyone who resists consequentialism seems committed to the claim that morality tells us to do less good than we are in a position to do, and to prevent less evil than we are in a position to prevent.'[29]

The basic response is that to conduct moral enquiry on the basis of

---

[28]Bernard Williams, 'A Critique of Utilitarianism' in J. J. C. Smart and Bernard Williams, *Utilitarianism: For and Against* (Cambridge: CUP, 1973), p137.
[29]Samuel Scheffler, 'Introduction' in Samuel Scheffler (ed.), *Consequentialism and Its Critics* (Oxford: OUP, 1988), p1.

consequences alone is totally inadequate. As noted already, consequentialism is not able to give a coherent account even of relatively straightforward moral questions. To weigh the potentially 'beneficial' consequences of torturing babies (perhaps the babies of an evil dictator - who might relent of evil in the face of such torture) against the 'negative' consequences (including those for the babies) of the torture, involves the assumption that there is nothing intrinsically wrong with such torture in itself. Such an assumption is inadequate, because it denies the moral seriousness of the view that certain actions are in and of themselves wrong.

It should be noted in passing that Scarre's broad utilitarianism does seem to accept without question the wrongness of certain classes of action, such as cruelty or rape:[30] and, he says, 'we do not need any rules to explain the wrongness' of such actions (p132). Here Scarre appears to approve of the very thing for which he elsewhere criticises any approach with deontological elements, namely those 'which forbid any exception to...rules even *in extremis*' (p154). Presumably Scarre's inconsistency here arises from the fundamental problem that he can offer no ultimate justification for taking the maximisation of general utility as *the* criterion for moral reasoning, and is therefore forced to resort to unsubstantiated assertions.

Returning to the thrust of the first challenge posed by utilitarianism, the basic issue is the extent to which a Christian conception of justice can be founded with sufficient solidity that it avoids *both* being reduced to a merely consequentialist conception, *and* being incompatible with the promoting of good and the countering of evil. Again, the basic response is that the Christian faith is the perspective *best* placed to deal with the evaluation of how to do good and to counter evil, both as regards matters of justice and as regards moral issues more generally. Nevertheless the task of articulating a Christian conception of justice is far from completed.

The deeper answer to these questions, in principle at least, must lie in God himself, in his very character and nature as good. He is the 'absolute standard' of goodness; and, as the one who is the God of justice, then he is, and defines, the standard of justice. But it is a further task to move *from* such statements *to* detailed responses to the challenges just raised.

The second serious challenge posed by utilitarianism is this: what is the basic shape of a Christian notion of justice? As shown earlier, Mill conceives justice in terms of rights residing in individuals. Moreover, his approach also has the advantage - compared with those which present rights as absolutes, and thus have no means of resolving conflicts between different rights - of providing an overarching framework by means of which clashes between the different rights of different people may be resolved: this is done, as seen earlier,

---

[30]Scarre, *Utilitarianism,* pp129,132.

on the basis of maximising general happiness, or social utility.[31]

As shown already, the means by which utilitarianism seeks to conduct such resolutions is deeply flawed: the challenge is whether a Christian understanding can succeed here. Miller demonstrates one aspect of utilitarianism's failure in this regard. Miller's critique is in the context of his attempt to separate the common notion of social justice into three elements: rights, deserts, and needs.[32] He argues that each of these forms part of that notion, and that each of them is *ir*reducible to the others.[33] The problem with utilitarianism - as with other approaches - he argues, is its failure to synthesise the conflicting claims of justice (rights, deserts, needs) into either a single principle or a consistent set of principles.[34] Miller tries 'to bring out as clearly as possible the contrast between aggregative and distributive principles, and the reasons why an *aggregative* principle such as utility cannot accommodate the *distributive* principles of social justice.'[35] Essentially, the aggregate criterion must always take precedence - when such a choice has to be made - over any distributive criterion.

Nevertheless the utilitarian framework still poses a serious challenge to any attempt to found a Christian conception of justice. What, then, is the appropriate shape of justice? Is it aggregative or distributive? Is it based on rights, or on the general good? Whatever the solution, the challenge remains to overcome the various weaknesses exposed above.

A basic response, in Christian terms - as set out in the previous two chapters - is that justice is, at heart, about the appropriate treatment of people; and thus it concerns *right relationships.* Even if this is right and true, however, the challenge that remains is to articulate such an approach sufficiently that it generates a shape which is both an adequate alternative to the utilitarian approaches, and an adequate response to the utilitarian challenge.

Contractarianism and Justice: Especially Rawls' *A Theory of Justice* [36]

In this section, the foundational framework adopted by John Rawls, and the particular theory of justice he puts forward, are explained. This is followed by a

---

[31]The literature on consequentialism also makes significant use of the idea of rights (see, e.g., Scanlon's paper in Scheffler's book).

[32]David Miller, *Social Justice* (Oxford: Clarendon, 1976); in particular, Part I.

[33]*Ibid.*, p151.

[34]*Ibid.*

[35]*Ibid.* (emphasis added).

[36]John Rawls, *A Theory of Justice* (Cambridge, MA: Harvard University Press, 1971/ Oxford: OUP, 1972). In subsequent literature Rawls has extended, clarified, and sometimes amended the material in that book. This development is helpfully surveyed by Chandran Kukathas and Philip Pettit, *Rawls: A Theory of Justice and its Critics* (Cambridge: Polity, 1990), *passim*.

critical appraisal of his conception of justice;[37] and finally by an outline of the challenges posed by Rawls' approach for a biblically-rooted conception of justice.

Rawls' Foundational Framework for Justice

There are a number of central, and related, points to make concerning Rawls' foundational framework. First, there is no doubt that the utilitarian understanding of justice is one of the main approaches to which Rawls is responding, and from which he intends to distinguish his own approach.[38] A key distinction he draws is that, whereas utilitarianism is a teleological framework - in which the Good is prior to, and defined independently of, the Right - Rawls' approach regards the Right as prior to the Good (and is thus, in part at least, deontological).[39] For utilitarianism, the main idea 'is that society is rightly ordered, and therefore just, when its major institutions are arranged so as to achieve the greatest net balance of satisfaction summed over all the individuals belonging to it' (p22). Thus the Right, or the just outcome, is whatever maximises the Good.[40] What Rawls objects to about this utilitarianism is not that it has some notion of the Good, but that this understanding of justice allows things to happen, potentially at least, which Rawls thinks are generally regarded as *unjust*. This is why he proposes a foundational framework in which, instead, actions that would be generally regarded as unjust are disallowed: this is a framework, therefore, in which what is Good depends on a prior understanding of what is Right and just and fair. Hence his name for this overall framework is 'justice as fairness'.

Secondly, Rawls is not only concerned with the desirability of justice as fairness, but also its feasibility. It is not enough to demonstrate that it is more desirable than, in particular, a utilitarian conception: he seeks to show also that it is feasible, especially in the sense that it is stable and will therefore continue to be accepted by future generations.[41] The particular mode of analysis presented in *A Theory of Justice* - notably the related devices of the veil of

---

[37]The critique offered below (in sub-section 3) focuses on Rawls' actual conception of justice, rather than on his theory as a whole: a critical appraisal of the latter is far beyond the present remit, would be a mammoth undertaking, and in any case has been the focus of a huge swathe of literature, as indicated by the hundreds of references cited by Kukathas and Pettit, *Rawls*.

[38]See, e.g., p22 of Rawls, *A Theory of Justice*.

[39]*Ibid.*, p30.

[40]As noted in section A, mainstream utilitarianism refuses to disallow *any* act on the grounds simply that such an act is in itself wrong: it refuses all deontological claims.

[41]Kukathas and Pettit, *Rawls* (chapter 1) argue that the landmark nature of Rawls' book was in no small measure due to his recombination of these two criteria, criteria which had for decades been analysed in largely separate parts of academia.

ignorance and the original position - is primarily a relatively rigorous means of attempting to demonstrate that justice as fairness is both desirable and feasible.[42]

Thirdly, the question now arises as to the underlying moral and philosophical justification for justice as fairness, in the sense of how Rawls can claim that this is what is right - the kind of right that is prior to the good. Rawls explicitly eschews any derivation of justice from any external given (such as a divine being). With regard to his two particular principles of justice - which effectively embody the underlying notion of justice as fairness - he says the following:[43]

> I do not claim for the principles of justice proposed that they are necessary truths or derivable from such truths. A conception of justice cannot be deduced from self-evident premises or conditions [or] principles; instead its justification is a matter of the *mutual support of many considerations*, of everything fitting together into one coherent view.

Of these considerations, a central one concerns what Rawls often describes with such phrases as 'our considered judgments of justice', or conditions that 'we are ready upon due consideration to recognise as reasonable' (p21). He is careful to distinguish his approach from any kind of 'intuitionism', and thus it is clear that he is not referring here to any unreflective intuition or sense of justice. Rather, he is - as he states explicitly (e.g. p11) - operating in this regard in the Kantian tradition of reason and rational argument. Rawls' ultimate justification for justice as fairness, therefore, is simply that it is, at least in broad terms, the best available and the most coherent presentation of what we consider justice to be, given that we reason as carefully as we can from what we know about justice. There is no more ultimate justification than this.

Fourthly, the identity of the 'we' who reason carefully and rationally requires to be recognised. Although the literature which ensued from *A Theory of Justice* found this identity to be less than clear, his subsequent work has made it plain. Rawls intends to refer to modern, liberal, democratic societies - such as the USA. This is clear from his Dewey Lectures (published in 1980[44]),

---

[42]This can be seen by noting that, as a matter of logic, those devices cannot by themselves generate any proof of any proposition concerning justice. The conclusions about what might be chosen behind the veil of ignorance depend entirely upon the assumptions made regarding individuals in that original position. See further Kukathas and Pettit, *Rawls*, chapter 3. A more detailed account of Rawls' mode of analysis is given in the following sub-section.

[43]Rawls, *A Theory of Justice*, p21 (emphasis added). These two principles are described and assessed in the following sub-section.

[44]John Rawls, 'Kantian Constructivism in Moral Theory', *The Journal of Philosophy*, 1980, 88, 515-72.

where he stated that his concern in developing a Kantian conception of justice was to address 'an impasse in our recent political history', regarding two centuries of disagreement in the USA 'on the way basic social institutions should be arranged if they are to conform to the freedom and equality of citizens as moral persons'.[45] The disagreement concerns what seems to be a clash between freedom and equality; but the main point here is that Rawls' concern 'is to find, not universal principles of justice, but principles appropriate for modern societies like the United States'.[46] Thus, according to Rawls, 'we are not trying to find a conception of justice suitable for all societies regardless of their particular social or historical circumstances... How far the conclusions we reach are of interest in wider context is a separate question.'[47]

The fifth and final point about Rawls' foundational framework for justice is that it is explicitly in the contractarian tradition of Locke, Rousseau and Kant.[48] The particular mode of analysis - involving a veil of ignorance in an original position - is discussed in the next sub-section, but it is important, first, to recognise how central the idea of a social contract is to Rawls' proposed conception of justice, and therefore to the two specific principles he develops:[49]

> These principles rule out justifying institutions on the grounds that the hardships of some are offset by a greater good in the aggregate.[50] It is expedient *but it is not just* that some should have less in order that others may prosper...The intuitive idea is that since everyone's well-being depends upon a scheme of cooperation without which no one could have a satisfactory life, the division of advantages should be such as to *draw forth* the willing cooperation of everyone taking part in it, including those less well off.

Thus the contractarian approach, when combined with an appropriate - modern, liberal, democratic - notion of justice, is a very helpful means of achieving the twin goals, already explained, of desirability *and* feasibility. For if the social contract failed on the criterion either of desirability (because it was not just) or of feasibility (because not everyone took part) then it would not be a social contract. This is the heart of Rawls' conception of justice.

Rawls' Specific Theory of Justice

In Rawls' conception of justice

---

[45]*Ibid.*, p517. See also Kukathas and Pettit, *Rawls*, p123,
[46]Kukathas and Pettit, *Rawls*, p123.
[47]Rawls, 'Kantian Constructivism', p518.
[48]*A Theory of Justice*, p11.
[49]*Ibid.*, p15 (emphasis added).
[50]The contrast with utilitarianism is evident here.

the guiding idea is that the principles of justice for the basic structure of society are the object of the original agreement. They are the principles that free and rational persons concerned to further their own interests would accept in an initial position of equality as defining the fundamental terms of their association...This way of regarding the principles of justice I shall call justice as fairness.[51]

It is important to note here that - as in the passage just quoted - Rawls assumes that people are rational not only in that they reason sensibly, 'taking the most effective means to given ends' (p14), but also in that they act only in their own interests. His theory neither requires nor contains any assumption that people are in any way altruistic. Rather, one feature of his approach is to think of the parties - at least in the initial situation (see below) - 'as rational and mutually disinterested. This does not mean that the parties are egoists, that is, individuals with only certain kinds of interests, say in wealth, prestige and domination. But they are conceived as *not taking an interest in one another's interests.*'[52]

Note also that, prior to presenting the essentials of his specific theory of justice, Rawls has already stated that the *general* subject area covered by *any* concept of justice[53] comprises two aspects: (1) assigning rights and duties; (2) defining the appropriate division of social advantages (p10). Together these two aspects form 'the basic structure of society' (p10); and any particular conception of justice - such as his 'justice as fairness' - is to address this basic structure.

Rawls' use of a hypothetical 'initial situation' or 'opening position', featuring a universal veil of ignorance regarding the actual socio-economic position of all agents, is well known, and the principles of justice he then develops require serious appraisal.[54] His initial statement of the two principles is as follows (pp14f):

the first requires equality in the assignment of basic rights and duties, while the second holds that social and economic inequalities, for example inequalities of

---

[51] *Ibid.*, p11.

[52]*Ibid.*, p13. Later on Rawls notes (p264) that this strongly individualistic assumption requires some modification if the theory of justice as a whole is to succeed. What is needed is an explanation of 'the value of community'. He claims to show (pp440ff) that this explanation will be found in terms of self-respect. Whether this attempt is successful is assessed below.

[53]Hence this *general concept* of justice is clearly distinguished by Rawls from *particular conceptions* of justice - such as his own.

[54]Whatever the flaws in the methodology (see, for example, the papers in J. Angelo Corlett (ed.), *Equality and Liberty: Analyzing Rawls and Nozick*, Houndmills, Basingstoke: Macmillan, 1991), it is obvious that the two principles are those which Rawls himself believes in. The very substantial influence of his book is surely due, in significant measure, to the large number of people who find themselves in broad agreement with Rawls' basic conception of justice.

wealth and authority, are just only if they result in compensating benefits for everyone, and in particular for the least advantaged members of society.

A more precise formulation appears on p60:

> First: each person is to have an equal right to the most extensive basic liberty compatible with a similar liberty for others.[55]
> Second: social and economic inequalities are to be arranged so that they are both (a) reasonably expected to be to everyone's advantage, and (b) attached to positions and offices open to all.

There is a lexicographic ordering (p61) to these principles or conditions. The first must be met before the second can be applied, for 'a departure from the institutions of equal liberty...cannot be justified..., or compensated for, by greater social and economic advantages'. And within the second principle, (b) must be met before (a) can be applied.[56]

This formulation appears, at first sight, to lack the particular reference (in the initial statement) to the least advantaged persons. However, this apparent disparity is removed as soon as Rawls explains the phrases 'everyone's advantage' and 'equally open to all'.[57] He suggests that each of these phrases can be interpreted in two ways. The table below (from p65) displays the four possible different systems that therefore emerge:

---

[55]Subsequently Rawls revised this first principle slightly. In the initial formulation, he appeared to favour *both* the requirement of certain basic liberties - for all - *and* a principle of 'greatest equal liberty'. He was criticised for this apparent ambiguity (see Kukathas and Pettit, *Rawls*, p130), and responded by stating that he wished only to defend certain basic liberties (such as freedom of speech and the right to vote), and not the principle of liberty as such. Thus the revised first principle now reads: 'Each person has an equal right to a fully adequate scheme of equal basic liberties which is compatible with a similar scheme of liberties for all' (John Rawls, 'The Basic Liberties and Their Priority', in S. MacMurrin (ed.), *The Tanner Lectures on Human Values* (Cambridge: C.U.P., 1982), p5).

[56]See also Brian Barry, *The Liberal Theory of Justice: A Critical Examination of the Principal Doctrines in* A Theory of Justice *by John Rawls* (Oxford: Clarendon, 1973), pp51-2.

[57]With great candour he describes these phrases as ambiguous - even though ambiguity is perhaps a surprising characteristic of such a crucial matter as the formulation of one's two key principles.

"Everyone's advantage"

"Equally open"	Principle of efficiency	Difference principle
Equality as careers open to talents	System of Natural Liberty	Natural Aristocracy
Equality as equality of fair opportunity	Liberal Equality	Democratic Equality

The first (weaker) understanding of 'equally open' is 'careers open to talents', i.e. that 'positions are open to those able and willing to strive for them' (p66); 'all have at least the same legal rights of access to all advantaged social positions' (p72). In consequence, the initial distribution of assets for any period of time is strongly influenced by natural and social contingencies.

The stronger understanding adds the further condition of the equality of fair opportunity, i.e. that all people should have a fair chance to attain any given position. Essentially this means that class barriers should be 'evened out' - by which Rawls presumably means removed (p73).

The criterion of 'everyone's advantage' also has a weaker and a stronger interpretation. The weaker is the Pareto efficiency criterion prominent in welfare economics: this allows a range of possible outcomes - with varying trade-offs between equality and aggregate welfare/income - each of which is efficient in the sense that any further addition to any individual's income can be attained only if at least one other person's income decreases. Each of those possible outcomes is deemed efficient.

If this principle of efficiency is combined with 'careers open to talents', then we have a system of 'natural liberty'. If instead it is combined with the stronger version of equality - fair opportunity - then the resultant system is 'liberal equality'. Rawls is dissatisfied with both these systems. He claims that 'the liberal conception [liberal equality] seems clearly preferable to the system of natural liberty...'[58] Nevertheless, the liberal conception

---

[58]Rawls, *A Theory of Justice,* p73. In particular, it seeks 'to mitigate the influence of social contingencies and natural fortune on distributive shares' - and does so by setting free market arrangements 'within a framework of political and legal institutions which regulates the overall trends of economic events and preserves the social conditions necessary for fair equality of opportunity' (p73). Note that, in his theory of justice,

still appears defective...[It] still permits the distribution of wealth and income to be determined by the natural distribution of abilities and talents. Within the limits allowed by the background arrangements, distributive shares are decided by the outcome of the natural lottery; *and this outcome is arbitrary from a moral perspective*...Furthermore, the principle of fair opportunity can be only imperfectly carried out, at least as long as the institution of the family exists...[59]

Even though both natural liberty and the 'liberal conception' [liberal equality] do attempt to go beyond the principle of efficiency - they moderate its scope of operation, and constrain it by certain background institutions - they leave the rest 'to pure procedural justice' (p79). But this fails to deal with distributive injustice.

Rawls then introduces the stronger version of the 'everyone's advantage' principle, namely the 'difference principle' (p75):

This principle removes the indeterminateness of the principle of efficiency by singling out a particular position from which the social and economic inequalities of the basic structure are to be judged...[The] higher expectations [prospects] of those better situated are just only if they work as part of a scheme which improves the expectations of the least advantaged members of society.

When the difference principle is combined with 'careers open to talents', the resultant system is 'natural aristocracy': equality of opportunity exists only in the formal sense, 'but the advantages of persons with greater natural endowments are to be limited to those that further the good of the poorer sectors of society' (p74). Rawls spends little time on this particular formulation of the 'aristocratic ideal', but he does claim that it is 'unstable', by which he seems to mean that it is morally arbitrary to allow either social contingencies or natural chance to determine distributive shares (p75).

Thus Rawls comes to the fourth possible system, that of 'democratic equality' - the one he proposes to defend - which combines fair equality of opportunity with the difference principle. As already noted, Rawls assumes a basically free market economy. In order for 'democratic equality' to work, therefore, he further assumes that the economy is able to operate in such a manner that the efforts of entrepreneurs lead to the spread of material benefits 'throughout the system and to the least advantaged' (p78). Rawls models society here in terms of representative individuals by reference to whose

---

Rawls assumes an economic system of free markets, in which prices are freely determined by the forces of supply and demand (see, e.g., p270). Also, although he assumes that the ownership of production is largely in private hands he states that the system of ownership - so long as prices are determined by supply and demand - is not a central matter in his theory of justice (pp265-274).

[59]*Ibid.*, pp73-4 [emphasis added].

expectations (prospects) the socio-economic distribution can be judged. He argues that, even when 'the social injustices which now exist are removed' - referring to social and natural contingencies - it remains the case that 'those starting out as members of the entrepreneurial class[60]...have a better prospect than those who begin in the class of unskilled labourers.'[61] The key question is this: 'What...can possibly justify this kind of initial inequality in life prospects? According to the difference principle, it is justifiable only if the difference in expectation is to the advantage of the representative man who is worse off, in this case the representative unskilled worker' (p78). Hence the difference principle has come to be known as a 'maximin' principle: for, strictly speaking, inequalities are permitted only if they enable the maximization of the expectations of the person in the minimum (least well-off) position.

Rawls regards this system of democratic equality - the system he both favours and thinks would be favoured by those in the opening position - as strongly egalitarian, at least in one sense. The key factor here is the difference principle.[62] According to Rawls,

> the difference principle represents, in effect, an agreement to regard the distribution of natural talents *as a common asset* and to share in the benefits of this distribution whatever it turns out to be. Those who have been favoured by nature...may gain from their good fortune only on terms that improve the situation of those who have lost out.[63]

Thus Rawls claims that, under justice as fairness, the 'social order can be justified to everyone, and in particular to those who are least favoured; and in this sense it is egalitarian.'[64] He also claims, in a short excursus on the difference principle (pp76-78), that, by contrast with this principle, a classic utilitarian approach is significantly less egalitarian. This is because a classic utilitarian 'is indifferent as to how a constant sum of benefits is distributed'; the point here is that the utilitarian does *not* insist that a more favoured person may gain *only* if every person gains. Rather, the utilitarian will allow - indeed insist - that a more favoured person will grow considerably more wealthy, even if others do not gain (or if they lose), if that greater wealth - or, more precisely, the greater utility which ensues - results in a better overall social utility. By contrast, 'the difference principle is a strongly egalitarian conception in the

---

[60]For everyone must start somewhere - at least in Rawls' scenario.

[61]Any readers of Rawls who might have suspected Marxist underpinnings will by this point have had those suspicions removed.

[62]Interpreted, as above, in terms of democratic equality.

[63]*Ibid.*, p101 (emphasis added). By making this assumption that natural talents are a common asset, Rawls evidently stakes out ground distinct from that of libertarians. (See the following section, on Robert Nozick.)

[64]*Ibid.*, p103.

sense that unless there is a distribution that makes both persons better off [Rawls is here assuming a simple, two-person world], an equal distribution is to be preferred.'[65]

The claim that the system is, in the above sense, egalitarian faces a difficulty. In an extreme case, suppose the prospects are for one entrepreneur to gain millions of pounds, whilst everyone else (including the least advantaged) expects to gain only one pound each. Such a prospect would be permitted by 'democratic equality'. Clearly this poses a serious problem for Rawls: is such a prospect compatible with any meaningful conception of equality? He tries to deal with this by distinguishing two cases (pp78f). In the first, the expectations of the least advantaged are maximized: no changes 'in the expectations of those better off can improve the situation of those worst off. The best arrangement obtains, what I shall call a perfectly just scheme' (p78).[66]

The second case

> is that in which the expectations of all those better off at least contribute to the welfare of the more unfortunate. That is, if their expectations [those of the better off] were decreased, the prospects of the least advantaged would likewise fall. Yet the maximum is not yet achieved. Even higher expectations for the more advantaged would raise the expectations of those in the lowest position. Such a position is, I shall say, just throughout, but not the best just arrangement.[67]

This second case appears to be Pareto-*in*efficient, and would seem therefore to be only second best.

Rawls then seeks to distinguish this second case from a third sort of possible scheme (p79):

> A scheme is *unjust* when the higher expectations, one or more of them, is excessive.[68] If these expectations were decreased, the situation of the least favoured would be improved. *How unjust* an arrangement is depends on how excessive the higher expectations are and to what extent they depend upon violation of the other principles of justice, for example, fair equality of

---

[65]*Ibid.*, p76. Note that the hypothetical initial arrangement has an equal distribution of all the social primary goods (such as freedom of speech and opportunity, and self-respect), *and* an equal sharing of income and wealth. In explaining his general conception of justice, Rawls takes this state of affairs as 'a benchmark for judging improvements. If certain *inequalities* of wealth and organizational powers would make everyone better off than in this hypothetical starting situation, then they accord with the general conception' (p62; emphasis added).

[66]This seems to mean the most egalitarian option drawn from the range of Pareto-efficient possibilities.

[67]*Ibid.*, pp78-9.

[68]This seems to refer to the expectations of one or more of those individuals in the 'better off' category.

opportunity; but I shall not attempt to measure in any exact way the degrees of injustice.[69]

It is this third type of case which seems to enable Rawls to avoid the extreme 'trickle down' possibility. He can avoid it *if* in such an extreme case, it would be possible to rearrange matters in such a way that the expectations of the better off could be lowered to the benefit of the worst off: i.e. if the 'extreme trickle down' scenario is 'unjust' as defined here by Rawls. If, on the other hand, no such rearrangement were possible - if 'extreme trickle down' is the only way for the economy to develop - then that is too bad; but not unjust. However, that degree of rigidity is at odds with Rawls' type of approach, which assumes there are genuinely alternative ways in which the economy might develop.

The reason why Rawls distinguishes between these three cases is to show that 'while the difference principle is, strictly speaking, a maximizing principle, there is a significant distinction between the cases that fall short of the best arrangement' (p79). If, then (for some unstated reason) the first case - perfect justice - is unattainable, then society should avoid the third type of case, and instead choose the second. For, comparing those two cases, then in the third the 'even larger difference between rich and poor makes the latter even worse off, and this violates the principle of mutual advantage as well as democratic equality' (p79).

Finally, it should be noted both that a perfectly just system (i.e. democratic equality) is also efficient (p80); but also that, if one starts from a position where the basic structure is unjust, then the operation of Rawls' two principles 'will authorize changes that may lower the expectations of some of those better off' (p79).

Weaknesses in Rawls' Conception of Justice

Rawls requires that any gain for the rich be accompanied by at least some gain to everyone else. This is his fundamental conception of justice. Particularly in the light of the biblical conception developed in the previous two chapters, one fundamental problem with Rawls' conception is that it says little or nothing about relationships. Utilitarianism has the same weakness: and that linkage is not surprising, since Rawls' theory is in significant measure a response to utilitarianism; and since both frameworks share an individualist model of society.[70]

The non-relational nature of Rawls' approach can be seen by noting that, in his system, the better off have no actual responsibility towards the less well off. The requirement that the least advantaged should gain (when others do) is

---

[69]*Ibid.*, p79 [emphasis added].
[70]This point is discussed further in the following chapters.

simply stated as a principle. Egalitarianism - within the constraints of 'real life' - is his axiomatic commitment.

A second fundamental problem, again brought out in the light of the biblical conception of justice, is an inadequate view of the person. For example, the least advantaged individuals have no stated or explicit needs: they are given attention simply because they are at the bottom of the pile, not because being at the bottom of the pile causes them any particular hardships or difficulties. They are not 'poor and needy'. A deeper analysis, by contrast, would draw attention to the actual people involved and the personal aspects of their life situation.[71]

Another class of problems concerns Rawls' more detailed interpretation of his principles of justice. Two particular practical difficulties are discussed here. First, the difference principle requires the maximization of the social and economic interests of the 'least advantaged' (given that Rawls' first principle has been thoroughly applied, i.e. that 'equal citizenship' - in terms of civil and political rights - has been established). Such interests involve, essentially, the 'primary goods' of wealth and power. But what is the precise definition of 'least advantaged'? Recall that Rawls assesses the outworking of the difference principle by means of 'representative individuals'. This in turn requires a definition of the least fortunate group, i.e. the group of which the least advantaged 'representative man' is a member. Rawls calls this question of definition a 'serious difficulty' (p98) - although, as Barry observes, to this serious difficulty Rawls then 'devotes a little under one page out of six hundred', and hence 'his treatment of it can only be described as offhand'.[72] Rawls offers two different indices or definitions for the 'worst-off representative man' (p98). His approach, which relies on averages, aggregations and representative individuals, means that the people who are actually worst off might not be bettered at all by the application of Rawls' principles. This characteristic of Rawls' model seems to invite Barry's charge that Rawls is 'an unreconstructed Gladstonian liberal' (p50). Lest we think that this 'averaging' is a quirk of Rawls' specific model, and not a more general feature of his thinking, Rawls' account - which spells out the process by which, behind the 'veil of ignorance' in the 'original position', the principles of justice are supposedly agreed upon - clarifies the matter:

> In any case we are to aggregate to some degree over the expectations of the worst off...Yet we are entitled at some point to plead practical considerations in formulating the difference principle...I assume therefore that the persons in the original position understand the difference principle to be defined in one of these [two] ways. They interpret it from the first as a limited aggregative principle and assess it as such in comparison with other standards. *It is not as if they agreed to think of the least advantaged as literally the worst off individual and then in order*

---

[71]This point also is discussed further in the chapters which follow.
[72]Barry, *The Liberal Theory of Justice,* p49.

to make this criterion work adopted in practice some form of averaging. Rather it is the practicable criterion itself that is to be evaluated from the perspective of the original position.[73]

It is not entirely clear why Rawls leaves behind, once he gets down to details, the 'literally' least advantaged. He gives no principled reason for doing so; and, as already noted, his discussion here is remarkably brief and casual. The above-quoted paragraph, however, carries a hint that it is a matter of what is a 'practicable criterion'. To interpret this further is guesswork, but perhaps Rawls thinks it is somehow infeasible to focus efforts on that small number of individuals who are literally the worst off - and that it is more 'practicable' to devote energies to a wider group of people, as a group, even if some of the 'literally' worst off fail to benefit in the process.

Even if that conjecture were right, Rawls would be on shaky ground in having such a view of what is practicable. As Barry comments, research suggests that the sources of poverty include such things as having children, being sick or unemployed for a long period, and being old or disabled. Another source is the low pay awarded (in many countries, including industrial ones) to agricultural work and to jobs done almost exclusively by women. 'These causes of poverty could remain untackled while either of Rawls's indices for the "worst-off representative man" were maximized'.[74]

The second practical difficulty is that Rawls' 'justice as fairness' seems ill-equipped to cope with the complex distributive questions posed in modern societies.[75] On the one hand, his principles - perhaps strangely - lack the simplicity and conviction to get him very far once things become more complex. On the other hand, they are, at root, too simple. This somewhat paradoxical matter can be explained in the following way. The *lack* of simplicity and conviction is revealed in Rawls' statement on p158:

> [There] is no objection to resting the choice of first principles upon the general facts of economics and psychology...[The] parties in the original position are assumed to know the general facts about human society...their choice of principles is relative to these facts. What is essential, of course, is that these premises be true and sufficiently general.

Whilst the role of empirical data in moral reasoning undoubtedly requires careful deliberation, Rawls' particular stance here places excessive emphasis upon 'the facts', and too little upon the integrity and coherence of his own 'first principles'. In particular, 'the facts' do not back him all the way: as noted earlier, persistent poverty is a reality. Rawls' model, by contrast, assumes that,

---

[73]Rawls, *A Theory of Justice,* p98 [emphasis added].
[74]Barry, *The Liberal Theory of Justice,* pp51-2.
[75]Cf. Barry, *ibid.,* pp112-5.

in maximizing the interests of the least advantaged, everyone benefits. (See his discussion of 'chain connection' - 'trickle down' by another name - on pages 80-83.) It is really no surprise that, in such a (prospective) world, rational agents behind the veil come to agree (according to Rawls) upon a system of democratic equality - especially when it is recalled that the maximization of the benefits of the least advantaged might well involve substantially greater increases in income (compared with those for the poorest) for those already expecting to be the most well off. The problem for Rawls is that, in a world where Panglossian 'chain connection' does not hold, then there is no reason to believe that 'democratic equality' will win wide agreement. His kind of justice is far from an absolute requirement - rather, it has to be affordable.

On the other hand, Rawls' principles, despite a lack of simple conviction, are *too simple*, almost to the point of naivete. Barry argues that questions of distributive justice require a whole mass of different measures.[76] He concludes that 'egalitarianism as an actual belief is not to be identified simply as a belief about the desirable extent of deviation about the mean but is a much more complex distributive doctrine' (p115). 'Justice as fairness', however - despite the length of the book - barely seems to make a start on such matters.

Challenges Posed by Rawls for a Biblically-rooted Conception of Justice

Despite Rawls' weaknesses, he poses some serious challenges for a biblical understanding of justice.[77] First, is something like the maximin (difference) principle a necessary ingredient of justice? Those who perceive in Scripture a 'bias to the poor' clearly answer 'yes', but is this so? And if it is, then the two weaknesses in Rawls discussed in the previous few paragraphs will need to be overcome. If, on the other hand, it were argued that a biblical understanding of justice entails *nothing* so specific as the difference principle, then the difficulty would be that such an understanding was somewhat vacuous: it would be a very general understanding, but with little operational significance.[78]

Secondly - and related - does a biblically-rooted conception of justice have anything to say about the extent to which justice is egalitarian? If so, is it more egalitarian, or less egalitarian, than Rawls' conception? If it has nothing to say on this, can it claim with any conviction to have relevance to contemporary debates? Alternatively, it might be argued that the egalitarian scale of

---

[76]*Ibid.*, p114.

[77]These challenges need be stated only briefly here: they are discussed at length in the following chapter.

[78]Such a general understanding allows Christians who actually have conflicting interpretations of justice to *appear* to be in agreement; but this agreement is a mirage. (For related weaknesses with contemporary Christian thought regarding justice, see chapter 1, above.)

assessment is simply inappropriate in terms of a biblical-rooted conception of justice. But if that is the case, then there would seem to be a requirement for some other scale(s) of assessment to be articulated, in order for the conception of justice to have significant applicability.

Thirdly, does a biblically-rooted conception of justice require a greater emphasis on heterogeneity than that offered by Rawls? For example, to what extent do the doctrines of creation and Fall imply a greater degree of heterogeneity and variety than that assumed, and thought acceptable, by Rawls?

Fourthly, Rawls' work, which is dismissive of a meritocratic emphasis, raises the question of whether a biblically-rooted conception is similarly dismissive. Does a biblical framework have the capacity to appraise whether Rawls is correct to view the natural endowment of talents[79] as a common pool, or whether a more meritocratic view - with reward for effort much more prominent - is a correct understanding of justice?

Libertarianism and Justice: Especially Nozick's Entitlement Theory

The substantive task of this section is to offer an appraisal of Nozick's theory of justice. The section closes by briefly identifying the challenges posed by Nozick's theory for a biblical understanding.[80]

Nozick's Theory of Justice

In *Anarchy, State and Utopia*[81] Nozick argues for a minimal state: the state which governs a country should, on the one hand, have greater powers than a proponent of anarchy would accept; on the other hand, its powers should be strictly limited to the protection of people's property rights - protecting people against force, fraud and theft, and enforcing mutually-agreed contracts.[82] According to Nozick, his entitlement theory of justice demonstrates that any state which has more than minimal powers (as defined above) necessarily behaves unjustly. Thus the many modern, more extensive, states which seek to distribute resources from better off to worse off individuals are unjust.

Nozick does not ignore distributive justice. Rather he develops a theory of holdings (entitlements) in which the state is not needed in order to ensure that everyone gets their rightful share of resources. 'If the set of holdings is properly

---

[79]Typically regarded as unequal - as by Rawls.

[80]This section is considerably shorter than the previous two, primarily because Nozick's theory of justice - although influential - is substantially less complex than that of Rawls, and the issues raised are less complex than those raised by utilitarianism. Simplicity and profundity are not, of course, incompatible.

[81]Oxford: Blackwell, 1974.

[82]Nozick, *Anarchy, State and Utopia*, p.ix.

generated, there is no argument for a more extensive state based upon distributive justice.'[83] Obviously this implies a radically different understanding of justice from that (or those) underpinning most modern states: in contrast to the notion that there is some social 'cake' to which everyone should be allocated, as of right, some share or other, Nozick focuses upon 'justice in holdings'[84]. If someone's holding of a particular property is just, then the state would violate that person's rights if it sought to tax or remove that property, in order to distribute to someone else. A related feature of Nozick's theory is that it takes account of past actions and circumstances - in contrast to those that focus solely on the current structure of distribution.[85] The latter are termed 'end-state' or 'time-slice' theories.

Nozick argues as follows:

> If the world were wholly just, the following inductive definition would exhaustively cover the subject of justice in holdings.
>
> 1.   A person who acquires a holding in accordance with the principle of justice in acquisition is entitled to that holding.
>
> 2.   A person who acquires a holding in accordance with the principle of justice in transfer, from someone else entitled to that holding, is entitled to the holding.
>
> 3.   No one is entitled to a holding except by (repeated) applications of 1 and 2.
>
> The complete principle of distributive justice would say simply that a distribution is just if everyone is entitled to the holdings they possess under the distribution.[86]

To the above two principles of justice in acquisition and justice in transfer must be added justice in rectification - in order to repair the effects of past injustices in acquisition and transfer. What does Nozick means by such 'injustices'?

> Not all actual situations are generated in accordance with the two principles of justice in holdings... Some people steal from others, or defraud them, or enslave them, seizing their product and preventing them from living as they choose, or

---

[83]*Ibid.*, p230.

[84]*Ibid.*, p150.

[85]*Ibid.*, p153.

[86]*Ibid.*, p151. In contrast to his fellow libertarian Hayek - whose major concern with regard to many notions of distributive justice and social justice was to demolish them - Nozick seeks to construct a positive libertarian account of what makes a distribution just. Hayek puts his case in *The Mirage of Social Justice* [1976]; Vol. 2 of F. A. Hayek, *Law, Legislation and Liberty: A new statement of the liberal principles of justice and political economy* (London: Routledge and Kegan Paul, 1982).

forcibly exclude others from competing in exchanges. None of these are permissible modes of transition from one situation to another.[87] And some persons acquire holdings by means not sanctioned by the principle of justice in acquisition.[88]

Given some means of discerning and rectifying such injustices, Nozick is able to state the general outlines of his theory as follows: 'the holdings of a person are just if he is entitled to them by the principles of justice in acquisition and transfer, or by the principle of rectification of injustice (as specified by the first two principles).[89]

Given this entitlement theory of justice, Nozick offers his 'Wilt Chamberlain' example (pp161-164).[90] This is designed to demonstrate that liberty and equality are *not* compatible goals; i.e. one can enforce some particular notion or degree of equality only by infringing upon the liberty of a smaller or larger number of people. As Wolff points out, however, liberty is not - even for Nozick - the pure or unrestrained thing that one might initially assume it to be. 'Liberty is merely the right to do what you have a right to do.'[91] In particular, to say that liberty includes the freedom to use and enjoy one's private property entirely as one wishes is predicated upon the understanding that ownership of private property includes the right to the use of that property. The liberty of some other person, on this understanding, does *not* include the right to use the first person's property. Why not? Because of the prior understanding of what rights are about.

To establish his view, Nozick has to go further back and argue the case for justice in acquisition. If a just acquisition does entail an absolute right to use of property, then he has a case for his view of justice in transfer. To establish this requires one in turn to go back to a time in history when the earth's resources had not been appropriated by anyone. However, a libertarian has a serious problem here: prior to such appropriations, everyone had a right of use (e.g. to walk across or around a particular area of land); after it, this right is gone; hence everyone's liberty is diminished, except that of the appropriator. How can such acquisition be just?

Perhaps surprisingly, Nozick offers no formulation of this principle of justice in acquisition. He does, however, seek to provide some relevant insights

---

[87]I.e., they are injustices in transfer.

[88]*Ibid.*, p152.

[89]*Ibid.*, p153.

[90]In which a famous basketball player becomes extremely wealthy, on the back of (relatively) very small entrance fees paid by a very large number of admiring, and relatively poor, spectators; and hence the initial income distribution is made considerably more unequal.

[91]Jonathan Wolff, *Robert Nozick: Property, Justice and the Minimal State* (Cambridge: Polity Press, 1991). p100.

here, based on Locke's attempt to specify a principle of justice in acquisition.[92] 'Locke views property rights in an unowned object as originating through someone's mixing his labour with it.'[93] There are considerable practical difficulties with this approach, however, and these lead Nozick to add the following 'Lockean proviso': 'A process normally giving rise to a permanent bequeathable property right in a previously unowned thing will *not* do so if the position of others no longer at liberty to use the thing *is thereby worsened*.'[94] Thus Nozick's argument is that, when someone appropriates some previously unowned property, no one else's situation must thereby be actually worsened, all things considered. (Nozick wants such 'all things' to include the possibility that the owner of the property is the person able to make the most efficient use of it; in which case, his ownership may produce *benefits*, rather than losses, for others.) Nozick argues that one person's appropriation should still leave others enough to *use*, even if not enough to *take* or *own* (p176). Without some such Nozickian proviso, others could object, rightly, that the action of the first party was in some sense unjust or unfair.

Nozick's approach faces substantial difficulties, however. If justice in acquisition depends on matters of relative efficiency, the task of verifying such justice can never be done at the time, but, at best, only later (how much later?). Is inheritance an adequate basis for handling the transfer of property across generations? Surely my rights are not preconditioned by apparently random factors regarding who 'first discovered' different sections of land centuries earlier? It may also be doubted whether Nozick's discussion is an adequate response to the initial problem of liberty-reduction for everyone except the appropriator.

It would appear, then, that Nozick takes it as his fundamental axiom that property ownership brings absolute rights. He does not defend this because he cannot defend it. All he can offer is an assortment of suggestions, none of which makes a convincing argument. Thus Nozick's first principle - that of justice in acquisition - is significantly lacking in rigour. Nevertheless he argues that a valid theory of justice in holdings is constituted by this principle, combined with the second - justice in transfer. Thus, with regard to claims for a state more extensive than the minimal state, Nozick argues as follows:

> According to the entitlement conception of justice in holdings that we have presented, there is no argument based upon the first two principles of justice...for such a more extensive state... (Nor...will the Lockean proviso actually provide occasion for a more extensive state.)[95]

---

[92]Nozick, *Anarchy, State and Utopia*, p174.
[93]*Ibid.*, p174.
[94]*Ibid.*, p178 [emphasis added].
[95]*Ibid.*, p230.

If, however, the first two principles are violated, Nozick's third principle - that of rectification - comes into play.[96] And with it comes a case for a more extensive state. As Wolff points out, for a libertarian to *ignore* past injustices - according to libertarian criteria for justice in acquisition and in transfer - will not do:

> Part of the libertarian position involves treating property rights as natural rights, and so as being as important as anything can be. On the libertarian view, the fact that an injustice is old, and, perhaps, difficult to prove, does not make it any less of an injustice. Nozick, to his credit, appreciates this, and implies that in all cases we should try to work out what should have happened had the injustice not taken place. If the present state of affairs does not correspond to this hypothetical description, then it should be made to correspond.[97]

Such justice in rectification, however, appears utterly infeasible. The number and extent of past injustices are surely incalculable, let alone their consequences. All state-imposed transfers are unjust (on Nozick's view), for a start. And private individuals have, on any account, committed many, many injustices, but whose precise details are, centuries later, impossible to assess.

What, then, can be done? Remarkably, Nozick concludes by abandoning his earlier opposition to patterned approaches to distribution, and by adopting a Rawls-type criterion:

> Perhaps it is best to view some patterned principles of distributive justice as rough rules of thumb meant to approximate the general results of applying the principle of rectification of injustice. For example, lacking much historical information, and assuming (1) that victims of injustice generally do worse than they otherwise would and (2) that those from the least well-off group in the society have the highest probabilities of being the (descendants of) victims of the most serious injustice who are owed compensation by those benefited from the injustices..., then a *rough* rule of thumb for rectifying injustices might seem to be the following: organise society so as to maximise the position of whatever group ends up least well-off in society. (pp230-1)

Nozick goes on to suggest that 'past injustices might be so great as to make necessary in the short run a more extensive state in order to rectify them' (p231). Clearly he ends up with the view that the world is messy, and that the only solutions possible are - especially in the light of his initial pure, untarnished liberty - messy. He is in the same pragmatic boat as most other political philosophers. His libertarian project seems to have failed.

---

[96]*Ibid.*
[97]Wolff, *Robert Nozick*, p116.

Challenges Posed for a Christian Understanding of Justice

Nozick's work poses two main challenges. These need be stated only briefly here, since they are taken up in the following chapter. First, what rights, if any, are involved in relation to the ownership and/or use of property? How do these rights (if any) relate to liberty? Or - using the language of justice/injustice, rather than that of 'rights'- how does justice apply to the ownership and/or use of property? How does liberty in this area relate to justice? Secondly, in what ways, if any, can state-enforced transfers of income, wealth and property be justified? Although Nozick has not successfully made a positive libertarian case, his negative critique of standard assumptions about the legitimacy of government socio-political action is extremely important, and needs a response.

Justice: Recent Roman Catholic Teaching

In the remaining sections of this chapter, three Christian treatments of justice are appraised, on the basis of the biblical account developed in chapters 2 and 3, and in terms of whether they respond adequately to the challenges posed by the three secular conceptions already examined.

With regard, first, to Roman Catholic social teaching on justice, attention will be paid to documents issued during the last hundred years or so, i.e. from *Rerum Novarum* (1891) onwards. Some attention will also be given to the joint pastoral letter published in 1986 by the U.S.A.'s Roman Catholic bishops, *Economic Justice For All*.[98] The first sub-section offers a brief account of Roman Catholic social teaching in regard to justice. The second sub-section presents a critical appraisal, especially with relation to the extent to which this teaching is an adequate response to the challenges posed by the secular theories of justice already considered. The final sub-section notes briefly the challenges that the Roman Catholic social teaching itself poses, especially for the attempt to construct a biblically-rooted understanding of justice.[99]

An Account of the Roman Catholic Social Teaching on Justice[100]

Developments in the official teaching over the last hundred years or so have

---

[98]National Conference of Catholic Bishops, *Economic Justice For All: Pastoral Letter on Catholic Social Teaching and the U.S. Economy* (Washington, D.C.: United States Catholic Conference, 1986).

[99]This last sentence implies that the Roman Catholic teaching does not in practice fall fully within the parameters of what it means to be biblically-rooted. It will be argued in due course that this is indeed the case.

[100]There is no intention in this section of providing a survey of this teaching. Rather, the aim is simply to highlight some key contributions, thus conveying a sense of the overall thrust of Catholic social teaching on justice.

brought a clear emphasis upon, and call for, a preferential option for the poor. This process - up to Vatican II - is briefly surveyed in the following paragraphs. From that point, when the flow of relevant encyclicals and other official documents increased substantially, the social teaching will be largely taken as summarised in the recent *Catechism of the Catholic Church*[101] - 'a statement of the Church's faith and of catholic doctrine, attested to or illumined by Sacred Scripture, the Apostolic Tradition and the Church's Magisterium' (according to Pope John Paul II, on p5 of that *Catechism*).

The process towards proclaiming a 'preferential option for the poor' began with Leo XIII's *Rerum Novarum* (*RN*: 1891[102]). The socio-economic context here comprised the patterns now well-established by the Industrial Revolution, and Leo's primary concern was for the plight of those at the bottom of the social scale who, for the most part, 'are tossed about helplessly and disastrously in conditions of pitiable and utterly undeserved misery'. Ownership patterns were such that 'a tiny group of extravagantly rich men have been able to lay upon a great multitude of unpropertied workers a yoke little better than that of slavery itself.'[103] Leo rejected socialism as a false remedy, but called upon both owners and workers to fulfil their 'obligations in justice' to one another (*RN* 16), and argued in particular that 'the rich employer must not treat his workers as though they were his slaves, but must reverence them as men who are his equals in dignity...' (*RN* 16).

This was extended forty years later by Pius XI's *Quadragesimo Anno* (*QA*[104]), which offered an updated and more detailed analysis of socio-economic behaviour and structures, and was again fiercely critical both of economic liberalism and of Socialism (in both its Communist and less radical forms). He introduced the term 'social justice' to Catholic social teaching, and linked it with Leo XIII's emphasis on the common good, arguing as follows:

> Wealth...must be so distributed amongst the various individuals and classes of society, that the common good of all...be thereby promoted... By these principles of social justice, one class is forbidden to exclude the other from a share in the profits.[105]

Thirty years further on, Pope John XXIII's *Mater et Magistra* (1961), whatever its 'lack of understanding for the positive role of money, banking and

---

[101]Published (in Latin) in October 1992, and in English in 1994 (London: Geoffrey Chapman, 1994).

[102]Leo XIII, *Rerum Novarum* [1891], tr. Joseph Kirwan (London: Catholic Truth Society, 1991).

[103]*Ibid.*, #2.

[104]Pius XI, *Quadragesimo Anno* (London: Catholic Truth Society, 1931).

[105]*Ibid.*, p27.

financial markets',[106] argued that a greater involvement of the State in economic and social life, compared with earlier years, was now necessary. In Dorr's words, this was 'because in modern Western life human interdependence is possible only by going beyond one-to-one relationships and those of the small community; life is lived on a scale that requires the massive apparatus of the State to be actively involved in directing and controlling the economic and social life of the people'.[107] Shortly after that, the work of Vatican II, notably *Gaudium et Spes* (*GS*, 1965), laid a significant new emphasis on the rights of the world's poor in terms of *social justice*. Note especially the following:

> God intended the earth and all it contains for the use of all men and peoples...
> [E]verybody has a right to a share of the earth's goods sufficient for himself and
> his family. [H]e who is in extreme need has a right to supply this need from the
> riches of others. Since so many people in the world suffer from hunger, the
> Council urges men and authorities to remember that saying of the Fathers: 'Feed a
> man who is dying from hunger - if you have not fed him you have killed him.'[108]

By the early 1990s, a number of other official publications[109] had served to extend further the Catholic social teaching with regard to justice, so that the *Catechism of the Catholic Church* was able to bring together a number of significant points, in its section on 'the seventh commandment'.[110] This section contains six main themes, the first of which is 'The Universal Destination and the Private Ownership of Goods'. Secondly, 'Respect for Persons and Their Goods' requires (amongst other things) 'the practice of the virtue of *justice*, to preserve our neighbour's rights and render him what is his due; and the practice of *solidarity*'.[111] Third comes 'The Social Doctrine of the Church', which rejects both regulation by centralised planning, and regulation solely by the law of the marketplace, since the latter 'fails social justice, for "there are many

---

[106]Dennis P. McCann, 'The Church and Wall Street', *America*, 158, no.4, Jan.1988, 85-94; repr. in Max L. Stackhouse *et al* (eds.), *On Moral Business: Classical and Contemporary Resources for Ethics in Economic Life*, (Grand Rapids, MI: Eerdmans, 1995); p622 [page reference from the latter]. McCann argues that previous contributions to Catholic social teaching were similarly lacking in understanding.

[107]Donal Dorr, *Option for the Poor: A Hundred Years of Catholic Social Teaching*, (rev. ed., Maryknoll, N.Y.: Orbis, 1992), p137.

[108]Paul VI and the Fathers of the Sacred Council [Second Vatican Council: Pastoral Constitution on the Church in the World of Today], *Gaudium et Spes*, tr. William Purdy (London: Catholic Truth Society, 1966), 69.

[109]Notably John Paul II's encyclicals *Laborem Exercens* (*LE*, 1981) and Centesimus Annus (*CA*, 1991).

[110]This commandment - 'You shall not steal' - is regarded by Protestants as the eighth.

[111]*Catechism of the Catholic Church*, op.cit., p514, #2407.

human needs which cannot be satisfied by the market"'.[112] Fourthly, under the heading of 'Economic Activity and Social Justice', the *Catechism* states the following (p518, #2426):

> The development of economic activity and growth in production are meant to provide for the needs of human beings... Economic activity, conducted according to its own proper methods, is to be exercised within the limits of the moral order, in keeping with social justice so as to correspond to God's plan for man.

The term 'social justice' does not appear again under this heading, but it seems clear that what follows is intended to elucidate what is meant by 'social justice'. Thus it is stated that everyone has the right of economic initiative, whereby 'everyone should make legitimate use of his talents to the abundance that will benefit all, and to observe the just fruits of his labour' (p519, #2429). It is also stated that those responsible for business enterprises 'have an obligation to consider the good of persons and not only the increase of *profits*.'[113] In addition, the *Catechism* says that a just wage 'is the legitimate fruit of work... In determining fair pay both the needs and the contributions of each person must be taken into account' (p520, #2434). It then adds (quoting from *GS* 67):

> Remuneration for work should guarantee man the opportunity to provide a dignified livelihood for himself and his family on the material, social, cultural and spiritual level, taking into account the role and the productivity of each, the state of the business, and the common good.

It concludes the paragraph by stating that agreement between the parties 'is *not* sufficient to justify morally the amount to be received in wages'.[114]

Fifthly, 'Justice and Solidarity Among Nations' claims that rich nations 'have a grave moral responsibility towards those which are unable to ensure the means of their development by themselves or have been prevented from doing so by tragic historical events. It is a duty in solidarity and charity; it is also an obligation in justice if the prosperity of the rich nations has come from resources that have not been paid for fairly'.[115]

It is worth noting here that the use of the term 'solidarity' is particularly prominent in the papal encyclical *Laborem Exercens* (*LE*, 1981)[116]. For

---

[112]*Ibid.*, p518, #2425; the phrase it quotes comes from *CA* 34.

[113]*Ibid.*, p520, #2432 (emphasis in the original).

[114]*Ibid.* (emphasis added).

[115]*Ibid.*, p521, #2439. It would be unreasonable to conclude from this last sentence that solidarity and justice are independent criteria, with justice *not* included in solidarity. The following paragraphs in the text indicate why that would be unreasonable.

[116]John Paul II, *Laborem Exercens* (London: Catholic Truth Society, 1981).

example, in a paragraph dealing with the need for new movements of solidarity of and with those who are degraded and exploited, John Paul II writes: 'The Church is firmly committed to this cause, for she considers it her mission, her service, a proof of her fidelity to Christ, so that she can truly be "the Church of the poor"'.[117] Thus solidarity is not a matter only for the poor and exploited themselves, but is also a matter of the Church's duty. The call is for an active involvement that accepts the need for some confrontation but which is well short of a revolutionary-type struggle.[118]

Finally, under 'Love for the Poor', it is stated that giving alms to the poor is not only 'one of the chief witnesses to fraternal charity', but 'is also a work of justice pleasing to God' (p523; #2447). Moreover, in line with the example of Christ the Saviour, who identified himself with the least of his brethren, so 'those who are oppressed by poverty are the object of *a preferential love* on the part of the Church which...in spite of...failings...has not ceased to work for their relief, defence and liberation, through numerous works of charity...'[119]

A Critical Appraisal of the Recent Roman Catholic Social Teaching on Justice

This sub-section seeks to assess the overall contribution of the recent Roman Catholic teaching, taken cumulatively, especially with regard to the extent to which it offers an adequate response to the challenges posed by the secular theories of justice considered previously. It will be argued that the major weakness in the teaching is that inadequate attention is given to the task of defining the notion of justice. There are two aspects here. First, justice is given insufficient theological underpinning. Secondly, there is no thorough account of justice in philosophical terms. So, at a practical level, the Roman Catholic social teaching seems to assume that everyone knows what justice is - and that the only real questions concern whether or not the Church will or should get its hands dirty and do something about it.[120] But that can properly be considered only after clear theological and philosophical foundations have been laid. These two aspects - theological and philosophical - will be considered in turn.

THEOLOGICAL BASIS

One of the clearest recent theological treatments is in Pope Paul VI's Apostolic

---

[117]*Ibid.*, #8.

[118]Cf. Dorr, *Option for the Poor*, pp309-315.

[119]*Catechism of the Catholic Church*, p523, #2448 (emphasis in the original).

[120]The recent *Catechism of the Catholic Church* contains material on economic activity and social justice, as noted earlier. The point here, however, is that, despite the various references to justice and social justice, there is little attempt to say what is actually meant by these terms.

Exhortation *Evangelii Nuntiandi* (*EN*, 1975).[121] This was published, at least in part, in response to the document *Justice in the World* issued by the Third General Assembly of the Synod of Bishops in 1971.[122] The latter had argued that action to promote justice and transform the world are 'a constitutive dimension' of the preaching of the Gospel and of the mission of the Church to bring redemption and liberation from oppression.[123] The word 'constitutive' is significant here. Some critics sought to replace it with 'integral', and thus tone down the social commitment. In this context, the pope made three key statements on the Kingdom, evangelization, and liberation. On the Kingdom, he wrote (*EN* 8):

> As an evangelizer, Christ first of all proclaims a kingdom, the Kingdom of God; and this is so important that, by comparison, everything else becomes 'the rest', which is 'given in addition'. Only the Kingdom therefore is absolute, and it makes everything else relative.

The implication is that Kingdom work is not confined to what might be termed 'churchy' activities (e.g. services of public worship, and the work performed by the institutional church); and thus the pope's affirmation means that what might be termed 'secular' activities - such as the overcoming of oppression - are, or can be, a constitutive part of the absolute task of seeking the Kingdom.

Secondly, on evangelization, the pope wrote as follows regarding the *witness* of life and the *word* of life (*EN* 21-22):

> Above all the Gospel must be proclaimed by witness...[a] witness which involves presence, sharing, solidarity, and which is an essential element, and generally the first one, in evangelization...

> Nevertheless...even the finest witness will prove ineffective in the long run if it is not explained, justified...and made explicit by a clear and unequivocal proclamation of the Lord Jesus. The Good News proclaimed by the witness of life sooner or later has to be proclaimed by the word of life.

Thus Christian living is as important as verbal preaching - a new emphasis compared with Vatican II.[124] But the pope went further, and argued that action for justice should be given a privileged place, over and above many other kinds of secular work. This brings us, thirdly, to the matter of liberation. The pope said that the two words which provide the key to understanding the evangelization of Christ are 'Kingdom' and 'salvation' (*EN* 10). Christ came to

---

[121]Paul VI, *Evangelii Nuntiandi* (London: Catholic Truth Society, 1990).
[122]*EN* #2.
[123]Cf. Dorr, *Option for the Poor*, p238.
[124]Dorr, *Option for the Poor*, p243.

bring the Good News of the Kingdom of God, that 'good news to the poor' foretold by Isaiah.[125] The pope summarized the content of the Good News as follows (*EN* 9):

> As the kernel and centre of his Good News, Christ proclaims salvation, this great gift of God which is liberation from everything that oppresses man but which is above all liberation from sin and the Evil One, in the joy of knowing God and being known by him, of seeing him and of being given over to him.

Thus evangelization and liberation are linked: '...evangelization would not be complete if it did not take account of the unceasing interplay of the Gospel and of man's concrete life, both personal and social... [E]vangelization today involves an explicit message, adapted to the different situations constantly being realized, about...international life, peace, justice and development - a message especially energetic today about liberation' (*EN* 29). Further (#31):

> Between evangelization and human advancement - development and liberation - there are in fact profound links. These include links of an anthropological order...They also include links in the theological order, since one cannot dissociate the plan of creation from the plan of Redemption. The latter plan touches the very concrete situations of injustice to be combatted and of justice to be restored.

These are substantial claims, and they bear considerable similarity with some of the arguments presented in chapter 3. What, then, is inadequate, in the context of a discussion about justice, about all this? It is not, fundamentally, that the Roman Catholic teaching is too optimistic about the scope for transformation in this world - although that is a major weakness that runs through many of the official documents of this century.[126] Nor is it that the relationship between the 'spiritual' and 'social/secular' aspects of reality is inadequately addressed - although that is again a weakness.[127] One fundamental inadequacy is the lack of a Christological understanding of the Good News. Christ is mentioned, as the one who brings the Good News, and who is proclaimed by it, but no further Christological content is given. The consequence, in terms of justice, is that the relationship of Christ himself to oppression, and to the bringing of justice, is simply not addressed. A second

---

[125]*Evangelii Nuntiandi*, 6,10.

[126]This point might be an example of the long-established divergence between Roman Catholic and Reformed theology on whether grace 'perfects nature' or, alternatively, radically breaks with it and only then can begin to produce something glorifying to God.

[127]It hardly seems sufficient to say that both aspects are somehow present: e.g. to leave it there begs the question of whether it is meaningful and truthful to divide those two aspects in the first place. A more thorough theology of creation, for one thing, is needed here.

fundamental lack is a treatment of the radical conflict, taught throughout the New Testament, between the kingdom of God and the kingdom of darkness (e.g. Mt. 13:24-30; 36-43; Col. 1:13f). Such a treatment, if offered, would make it difficult to speak, as does the pope, of something so ill-defined and general as the renewal or transformation 'of *humanity*' (*EN* 18). Whilst there is undoubtedly in *EN* a significant emphasis on interior change in those who choose to adhere to Christ (e.g. #18), it is much less clear how those who make no such confession can be changed. At root, the problem here may be that the Roman Catholic teaching has not grappled adequately with the seriousness of sin.

A more robust theological account would begin with a recognition that the kingdom of God means the saving rule of Christ as Lord (Acts 2:36-40; 4:10-12; 5:30-31). That is, his rule is a *saving* one; and this salvation from sin comes about only where *he rules*.[128] Without such emphases, the Roman Catholic teaching is exposed to the danger of becoming a vague gospel, in which the kingdom of God somehow expands in the world, as people bring a measure of justice, even though the Lordship of Christ might not have been recognised and acknowledged by those who have supposedly come, as now-liberated people, to enjoy its benefits.

PHILOSOPHICAL BASIS

As noted earlier, one reason for examining Roman Catholic social teaching is to examine the extent to which it is an adequate response to the challenges posed by secular theories of justice. The contributions of Mill, Rawls, and Nozick, together with the ensuing literature, make it clear that the question of the philosophical basis for justice is very far from resolved. Indeed, what justice *is* has become a matter of increasing controversy. Mill's attempt to locate justice within social utility is fraught with problems. Rawls' apparent focus on the needs of the least well-off - whilst at first sight sharing some similarity with the Roman Catholic emphasis on the poor - is again fundamentally flawed, in philosophical terms (see pp154-7 above). Nozick's theory, too, fails. Yet the Roman Catholic teaching, for the most part, seems to assume away these problems. It is taken as read that the meaning of justice as 'liberation from oppression' is clear and unproblematic. But it is not. Sometimes 'oppression' is put in terms of gross inequality: but how gross is gross? Sometimes injustice is seen in terms of being paid a 'living wage': but this seems to involve some notion of a 'just wage' that has simply not been spelt out at all;[129] and thus it

---

[128]Obviously much more detail is needed for a proper treatment - especially regarding the centrality of Christ's death and resurrection. Some additional detail was offered in chapters 2 and 3. The comments in the text are only indicative.

[129]Clearly it is not intended to limit injustice only to cases where people actually die through maltreatment.

seems to be a circular definition. Sometimes justice is seen in terms of 'rights', but once again without serious definition - and, in any case, the critiques offered by Rawls and Nozick expose the inadequacy of rights as a foundation.

One document that does attempt a somewhat sharper philosophical focus is the U.S. Catholic Bishops' Pastoral Letter, *Economic Justice For All*, which attempts (*inter alia*) to amalgamate philosophy and Roman Catholic teaching.[130] This makes (in Lebacqz's summary) the following definitional claim: justice 'is not simply a matter of proper distribution of goods (distributive justice) but also of permitting and indeed requiring each person to participate in the production of those goods (social justice)'.[131] It also claims the following:

> Biblical justice is the goal we strive for. This rich biblical understanding portrays a just society as one marked by the fullness of love, compassion, holiness and peace. On their path through history, however, sinful human beings need more specific guidance on how to move toward the realization of this great vision of God's kingdom. This guidance is contained in the norms of basic or minimum justice. These norms state the *minimum* levels of mutual care and respect that all persons owe to each other in an imperfect world.[132]

Catholic teaching, along with much philosophical reflection, identifies three dimensions of 'basic justice': commutative, distributive and social.[133] First, then:

> *Commutative justice calls for fundamental fairness in all agreements and exchanges between individuals or private social groups.* It demands respect for the equal human dignity of all persons in economic transactions, contracts or promises. For example, workers owe their employers diligent work in exchange for their wages. Employers are obligated to treat their employees as persons,

---

[130]National Conference of Catholic Bishops, *Economic Justice For All: Pastoral Letter on Catholic Social Teaching and the U.S. Economy* (Washington, D.C.: United States Catholic Conference, 1986). This Letter is discussed further in chapter 6 below, where the aim is to sharpen and clarify a biblically-rooted conception of economic justice by means of a conversation with that Letter. In the present chapter, however, the main purpose of considering the Bishops' Pastoral is different, namely to highlight the challenges that it poses for a biblically-rooted understanding. These two distinct purposes give rise to two distinct types of coverage in this book with respect to the material in the Letter.

[131]Karen Lebacqz, *Six Theories of Justice* (Minneapolis: Augsburg, 1986), p69.

[132]*Economic Justice For All*, p35 (emphasis in the original).

[133]*Ibid.* The lack of biblical argument for these categories, or for the definitions of them which follow - see the text - rather weakens the sense that it is actually *biblical* justice that is being sought in all this. Nevertheless the case presented is a substantial one, and merits careful reflection and appraisal.

paying them fair wages in exchange for the work done and establishing conditions and patterns of work that are truly human.[134]

This is unsatisfactory, however. In a world where there is no unanimity on what 'justice' or 'fairness' actually mean, it is inadequate simply to assert that wages should be 'fair'. This begs all the difficult questions.[135]
Secondly:

Distributive justice requires that the allocation of income, wealth and power in society be evaluated in light of its effects on persons whose basic material needs are unmet... Minimum material resources are an absolute necessity for human life. If persons are to be recognized as members of the human community, then the community has an obligation to help fulfill these basic needs unless an absolute scarcity of resources makes this impossible. No such scarcity exists in the United States today.[136]

Thirdly, justice 'also has implications for the way the larger social, economic and political institutions are organized' (p36). Thus:

Social justice implies that persons have an obligation to be active and productive participants in the life of society and that society has a duty to enable them to participate in this way. This form of justice can also be called 'contributive'... In the words of Pius XI, 'It is of the very essence of social justice to demand from each individual all that is necessary for the common good'... The meaning of social justice also includes a duty to organize economic and social institutions so that people can contribute to society in ways that respect their freedom and the dignity of their labour.[137]

At least three major practical conclusions are drawn by the Bishops from the foregoing understanding of basic justice and its three components. First, basic justice 'calls for the establishment of a floor of material well-being on which all

---

[134]*Ibid.*, pp35-6 (emphasis in the original).

[135]At the same time, since the above statement is unlikely to be disputed by anyone sympathetic to the United Nations Declaration on Human Rights, it is not clear that there is any particularly *biblical* understanding of justice here. It *might* be that, say, the UN Declaration (which the Letter refers to approvingly a little further on) happens to coincide with biblical categories for justice: but this would have to be demonstrated if one was to be convinced that it is *biblical* categories and norms which are the driving and determinative ones. Moreover, the total lack of any reference to God or Jesus Christ in these statements is somewhat disarming for anyone awaiting a *biblical* account. These weaknesses are symptomatic of the more general theological problems already observed with regard to Roman Catholic social teaching as a whole.

[136]*Ibid.*, p36 (emphasis in the original).

[137]*Ibid.*, pp36f (emphasis in the original).

can stand'.[138] Thus the 'fulfilment of the basic needs of the poor is of the highest priority'.[139] Here, it should be noted, the Bishops provide a clear contrast with Rawls: 'For Rawls, protection of the least advantaged is the result of a self-interested calculation under conditions of ignorance; for the bishops it is a result of acknowledgment of the presence and will of a loving God'.[140] The Bishops argue, further, that this duty 'calls into question extreme inequalities of income and consumption when so many lack basic necessities.'[141] This first major conclusion - the importance of a floor of adequate material well-being for all - follows directly from the Letter's definition of distributive justice. It is reinforced by reference to the second major conclusion, which concerns human rights - the protection of which is also stated to be part of basic justice.[142] It is asserted that a number of human rights are specifically economic in nature: that is, not only those 'indispensable to the protection of human dignity' (such as the right to life, food, shelter, medical care and education), but also those 'essential to...the integral development of both individuals and society' (such as a right to security in the event of sickness, unemployment and old age, the right to 'healthful working conditions', and the right 'to the possibility of property ownership').[143] It is striking that the Letter argues that any denial of these rights both 'harms persons *and wounds the human community*'.[144] Put slightly differently: '*The common good demands justice for all, the protection of the human rights of all.*'[145]

The third major practical conclusion concerns participation in production. 'Increasing active participation in economic life by those who are presently excluded or vulnerable is a high social priority.'[146]

In terms of the adequacy of all this to the challenges posed by secular theories of justice, there are some serious difficulties. First, whilst there is a clear attempt to articulate what a 'preferential option for the poor' means in practice - which may be seen as, at least implicitly, a response to Rawls' maximin/difference principle - the philosophical underpinnings of the Bishops' proposal seem very limited. Although it is claimed that human rights are God-given, and grounded in the nature and dignity of being human,[147] the detailing of these rights appears to be a matter of assertion rather than argument.

Secondly, the reliance on 'the common good', despite the strengths of this

---

[138]*Ibid.*, p38.

[139]*Ibid.*, p46.

[140]Lebacqz, *Six Theories of Justice*, p75.

[141]*Economic Justice For All*, p38.

[142]*Ibid.*, p44.

[143]*Ibid.*, pp41-2.

[144]*Ibid.*, p42 (emphasis added).

[145]*Ibid.*, p44 (emphasis in the original).

[146]*Ibid.*, p47.

[147]*Ibid.*, p41.

approach, has some serious limitations in practice, at least to the extent that others in society do not share a similar commitment to the common good. Whilst the Letter at some points argues uncontroversially for the meeting of basic *needs*,[148] and thus, as noted earlier, for a basic minimum floor of material well-being - with the better-off obliged to contribute - it also uses a different argument when tackling what it calls 'extreme inequality'. It sees 'extreme inequality as a threat to the solidarity of the human community, for great disparities lead to deep social divisions and conflict.'[149] The difficulty here is that the Letter relies on people as a whole accepting that same view. If, however, alternative and incompatible philosophies of society are held - for example that, assuming everyone's basic needs are met, then whatever income disparities the market generates are permissible, and indeed appropriate (on meritocratic grounds) - then the argument of the Letter at this point will simply be disregarded.

A related point is that the emphasis on *participation in production* cannot by itself succeed in providing a solid philosophical basis for justice. For one thing, it cannot apply to those whom the Bishops note are among the majority of the poor - children, the elderly, and others who cannot fully participate in production.[150] More fundamentally, the notion of 'participation in production', or of being 'active participants in the life of society',[151] is inadequate. For one thing, it cannot answer the question of what defines right relationships between people. It is good in that it affirms that human beings belong together, but it is silent on how they are to relate together, e.g. on what defines oppressive as opposed to non-oppressive behaviour. For another thing, however - and more fundamentally - it is not clear why participation *in the life of society* is such a desirable thing. The argument given in the Letter is that the *prime* purpose of the special commitment to the poor 'is to enable *all* persons to share in and contribute to the common good.'[152] Again, however, this can make sense only on the assumption that *the common good* - defined as something above and beyond the members - has a status sufficiently exalted to make such claims. This is in part a pragmatic difficulty: for, to the extent that others in the society are not persuaded to adopt the same ideas, then the appeal to the common good will fail. But the main point here is that the Letter is introducing a higher-order

---

[148]Few, if any, right-wing exponents would argue *against* some kind of safety net for those whose basic needs are unmet.

[149]*Economic Justice For All*, p438. In the Scriptures - see chapter 3 - the emphasis is not upon extreme inequality as a threat to the community's solidarity, but rather upon exclusion of the poor from God's blessings as something that is wrong in itself and displeasing to God.

[150]Lebacqz, *Six Theories of Justice* p76.

[151]*Economic Justice For All*, p441.

[152]*Ibid.* (emphasis in the original).

value for which it gives no adequate justification.[153]

Thus it cannot be said that Roman Catholic social teaching has as yet provided an adequate response to the challenges posed by secular theories of justice.

Challenges for a Biblically-rooted Understanding of Justice

With regard to the attempt to develop an understanding of justice founded on biblical teaching, the Roman Catholic social teaching poses at least three important challenges.[154] The first is very practical: a strength of the Roman Catholic teaching is the fact that the teachers have clearly paid close attention to what is actually happening 'out there', especially regarding the realities of the poverty and hardships faced by so many people. Serious attempts to understand the causes of poverty have been made. Detailed interaction with economic and political debates has occurred. No other denomination or grouping has attempted anything on this sort of scale, whilst seeking to retain a principled commitment to the teaching of the Scriptures. A second challenge is to formulate carefully the relationship between justice and some kind of preferential option for the poor. Precise nuancing will be extremely important here. A third challenge concerns the place of 'seeking justice' in relation to the proclamation of the Gospel of Christ. The Roman Catholic treatment of this may be lacking. But is it adequate to say in response, for example, that Christians should 'preach grace and do justice'? This also seems simplistic.

Justice: The Work of Reinhold Niebuhr

Three aspects of Niebuhr's work are addressed here. First, a brief account is offered of Niebuhr's understanding of justice. This is followed by a short critical appraisal of the main features of this understanding, including its adequacy as a response to the secular theories of justice already discussed. Finally, the challenges raised by Niebuhr's work for a biblically-rooted understanding of justice are assessed.

---

[153]A related weakness is in the way the Bishops seek to combine Scripture and philosophy. It is not at all clear that the particular understandings of justice proposed by philosophers are compatible with Scripture. Even if they might be, Lebacqz points out (*Six Theories of Justice*, p81) that the Pastoral Letter gives very little evidence to support their claim that reason and human experience confirm their theological reflections.

[154]These challenges will be put only briefly here, since they are taken up in the next two chapters.

Niebuhr's Notion of Justice

Central to his approach is a clear distinction between individuals and groups. Back in his *Moral Man and Immoral Society*[155] he argued that 'a sharp distinction must be drawn between the moral and social behaviour of individuals and of social groups, national, racial and economic; and that this distinction justifies and necessitates political policies which a purely individualistic ethic must always find embarrassing' (p.xi). Individuals, as individuals, are able to take into account the interests of others; they can have a measure of sympathy for other human beings. And their rational faculty 'prompts them to a sense of justice which educational discipline may refine and purge of egoistic elements until they are able to view a social situation, in which their own interests are involved, with a fair measure of objectivity. *But all these achievements are more difficult, if not impossible, for human societies and social groups.*'[156] Why is this? 'In every social group there is less reason to guide and to check impulse, less capacity for self-transcendence, less ability to comprehend the needs of others and therefore more unrestrained egoism than the individuals, who comprise the groups, reveal in their personal relationships.'[157]

It is not that individuals are free from sin. Niebuhr had a strong doctrine of sin (see below), and no human being (apart from Christ) is sinless. It is more that, in a fallen world, relationships between groups are always more distant than relationships between individuals; and it is only in a close setting that people can feel and act on the basis of *love*. Without that love, self-centredness always tends to predominate. 'Even a nation composed of individuals who possessed the highest degree of religious goodwill would be less than loving in its relation to other nations. It would fail, if for no other reason, because the individuals could not possibly think themselves into the position of the individuals of another nation in a degree sufficient to insure pure benevolence.'[158] In reality, of course, the 'Christian Realism' of Niebuhr and others[159] observed that groups and nations consist of individuals who do *not*, in the majority of cases, possess that high degree of goodwill. All the more so, then, the behaviour of groups and nations will always fall well short of the standard of love.

Niebuhr's notion of justice is closely linked to his understanding of love. He argues that from Jesus we receive the supreme ethical command: love. Thus

---

[155]First published in 1932; page references here are to the first British edition (London: SCM, 1963).

[156]*Moral Man,* p.xi (emphasis added).

[157]*Ibid.*, pp.xi-xii.

[158]*Ibid.*, p75.

[159]See Robin W. Lovin, *Reinhold Niebuhr and Christian Realism* (Cambridge: CUP, 1995).

'...religion absolutizes the sentiment of benevolence and makes it the norm and ideal of the moral life'.[160] Niebuhr claims that justice is linked to love dialectically. On the one hand, love requires justice: love for others will never be satisfied with anything less than the attainment of full justice for others. On the other hand, love transcends and judges justice, in the sense that whatever measure of justice is achieved *in this world* will never reach the goal set by perfect love.

There is some tension here in the way that Niebuhr uses the term 'justice'. In discussing the resources offered in support of justice by human reason (by contrast with religion), he says:

> The force of reason makes for justice, not only by placing inner restraints upon the desires of the self in the interest of social harmony, but by judging the claims and assertions of individuals from the perspective of the intelligence of the total community.[161]

Compared with justice in this sense, love is purer. 'Love meets the needs of the neighbour, without carefully weighing and comparing his needs with those of the self. It is therefore ethically purer than the justice which is prompted by reason.'[162] On the other hand, Niebuhr also refers to the justice which the kingdom of God, alone, can and will bring, in the age to come.[163] This justice can hardly be anything less than the perfection of absolute love. Lovin puts Niebuhr's position as follows: 'To do justice to another person, to render that person what is due, is, in the context of original righteousness, no less than to seek the person's good.' Given Niebuhr's vision of the perfect justice of the kingdom of God, in the age to come, then it follows that this absolute justice 'is identical with love'.[164]

Consistently with that perspective, Niebuhr is unwilling to offer a precise definition of justice, in philosophical or socio-political terms. Indeed his particular ideas about justice were formed not by abstract considerations of fairness, but in the context of specific grievances - especially in the car industry.[165] The implied goals (examples of middle axioms) are well worth fighting for; but they are always short of the ultimate standard set by love.

THEOLOGICAL UNDERPINNINGS
Niebuhr's scepticism about what can be achieved in this life reflects a Protestant theological emphasis. This contrasts both with the Roman Catholic

---

[160]Niebuhr, *Moral Man*, p57.
[161]*Ibid.*, pp30-31.
[162]*Ibid.*, p57.
[163]*Ibid.*, pp81-2.
[164]Lovin, *Reinhold Niebuhr,* p203.
[165]*Ibid.*, p209.

emphasis - which has tended not to grapple sufficiently with the seriousness of sin - and with the liberal Protestantism which was dominant at least during the earlier part of Niebuhr's lifetime, and which was typified in the 'Social Gospel' of Walter Rauschenbusch (1861-1918). For the latter, recent advances in scientific method, in relation to the Bible, had created an unprecedented opportunity for the Bible to be 'the people's book', as clear to us as to the original readers. And this had massive social implications:

> For the first time in religious history we have the possibility of so directing religious energy by scientific knowledge that a comprehensive and continuous reconstruction of social life in the name of God is within the bounds of human possibility.[166]

Niebuhr sought (at least once his pastoral ministry in Detroit removed any liberal optimism of his own) to oppose such optimism. His theology of sin - to be balanced by his work on grace - was vital in this task. He argued that sin in man is the inevitable, though not necessary, consequence of two other features of man, namely his finitude and his freedom.[167] Finitude and freedom combine to produce, in man, anxiety; and this anxiety is the occasion for sin.[168] Niebuhr regards falling into sin, given this psychological anxiety - together with the influence of the devil in actively suggesting evil to man - as therefore inevitable. Ideally we should, under these pressures, choose the option of faith; but we don't.[169] Niebuhr then applied his theology of sin to contemporary reality, especially in social and political terms, arguing that human nature and injustice made liberal optimism irrelevant, and that his realistic theology was far more appropriate.

In Volume II of *The Nature and Destiny of Man* Niebuhr again sought to relate biblically-based theology to contemporary reality, but here he focused upon grace. Later sections of that volume devoted considerable attention to providing a practically useful understanding, theologically grounded, of the possibilities for the growth of goodness *in society*, in the light of the atonement and justification by faith, but prior and inferior to the perfection that only the

---

[166]Walter Rauschenbusch, *Christianity and the Social Crisis* (NY: Macmillan, 1907/Louisville, Kentucky: Westminster/John Knox, 1991), p209. [The page reference is to the 1991 edition.]

[167]The paradox - if not contradiction - between 'inevitable' and 'not necessary' cannot be discussed in any detail here. Part of Niebuhr's treatment was an emphasis that man was held responsible for his sin, even if such sin was 'inevitable'. He also claimed Augustine and Calvin as allies in holding this tension between inevitability and responsibility. See his *The Nature and Destiny of Man: Vol.I: Human Nature*; London: Nisbet, 1941, pp256-8.

[168]*Ibid.*, p195.

[169]*Ibid.*, pp193,194.

parousia will bring. He argued that human society as well as the individual can know the sanctifying power of grace, although he was careful to say that 'social sanctification' is a less clearly defined experience than the equivalent for individuals.[170] Regarding love and justice, he continued to make the same kind of distinction as seen in *Moral Man and Immoral Society*. He argued that love is an end, while justice is a means. In Patterson's words: 'Love is the final goal towards which justice moves. Justice is not a fully satisfactory goal in itself because it falls short of love, being dependent upon coercive power on the one hand, and requiring rational calculations in the balancing of rights on the other.'[171]

Critical Assessment of Niebuhr's Understanding of Justice

With regard to Niebuhr's theological framework, there are two particular problems that bear on his understanding of justice. First, the notion of 'social sanctification' is problematic, in that it appears incompatible with Jesus' own emphasis on the absolute requirement to follow *him* if one is to be saved. Thus 'social sanctification' seems to involve an unnecessary blurring of the clear NT distinction between the kingdom of God and the kingdom of this world (e.g. Mt. 13:24-30, 36-43; 1 Cor. 15:23-24; Col. 1:12-14). Advances in the kingdom of God at the present time can undoubtedly bring indirect blessing to those who have not turned to follow Christ, but it is unhelpful to attach to this wider blessing the language of sanctification and holiness which the NT almost always restricts to those who confess Christ.[172]

Secondly, the criteria for what is 'just' - even given Niebuhr's limitations on the scope for justice in this life - tend to be given by contemporary consensus rather than by God's revealed word. Niebuhr does acknowledge that God's truth is transcendent (rather than merely consistent with whatever truth or understanding that human beings themselves discover). However, he does not provide a framework for clearly discerning these transcendent truths or for understanding how they might be implemented. Thus, effectively, the criteria for justice have to come entirely from within the current order. In practical terms, for example, the claim that, in a given context, justice requires a forty hour working week is something on which Niebuhr's framework can make no

---

[170]Bob E. Patterson, *Reinhold Niebuhr* (Waco: Word, 1977), p137.

[171]*Ibid.*, pp134-5.

[172] The one exception to this usage is 1 Cor. 7:14, where the 'unbelieving' spouse of a believing wife/husband is said to have been 'sanctified' through their believing spouse. Whatever the precise meaning of 'sanctified' here, however, it cannot mean confession of Christ, since the person 'sanctified' is plainly referred to as still 'unbelieving'. (See Gordon D. Fee, *The First Epistle to the Corinthians*, Grand Rapids, MI: Eerdmans, 1987, pp299-301.)

Christian comment. Thus there seems to be no observable difference between a secular understanding of the content of justice and a Christian understanding of the content of justice.

Each of these two problems illustrates Hauerwas' criticism of Niebuhr, that the latter permits Christianity to be policed and restrained by secular forces and, in particular, those of the 'liberal social orders':

> ...Niebuhr simply asserts that equality and freedom of the individual are the primary content of natural law. Why that should be the case he feels no need to explain. That he does not do so is but an indication that like Rauschenbusch he simply assumes that liberal social orders, with their commitment to freedom of the individual and equality, are normative for Christian presumptions about social relations. Therefore, the Christian quest for justice, which stands under the judgment of love, becomes the unending task of helping liberal social orders reconcile freedom with equality.[173]

Despite Niebuhr's professed desire to break with the false optimism of the 'Social Gospel', in practice he fails to do so; and he ends up supporting a 'justice' which the historic Gospel would rebuke. So, although Niebuhr included transcendent truths in his theological framework, he was not able to demonstrate the consequences of the implementation of those truths in terms other than those of liberal aspirations. As a response to secular theories of justice, therefore - such as those discussed earlier in this chapter - Niebuhr's work is, at this fundamental level of distinctives, thoroughly inadequate.

A second area of weakness, which relates to the above, concerns Niebuhr's deliberate unwillingness to define or even pin down what justice actually is. His emphasis on observing contemporary life, rather than merely calling for a standard of justice defined in a vacuum, is undoubtedly important. Christians do indeed need to understand the present. But this must be done in a Scriptural framework. Otherwise the definition of justice which is in fact used - and justice can never remain an esoteric, unapplied concept - will be given by the world, as appears to have happened with Niebuhr. Thus, given his unwillingness to give theologically-based content to the principle of justice, he was able to offer only secular-based criteria for justice. There is, of course, the danger of being too technical about justice, which would result in 'justice' losing its power. This is perhaps why 'justice' for Reinhold Niebuhr 'functions more as a principle of prophetic criticism of *any* stance taken than as a precise norm or philosophical category.'[174] Nevertheless, a principle must have some content to it, as a principle. This is what Niebuhr fails to provide. Instead he offers the following kind of criteria for justice: constitutional instruments to

---

[173]Stanley Hauerwas, *Dispatches From The Front* (Durham, N.C.: Duke University Press, 1994), p102.

[174]Lebacqz, *Six Theories of Justice*, p94.

guarantee the weaker nations their rights; equal rights in race relations; the principle of a 'living wage', provided it is generously interpreted, i.e. coupled with old age insurance and unemployment insurance.[175]

These things may well be desirable. But they come entirely out of the secular world, and no attempt at all is made to derive them from any theological-biblical principle(s). Middle axioms must enjoy some such derivation; otherwise there is no basis for a Christian to support them. The weaknesses of Niebuhr's work in this regard mean that his approach to justice has not provided an adequate response, in theological terms, to the challenges posed by secular conceptions of justice.

Challenges Raised by Niebuhr's Work

Nevertheless, Niebuhr's approach itself poses some significant challenges in the quest for a biblically-rooted conception of justice that can grapple with issues in the contemporary world. The first challenge thus posed is that a notion of justice, however well grounded theologically, is of little use if it is not applied to the contemporary world. Moreover, that application requires careful, consistent, detailed and attentive awareness of the contemporary world. Niebuhr's ministry certainly had this awareness; and it did not come easily.

Secondly, Niebuhr's work raises the challenge of how one should understand, theologically, strivings for and moves towards a greater measure of justice in this world. If 'social sanctification' is too vague an approach, is there a valid one?

Thirdly, how can something like a Christian 'theory of justice' be developed - with more detail than Niebuhr offered or wanted to offer - without being so esoteric and unapplied as to be of little practical value? To put this slightly differently: Niebuhr's theological framework recognised both the significance of historical existence (in concrete terms) *and* its limits; but he failed to unpack the contents of the divine element in the framework, and thus to provide an understanding of God's practical involvement in human historical reality. Is it possible for a theological framework to be developed which has a similarly balanced view of historical existence, but which also (unlike Niebuhr's framework) *is* able to discern how God's revealed truth concerning justice can be transposed into an understanding of the content of historical justice, in the contemporary context?

Liberation Theology: Its View of Justice

This section offers, first, a brief outline of liberation theology as developed in Latin America, especially in its approach to justice and injustice; secondly, a

---

[175]*Ibid.*, pp94-5.

critical appraisal of this approach, in the light of the biblical conception developed in chapters 2 and 3, and with particular regard to its adequacy as a response to the secular conceptions of justice considered earlier in this chapter; thirdly, a brief account of the challenges posed by liberation theology for a biblically-rooted understanding of economic justice.

Liberation Theology and its Approach to Justice

This sub-section offers a brief outline of some of the key features of liberation theology, especially with regard to its treatment of justice and injustice. The outline draws primarily on one of liberation theology's leading texts, *Liberation of Theology* by Juan Luis Segundo.[176]

One key feature of liberation theology is that its sense of justice and injustice is rooted in the actual life experience of people in Latin America: in particular, the experience of those in poverty. Justice is seen as a fundamental and vital issue, not because of what academic theology might have to say on the subject, but because of what the poor know about it.[177] For example Segundo, writing in the mid-late 1970s, illustrates the extent of the injustice felt by the poor in Chile, and observed by the Roman Catholic Church. He refers to the situation as it was some 10-15 years earlier: a degree of poverty and inequality which had by no means diminished over time.

> On various occasions, and especially in the early sixties, the bishops of Chile had denounced the profound injustice of the established capitalist system. Using official statistics, they pointed out a host of unpleasant facts: e.g., that ninety percent of the national income was distributed among only ten percent of the population. Whereas the per capita income of the vast majority came to about forty-five dollars a year, the privileged ten percent of the population had an annual per capita income of $3,500.[178]

Behind these statistics of severe poverty and extremely large inequality lies the reality of the lives of vast numbers of people oppressed and struggling to survive, with the powerful socio-economic structures seemingly against them. This is where liberation theology is rooted.

A second key feature of liberation theology is that its notions of what justice, injustice and oppression consist of are also rooted in the experience of the poor. The situation in Latin America is understood to be *unjust* - as opposed, say, to being merely unfortunate or difficult to bear - *not* because aspects of the

---

[176]*Liberation of Theology*, tr. John Drury (Dublin: Gill and Macmillan, 1977). This outline is not intended to be exhaustive, but only to give a sense of the whole with regard to liberation theology and justice.

[177]Segundo, *ibid.*, chapter 1.

[178]*Ibid.*, p130.

situation contravene particular criteria established by academic theology, but simply because the situation is felt on the ground to be patently unjust and oppressive. The role of theology here, it is felt, is not to establish some criteria for assessing what is just or unjust, but simply to explain that the contemporary situation of injustice is something to which God is opposed. Thus, in the same way that the Israelites in Egypt, prior to the Exodus, were blatantly being oppressed, so are the poor of Latin America. And God hears the cries now as much as He did then.

The third key feature is liberation theology's hermeneutic circle. In Segundo's account of this the force of the above two features is evident. Segundo's book is primarily an explanation and defence of the methodology and epistemology of liberation theology, and that is the setting for his account of hermeneutics. Segundo's hermeneutic circle - whereby 'each new reality obliges us to interpret the word of God afresh, to change reality accordingly, and then to go back and reinterpret the word of God again, and so on'[179] - has two preconditions: 'profound and enriching questions and suspicions about our real situation', and secondly 'a new interpretation of the Bible that is equally profound and enriching'.[180] Segundo places strong emphasis on these preconditions: where they are not accepted, he argues, 'theology is always a conservative way of thinking and acting'. And this is not so much because of its content but its method: for 'it lacks any *here-and-now* criteria for judging our real situation. It thus becomes a pretext for [e.g.] approving the existing situation...'[181] What Segundo is driving at, in particular, is the existing situation of Western capitalism and its impact on the poor in Latin America. If his charge - that academic theology is so enmeshed in that system as to be incapable of recognising the overall situation - is accurate, then it is a most serious charge; and some alternative methodology - such as his hermeneutic circle - would indeed be required.

Segundo proceeds to outline the four decisive factors in liberation theology's hermeneutic circle:

> *Firstly* there is our way of experiencing reality, which leads us to ideological suspicion. *Secondly* there is the application of our ideological suspicion to the whole ideological superstructure in general and to theology in particular. *Thirdly* there comes a new way of experiencing theological reality that leads us to exegetical suspicion that the prevailing interpretation of the Bible has not taken important pieces of data into account. *Fourthly* we have our new hermeneutic, that

---

[179]*Ibid.*, p8

[180]*Ibid.*, p9.

[181]*Ibid.* (emphasis in the original).

is, our new way of interpreting the fountainhead of our faith (i.e., Scripture) with the new elements at our disposal.[182]

It should be noted that Segundo's emphasis on ideological suspicion is by no means an uncritical or wholesale adoption of Marxist ideology, although it certainly embraces important elements of the thinking of Marx and his followers. Indeed, one of Segundo's criticisms is that Marx failed to get beyond the second stage of the hermeneutic circle: '...while Marx made a personal comitment to change the world, he never had a personal experience of theology... Moreover, Marx's act of will to abolish religion is not an act of will from within theology itself, an act of will that could signify a change in the way of treating problems theologically. It is rather an abandonment of them' [i.e. of treating problems theologically].[183]

The challenge of liberation theology, then, can be put like this: in the context of oppressive Western capitalism, *either* theology must press right on through all four stages of the hermeneutic circle, and emerge clearly opposed to capitalism and oppression (as Scripture would all along, it is said, have required of us); *or* theology will continue to exhibit merely passive acceptance of oppression. Opposition or acquiescence: these are the only two options.

Thus Segundo makes a clear call to take sides, to be partial: '...it is obvious that any "act of will" in the limited range of human possibilities comes down to taking a stand for some individual or community over against other individuals and communities. There is no help for it. Every hermeneutic entails conscious or unconscious partisanship.'[184] It is not possible, he argues, to adopt a universal perspective at each stage: partiality is essential. Nevertheless, since God is the liberating God, partiality is not ultimately opposed to universality:

> The universality that is renounced...is recovered in spades on a deeper level of the human condition - i.e. where it is revealed to us in an oppressed community that is still in need of liberation. In the process of liberation, *the one and only truth* is the truth of liberation itself as defined by the oppressed in their struggle.[185]

On Segundo's argument, then, 'it is quite clear that the Bible is not the discourse of a universal God to a universal man. Partiality is justified because we must find, and designate as the word of God, that *part* of divine revelation which *today*, in the light of our concrete historical situation, is most useful for the liberation to which God summons us.[186]

---

[182]*Ibid.* (emphasis in the original).

[183]*Ibid.*, p18.

[184]*Ibid.*, p25.

[185]*Ibid.*, p26 (emphasis added).

[186]*Ibid.*, p33 (emphasis in the original).

Critical Appraisal

The primary area of weakness, in the context of the present chapter, concerns the definition of justice. Although liberation theology - in its passionate concern for the plight of the poor, and its awareness of the crushing powerlessness they feel at the hands of capitalism - affirms something of vital importance, its method means that it leaves vital questions unanswered. It was noted earlier that Segundo does *not* simply adopt the Marxist ideology in a wholesale and uncritical manner. What he does do, however, is to accept uncritically a class-based conception of socio-economic oppression, injustice and liberation - with the correlate that all non-Marxist perspectives are on the capitalist side of the class struggle. Thus liberation theology renders itself unable to engage meaningfully with other conceptions of justice. In particular, liberation theology is unable to provide any kind of adequate response to the serious challenges posed by Mill, Rawls and Nozick.

The inability to engage with a Rawlsian conception of justice is a particularly serious weakness. What is the basis for saying (as Segundo does in his Chapter 3) that it is impossible to have any kind of 'third way' between capitalism and socialist-based revolution? He argues that 'the whole phenomenon of adopting "third ways" presents a profound methodological challenge to liberation and represents the ultimate consequence of *an erroneous way* of formulating the whole problem of the relationship between theology and politics'.[187] Yet Segundo's discussion (e.g. p92) makes clear his awareness that 'Western capitalism' is not one unchanging system that takes the identical form in each and every Western country. There is considerable variety between the forms and behaviour of both business and public sector organisations in different Western countries. And there is considerable variety, also, in the extent to which government policy in different countries seeks and achieves redistribution of income and wealth towards those who are less well-off. How is it, then, that Segundo is unable to advocate any kind of 'third way' exploration? It can only be that he has, from first principles, decided that liberation requires a socialist-based system. Hence his methodology prevents him from engaging with the broadly redistributive notion of justice proposed by Rawls.

Challenges Raised for a Biblically-rooted Understanding of Justice

Despite its own weaknesses, liberation theology itself poses some significant challenges to the quest for a biblically-rooted conception of economic justice that can engage with contemporary questions and issues. These challenges are put only briefly here, since they are taken up at greater length in the following

---

[187]*Ibid.*, p91.

chapters. First, a theology of justice has to hear the cries of those who are oppressed (however that term comes to be understood); it cannot be developed in insularity. Secondly, a biblically-rooted theology of justice has to specify clearly the relationship between the proclamation of the Gospel and the consequences of the Gospel for inter-human relationships. It is not sufficient - as is customarily done - to speak vaguely in terms of 'your life should bear fruit in good works', and then leave it at that. Thirdly, the sense in which the Gospel is 'good news to the poor' needs to be understood and articulated very carefully.

Conclusion

This chapter has demonstrated that the three secular theories of justice it has appraised - those proposed by Mill, Rawls and Nozick - pose, despite their serious weaknesses, a number of major challenges for the attempt to develop an understanding of justice that is both rooted in the Scriptures and able to grapple with contemporary questions and issues. This chapter has also demonstrated that the three Christian approaches to justice it has considered (those presented by recent Roman Catholic teaching, by Niebuhr, and by liberation theology) cannot be considered an adequate response to those challenges - even though they themselves have some significant strengths and pose some further challenges. The next task, therefore, in developing a biblically-rooted understanding of justice that engages with the contemporary world, is to consider how the approach to justice set out in chapters 2 and 3 can grapple with the challenges and issues presented above. This is the aim of the following two chapters.

CHAPTER 5

Biblical Justice for Contemporary Economic Life: Engaging with the Challenges Raised by Other Treatments of Economic Justice

Introduction

The previous chapter highlighted a number of substantial challenges posed by some recent treatments of justice in economic life. The remaining two chapters resume the task, begun in chapters 2 and 3, of developing a biblically-rooted conception of economic justice, and seek to do so in particular by engaging with, and responding to, the above-mentioned challenges. The intention is that, by means of this engagement, the biblically-rooted conception already outlined will be further sharpened and thus more fully equipped to address contemporary issues regarding economic justice.

The theological treatment in chapters 2 and 3 presented a biblical conception - founded upon the righteousness of God - which included four key aspects of economic justice. First, it was argued, justice means appropriate treatment, according to the norms commanded by God for each particular case - norms which also enable human flourishing. Secondly, God's justice, in terms of economic life, involves justice to the needy. Thirdly, economic justice is not only allocational, but also concerns the quality of relationships. Fourthly, justice in the allocation of resources means that everyone participates in God's blessing. It was also shown that those four aspects are indicative of a biblical conception only when understood in Christological terms, with the NT building on and fulfilling the OT. It is this conception which must now, in chapters 5 and 6, engage with the challenges highlighted in the previous chapter.

Those challenges relate to the notion of economic justice at a number of different levels.[1] Some concern justice as a moral conception - such as the question, raised by utilitarianism, of whether justice is to be conceived in terms of rights or in terms of the general good. A second type of challenge concerns justice as a political conception or theory - such as Nozick's argument about the notion of justice with respect to the ownership and use of property, and hence

---

[1] These levels overlap – there is no absolute distinction between them.

the question of how state-enforced transfers of property could ever be justified. A third type of challenge concerns justice as a socio-economic conception - such as the broadly egalitarian challenge posed (in different ways) by Rawls, Roman Catholic social teaching, and liberation theology. A final type of challenge concerns justice as a theological conception - such as Niebuhr's question concerning whether the pursuit of justice may be regarded as some kind of 'social sanctification'.

The discussion in the present and the following chapter will seek to address the notion of economic justice in all of these aspects, in the light of the biblical conception developed earlier, and thus to demonstrate the power and contemporary relevance of a biblical understanding of justice in economic life.[2] With regard to the challenges mentioned in the previous paragraph, chapter 6 will engage with those relating to justice in its moral, political and theological aspects. The present chapter focuses on the challenges regarding justice specifically as a socio-economic conception, and it considers the notion of justice in economic life under two conventional headings: commutative justice, and distributive justice. Commutative justice relates to justice in economic exchanges between individuals and/or parties. Thus it concerns, broadly, justice in production and exchange. Distributive justice relates to how income and wealth is allocated - deliberately or otherwise - across individuals, families, communities, institutions, and countries. Thus it concerns, broadly, justice in the allocation of the fruits of economic endeavour.[3] These two aspects of justice

---

[2]Whilst it is outside the scope of this book to construct a thoroughly comprehensive account or 'grand theory' of justice in all these aspects - a task cautioned against by Duncan Forrester, *Christian Justice and Public Policy* (Cambridge: CUP, 1997), e.g. ch.7 - the aim here is certainly to demonstrate that a biblical conception of economic justice is both coherent and incisive in the contemporary context.

[3]These categories of commutative and distributive justice, as presented in the text, are similar to - but by no means identical to - those categories as defined by the U.S. Roman Catholic Bishops in their Pastoral Letter *Economic Justice For All* (National Conference of Catholic Bishops, 1986) and by Roman Catholic social teaching more generally (see David Hollenbach, 'Modern Catholic Teachings Concerning Justice', in John C. Haughey (ed.), *The Faith That Does Justice: Examining the Christian Sources for Social Change*, New York: Paulist Press, 1977, especially pp219-222). That Letter also presents a third category, 'social justice', which they understand as implying '*that persons have an obligation to be active and productive participants in the life of society and that society has a duty to enable them to participate in this way*...The meaning of social justice also includes a duty to organize economic and social institutions so that people can contribute to society in ways that respect their freedom and the dignity of their labour' (National Conference of Catholic Bishops, *Economic Justice For All: Pastoral Letter on Catholic Social Teaching and the U.S. Economy*, Washington, DC: United States Catholic Conference, 1986), pp36-37 [emphasis in the original]. The present text does not utilize that type of conception of 'social justice': partly because detailed institutional analysis (the second aspect of social justice referred to in the Pastoral Letter) lies outside the scope of the book; partly because the idea of all

in economic life, which are interrelated,[4] will be examined in turn.[5]

Commutative Justice: Justice in Producing and Exchanging Goods and Services

Before proceeding with the attempt at a biblically-rooted account of commutative justice, some introductory points should be noted. First, mainstream economic analysis tends not to use the word 'justice' with regard to production and consumption. This does not mean, however, that the current chapter is calling for a totally novel kind of economic analysis.[6] For one thing, mainstream analysis does recognise that, at least on occasions, questions of 'fairness' - in the sense to be explained below - do arise in production/ consumption. One obvious example is monopoly power, e.g. in obtaining what are normally termed '*excess* profits'. 'Excess' implies that some norm has been broken, i.e. - in biblical terms - an injustice has occurred. Thus the biblical understanding of justice *is* connected with questions addressed by mainstream economic analysis.[7] Indeed it is generally recognised that, for 'actors' or 'agents' in economic life, their moral values are - amongst many other factors - relevant to their economic behaviour. What this chapter's emphasis on commutative justice does suggest is the need for a more explicit and better articulated account of the content of justice - in terms of appropriate treatment according to the norms commanded by God for each particular case - in the context of production and exchange.

Secondly, it must be acknowledged that, in settings which do fit the textbook criteria for competitive conditions (whether perfect or imperfect competition), economic agents have only a limited degree of choice as regards commutative

---

contributing, and being enabled to do so (the first aspect) is in *general* terms not problematic - all of the accounts considered in the previous chapter, for example, would accept such an idea - and partly because any *specific* issues relating to the nature of such participation can and will be dealt with here as aspects of commutative and/or distributive justice.

[4]What happens in production and exchange obviously affects the overall allocation of resources; and the extent of distributive justice also affects what happens in production and exchange, e.g. with regard to the relative bargaining power of the different parties in a given exchange relationship.

[5]Nozick's usage of the term 'distributive justice', in *Anarchy, State and Utopia* (Oxford: Blackwell, 1974), is different from its definition here. He combines justice in acquisition and justice in transfer - which are each aspects of *commutative* justice as defined here, under the one heading of 'distributive justice' (p151).

[6]Nor is it adopting a Marxian theory of labour value and thus of exploitation. For a critical account of the Marxian theory, see, e.g., Mark Blaug, *Economic Theory in Retrospect*, 4th ed. (Cambridge: CUP, 1985).

[7]Blaug offers a brief discussion of 'exploitation' in mainstream economic analysis, in *ibid.*, pp428-9.

justice. (These criteria include complete freedom for firms to enter and leave a market without restriction, and also perfect knowledge for all consumers and producers.) Thus a company in an industry which is perfectly competitive has very little choice in terms of pricing policy in the long run (assuming it wishes to remain in business): if it charges above the market price, it sells nothing and goes out of business; if it charges below the market price, it loses money on everything it sells, and will therefore soon go out of business.[8] For a firm in conditions of imperfect (or monopolistic) competition, in the long run it too has a rather limited degree of choice over pricing policy.[9] Firms have a somewhat greater degree of choice in the short run (i.e. during the period of time *before* new firms actually enter the market), but if the criteria for competition are met, then the short run is in turn fairly limited. In the contemporary economic world, however, there are many markets which do *not* meet the conditions for being competitive; in these settings, then, there is a substantial degree of choice for economic agents as regards commutative justice.

Finally, since biblical justice - including commutative justice - involves quality of relationship, then there are always, in any given economic setting, responsibilities on *both* (or *all*) sides to act justly: that is, to act appropriately, in accordance with the norms commanded by God. Justice is not one-sided, but mutual. This final point, like the other two, does not, of course, define in any detailed terms what commutative justice consists of. The chapter now turns to that task. Four propositions will be put forward, and then discussed, regarding the content of commutative justice.

(A.1) Mutual *agreement* between any two economic agents does *not* imply that the relation between them is one of justice.

(A.2) Even if both parties to an exchange do choose - in a meaningful sense - to agree to the particular exchange, exploitative behaviour is disallowed.

(A.3) Commutative justice with regard to the *level of wages* requires that, for a full-time job, the wage paid should *normally* be sufficient to ensure the livelihood of the employee and their household.

(A.4) An economic enterprise which has the sole aim of maximising the return to the owners of the enterprise's capital will tend to make at least some decisions which lie outside the boundaries set by a biblically-rooted understanding of commutative justice.

---

[8]Whether the market price in such circumstances should also be termed the 'just price' is not addressed in this book. The interest here is in situations where to do justice will make a difference.

[9]In the long run, such a firm can, at best, make only a normal level of profit, even when it follows the rule for profit maximisation (i.e. produce the level of output at which marginal cost equals marginal revenue). This is because, in the long run, new firms can enter the market, and they will thus be able, profitably, to charge a lower price than the existing firm if it is making more than normal profit.

Proposition (A.1)

The claim here is, in slightly more precise terms, that mutual agreement between any two (or more) agents - whether individuals, households, companies, governments, or other institutions - is neither sufficient nor necessary for the relation between them to be one of justice.[10] The foundation for this proposition is theological, namely that the norms for just behaviour are given and commanded by God, not by the parties to a relationship; therefore, agreement between two parties is not a sufficient condition for concluding that justice is being done. For example, suppose that a small supplier agrees with a large and aggressive monopolist company to a reduction in what was already a very low price for the items supplied (relative to that paid in other comparable industries); and suppose that the alternative was for the supplier to lose the business altogether. The claim here is that the agreement between the two agents to the exchange (transaction) is *not* a sufficient condition for concluding that the transaction is consistent with commutative justice.

The claim that mutual agreement is also not a *necessary* condition for commutative justice is relatively less important, but it still worth noting. One illustration would be where one party to an exchange is, to some extent at least, ignorant of some of the detail: thus a consumer who purchases a jar of coffee which is in fact a 'fairly traded' jar, but who is unaware of that fact, is still party to a transaction that is consistent with commutative justice. (This illustration evidently makes an assumption about the measurability of commutative justice: this assumption is spelt out, and discussed, below. The illustration also assumes that an agent in such a case bears some moral responsibility, even if they are less than fully informed.)

The claim of Proposition (A.1) is made, in part, in response to the libertarian challenge - notably that put by Nozick (examined in chapter 4) - regarding justice and choice. The claim here is evidently at substantial variance with the libertarian argument. Nozick's conception of justice in acquisition and justice in transfer is founded on choice. Thus, with regard to his 'entitlement' theory of justice (especially regarding transfers) - and in contrast to the maxims proposed by rival conceptions - he offers the following:

> From each according to what he chooses to do, to each according to what he makes for himself (perhaps with the contracted aid of others) and what others choose to do for him and choose to give him of what they've been given previously (under this maxim) and haven't yet expended or transferred.[11]

---

[10]Chapter 4 noted that the recent Roman Catholic Catechism made essentially the same claim, arguing - in the context of labour markets - that agreement between the parties 'is not sufficient to justify morally the amount to be received in wages' (*Catechism of the Catholic Church*, London: Geoffrey Chapman, 1994, p520, #2432.
[11]Nozick, *Anarchy, State and Utopia, op.cit.*, p160.

Noting wryly that the above has its defects as a slogan, Nozick then offers the following, 'as a summary and great simplification (and not as a maxim with any independent meaning):

From each as they choose, to each as they are chosen.[12]

Nozick does, as noted in chapter 4, list a number of transactions which he regards as *not* permissible, i.e. they are inconsistent with justice in acquisition and justice in transfer. He lists them thus: 'Some people steal from others, or defraud them, or enslave them, seizing their product and preventing them from living as they choose, or forcibly exclude others from competing in exchanges. None of these are permissible modes of transition from one situation to another' (p152) - and this is because each of them involves actions which prevent one party from making a free choice.

The claim made by this chapter with regard to Nozick's approach is that liberty is in reality an inadequate foundation for a conception of economic justice, and thus the approach is fundamentally deficient. Mutual agreement - the thing lacking in all the transactions proscribed in Nozick's list - is an inappropriate basis for understanding the content of economic justice. And this is demonstrated in the reality that Nozick's conception would permit the monopolist company - in the example given earlier - to pay a reduced price to the supplier: i.e. the mutual agreement is (for Nozick) a sufficient condition for justice. Thus the libertarian foundation gives rise to a range of outcomes that are not permitted by a biblically-rooted conception of justice. For the criteria which define economic behaviour that is acceptable are much less tight for the libertarian approach, compared with a biblically-rooted approach. The latter, for example, is inspired by the teaching of the Mosaic Law that proscribes oppression of any kind, whereas the list of actions proscribed by Nozick (see above) is substantially less restrictive. Put another way, the libertarian approach rests upon a notion of 'voluntary' that is extremely limited and thin: agents are presumed to 'agree' with other agents when in reality there is no alternative course of action. The biblically-rooted understanding offered here, by contrast, emphasizing the importance of relationships in line with God-given norms, provides a much firmer foundation.

Proposition (A.2)

The same example - the monopolist and the small supplier - can also be utilised in the presentation of the second proposition: namely, that commutative justice disallows various types of behaviour (which could be bracketed together as 'exploitative') in an economic exchange, even if both parties were to choose - in a meaningful sense - to agree to that particular exchange. It should be noted,

---

[12]*Ibid.* (Emphasis in the original).

as a matter of detail, that the rider concerning choice 'in a meaningful sense' is included here in order to make clear the contrast between the claim made here and that made by Nozick. Both views proscribe slavery - Nozick, for example, recognises the lack of any meaningful choice for a slave. Nozick, however, would permit the aggressive, price-lowering behaviour of the monopolist, since the supplier is not compelled to co-operate. The conception of commutative justice presented here, however, would not permit that behaviour.

Returning to the example, then, we suppose that the monopolist reduces the (already relatively low) price it pays for the goods supplied, in order to increase its own profits. Within the biblical conception of economic justice, this behaviour is exploitative, at least in the sense that the monopolist actively exploits the relatively weak economic position of its supplier, in order to further its own interests, at the expense of the supplier's interests.

Proposition (A.2) is founded on the biblical teaching that there are norms of fairness and justice, and of love, trust and faithfulness, in economic relationships. The Mosaic Law gave concrete examples of what the norms of justice mean in particular circumstances - such as the requirement to return, at the end of each day, a cloak taken in pledge (Dt. 24:13). Careful reflection on the biblical teaching, including such examples, will lead to increasingly clear awareness of what justice requires - and proscribes - in other settings. It is on this basis that the price-lowering behaviour of the monopolist, in the example given above, is recognised as exploitative and unjust. Justice, by contrast, would require the monopolist to be considerate, rather than aggressive, towards the supplying firm, on account of its relatively weak position. For the monopolist is in a relationship with that firm, a relationship to which the norms of justice apply.

This example also serves, then, to highlight the sense in which biblically-rooted economic justice is to do with *relationships*. The slogan that 'business is business' - meaning that business behaviour is free of the moral constraints that apply elsewhere in life - is never supported, only attacked, in the Scriptures.[13]

The above paragraphs do not imply, however, that competitive behaviour in economic life is in general incompatible with commutative justice. For any given individual, household or company, there is a positive and legitimate sense in which it is right to look to its own interests. There is nothing in the Scriptures to prohibit consumers from shopping around for bargains, or to stop sellers of purple cloth from ensuring that they obtain a decent return on their investments, or to prevent rival producers from seeking to improve their own products; and such patterns of behaviour necessarily have negative side-effects for other parties - initially, at least. In all these cases, however, there are boundaries - outer limits - to what is morally acceptable behaviour. And a major feature of these boundaries is that they apply in terms of the relationships in which the

---

[13]For one of many such attacks, see Mic. 2:1-5. Chapter 3 dealt at length with the biblical material here.

participants are involved. Put another way, economic behaviour is to be constrained by the norms of justice - including faithfulness and fairness. Within these boundaries, however, competitive behaviour is not only legitimate, but can also be recognised, within the providence of God, as part of the constructive orderliness of human life in this present world:[14] it would be difficult to deny, for example, that the impetus of competition underlies many of the improvements and innovations in the supply of goods and services in the 20th century.

Proposition (A.3)

The third proposition refers specifically to the link between the labour market and the household.[15] Commutative justice with regard to the *level of wages* requires that, for a full-time job, the wage paid should *normally* be sufficient at least to ensure the livelihood of the employee and their household, i.e. for them to earn a living.[16] (In a developed economy, this will mean not only that the basic needs of the household are met – the need for food, shelter and clothing – but also that the household is able to participate in the material blessings enjoyed in that society, and hence is able to have a reasonably dignified and flourishing life.) The basis for this understanding is the Scriptural teaching that in God's created order, as expressed in particular in the life of OT Israel, the labour of a household will generate sufficient income (whether in kind or in some monetary form) to provide for that household. The principle being put forward here derives from a combination of two things: first, the emphasis of the biblical conception of justice on *everyone* participating in God's material blessings; and, secondly, the importance of work in the biblical account of economic life (see Part I of chapter 3). Apart from those members of the community who were, of necessity, relatively dependent on others (section II.D of chapter 3), the norm established in the OT was that each household would, by means of productive work, be able to provide for itself, and thus participate in God's material blessings.[17] This, then, is the pattern and the norm for life in

---

[14]Paul Helm, having noted that God may not approve of all that he upholds, writes as follows regarding the orderliness and predictability which is relevant to all aspects of human life: 'Besides being in itself an important feature of God's providential rule, knowledge of the predictability of nature adds to a person's responsibility...Human activity is worthwhile because it takes place in a world that is so orderly that there is a reasonable chance of many plans and purposes being achieved' (*The Providence of God*, Leicester: IVP, 1993, p100). With regard to economic life and competition, this does not mean that there are no 'chance' elements, but it does mean that planning and progress are in general realistic and worthwhile.

[15]A household consists of one or more persons, living in one home.

[16]Exceptions to this norm are considered below. Roman Catholic social teaching offers a similar emphasis to that of (A.3), as noted in chapter 4.

[17]This seems to be assumed in, for example, the teaching of Lev. 19:13 about the wages

God's created order. Part of this pattern, consequently, is that if someone has the means to employ another person, and chooses to do so, then in doing so the employer takes on a share of responsibility, within God's created order, towards the person employed; and hence that responsibility includes paying a wage that is normally sufficient at least to ensure the livelihood of that person and their household.

Even if the apparent 'going rate' for a particular job is lower than will meet basic needs, the employer is *not* thereby permitted to pay only the going rate: the moral problem with such action is part of a wider moral problem, namely that those who are involved in choosing that particular 'going rate' have failed to adopt the standards set out in the previous paragraph. Two cases need to be distinguished here. First, where markets are competitive, it is clear that no individual economic agent can influence the market price (at least in the long run: see p203 above); for example, no individual employer can affect the market wage rate. Even in this case, however, the economic agents *collectively* share moral responsibility for a situation in which, for example, wages are – without good reason – below a rate compatible with proposition (A.3).[18]

The second case is more straightforward, and involves the large number of situations where markets are not competitive. Here it is clear that prices and wages are not given from on high, or somehow determined by forces external to the economic agents; rather, they are actually set by those who are market participants. Thus if no participants were prepared to accept a 'market' wage rate below, say, some subsistence level, the market would function with wages at or above that subsistence level.

There are questions concerning the feasibility, for the labour market as a whole, of a strategy which deliberately pays more than the 'market' or going rate. Will it attract too many people, for example, to low-skilled jobs - with the consequent disincentive to train to obtain additional skills - so that long-term productivity is hampered? A basic response here is that higher-skilled jobs will, in general, always attract higher wages - assuming that, as is certainly understood here, differential wages are not prohibited.[19] Moreover, supposing there were a *general* upward revaluation of labour - as employers in general repented, so to speak, of their previous underpayments, corporately, to the lower skilled workers. Then, although it might be feared that the economy as a

---

of a hired servant. The servant needs his wages, and they should not be held back overnight. The context is, by assumption, one where that servant's only job is with the employer concerned. (The world of multiple part-time jobs is a very recent invention!) This verse, incidentally, evidently does not *prove* the principle advocated in the text; but it does serve to illustrate the operation of that underlying principle.

[18] An individual firm which, whilst relatively powerless in this situation, still wanted to take seriously its moral responsibility, could, for example, seek to persuade other firms to co-operate on a joint strategy to increase wages towards a more adequate level.

[19] I.e. it is *not* required that the same wage is paid to each and every employee.

whole might become less able to compete internationally, it is easy to conceive of other shifts which could occur at the same time - such as a rise in productivity due to workers generally feeling better motivated, in view of their improved treatment - which would foster relatively *greater* international competitiveness, and hence offset the higher monetary cost of labour.

Finally, however, it must be recognised that commutative justice does *not* require that a wage paid must *always* be sufficient to ensure the livelihood of the employee and their household. Circumstances may be envisaged either where the employer is unable to pay an adequate wage, due perhaps to an adverse economic climate at the time; or where the basic needs of the employee are unusually great, so that the standard wage paid is insufficient to meet those needs. It follows from that caveat that any policy which sought to ensure that no wage is less than some stated minimum wage would have to allow for particular circumstances in which that minimum could not reasonably be paid. It should also be emphasised that nowhere in the above paragraphs has a minimum wage *policy* been advocated - in the sense of a policy enforced by the governing authorities. This does not mean that such a policy is without merits. Rather, the point is that the relation between, on the one hand, moral propositions regarding justice, and, on the other, the most appropriate means for achieving justice in practice, is a topic in its own right, and a topic that has not yet been addressed in this thesis in any detail.[20]

Proposition (A.4)

The fourth proposition is not so much a moral proposition as a statement about the likely moral consequences, with regard to economic exchange, if an enterprise pursues its own narrowly-defined end irrespective of other goals. The proposition is that an economic enterprise which has the sole aim of maximising the return to the owners of the enterprise's capital will tend to make at least some decisions which lie outside the boundaries set by a biblically-rooted understanding of commutative justice, decisions which therefore are incompatible with biblically-rooted moral principles.

This proposition might appear to imply that the vast majority of economic theorising about business enterprises is based on an assumption that is incompatible with moral values, namely the assumption that an enterprise exists to maximise the return to its owner(s), whether in the form of maximising profit, or in the form - more relevant to companies quoted on stock markets - of maximising shareholder wealth.[21] This implication, however, does not actually

---

[20]These issues will be addressed, at least in outline terms, in the following chapter.

[21]These two ways of articulating the maximisation of the return to the owners of capital are not mutually inconsistent. The latter, unlike the former, takes account of the particular form of ownership whereby a company is owned by those who hold shares, shares which are tradeable on a stock market. The latter also takes into account a longer-

follow. For one thing, economic analysis - as any other form of analysis - makes *simplifying* assumptions, and the standard maximisation assumption is in that sense a perfectly legitimate tool of analysis. For another thing, that assumption is compatible with enterprise behaviour which in practice pursues other goals *as well as* the interests of the owners of capital.[22] On the condition that such behaviour can be commensurate with commutative justice, then the maximisation assumption of economic analysis carries no necessary implication that business behaviour must break the boundaries of justice.

Returning to what is being claimed by proposition (A.4), it may be noted that this proposition is, at one level, no more than a reiteration of the theological truth that this present world is a sinful world, in which self-centred goals lead to sinful behaviour. If a particular enterprise pursues its own ends, totally disregarding the interests of everyone else, then unjust behaviour is inevitable.

At another level, however, more needs to be said. For proposition (A.4) is in direct opposition to the strongly held view that the true social responsibility of business is precisely to maximise profit/shareholder wealth, and that any supposed 'socially responsible' deviation from this single goal will, however well-intended, produce results that are *detrimental* for the society as a whole.[23] The underlying problem with this common view (termed here the 'business is business' view) is that it fails to take sufficiently seriously the sinfulness of this present world - which is why the theological underpinnings of proposition (A.4) need to be recognised (as noted in the previous paragraph). It might be possible to imagine a world in which one party, precisely by single-mindedly pursuing only its own interests, thus served the interests of others to the greatest possible extent.[24] This is not, however, the world we live in. The Scriptural account of reality teaches that, because of the Fall (see chapter 3 above), a

---

run time perspective - hence the emphasis on the maximisation of shareholder *wealth*.

[22]Such behaviour will no longer take the form of unconstrained maximisation of return to the owners of capital. But the simplifying assumption, mentioned in the text, may assist the economic theorist in understanding important aspects of the economic situation.

[23]For one statement of this general view, see, for example, Elaine Sternberg, *Just Business: Business Ethics in Action* (London: Little, Brown and Company, 1994). She argues 'that business organisations which seek anything but long-term owner value are guilty not of socialism, but of theft' (p6). Milton Friedman argued along broadly similar lines in *Capitalism and Freedom* (Chicago: University of Chicago Press, 1962).

[24]The theorising of Adam Smith in *The Wealth of Nations* [1776] (London: Methuen, 1961) comes readily to mind, of course. As is now generally recognised, however, the 'invisible hand' assumption of that book by Smith should - for a fair reading of his thought as a whole - be taken alongside the moral framework he advocated for human behaviour in *The Theory of Moral Sentiments* [1759] (in D. D. Raphael and A. L. Macfie (eds.), *The Glasgow Edition of the Works and Correspondence of Adam Smith*, Vol. I, Oxford: OUP, 1976).

universal feature of sinful human beings, in their rebellion against God, is to act self-centredly. Chapter 3's overview of the biblical material on justice in economic life demonstrated a number of ways in which the self-centredness of human beings in the context of economic behaviour results in harm to others. There is no absolutely no scope here for thinking that self-centred behaviour can be benignly regarded as the harbinger of the common good. Not surprisingly, then, it takes only a small amount of observation of the behaviour of those business enterprises driven solely by the maximisation of profit/shareholder wealth in order for this theological account of reality to be corroborated.

Nevertheless, the advocates of the 'business is business' persuasion draw attention to a related theological point, namely the reality of God's over-ruling in and over - but not necessarily approval of - all human affairs in this sinful world. God's present rule over the world takes account of the fact that human beings are sinful, and it also requires human society to make some recognition of this fact. Further, the interests of different parties often coincide to a far greater degree than is generally recognized. It can be argued, for example, that the introduction of better safety conditions into a workplace is sometimes driven not by social responsibility but by profit-maximisation: the owners' desire is to have its workers work harder and more efficiently (to the ultimate goal of higher profit), and if the greater assurance offered by improved safety, combined with fewer industrial accidents and therefore lower legal costs, help to bring this about, then the result will be satisfactory for all concerned. To say, however, that such an example proves the superiority of the sole goal of profit-maximisation, however, does not follow. What the example demonstrates, rather, is that the goals of higher profit and greater safety can coincide.[25]

It may be argued that, if the market for capital is competitive, a firm which – because of its pursuit of other goals alongside profit – does not strictly maximise the return to its shareholders (or suppliers of capital) may be unable to continue in business in its current state. Two cases may be distinguished. First, for a firm with shares which are publicly traded, if it makes a positive return on capital, but a return less than that required by the capital market, then the price of its shares will be driven down, which may ultimately result in the firm being sold, and put under new management (presumably with the mandate to maximise shareholder value). However, given the attention now paid in the business and financial world to social responsibility, it is not clear how frequent such an outcome would be in practice. If, for example, the majority of publicly quoted firms consider that *some* attention to social responsibility forms part of their corporate objectives, then the outcome sketched above is relatively less

---

[25]The example does not demonstrate, of course, that they will always coincide - and there is no reason to suppose that they will always do so. The lesson from this, however, is that one should seek such harmonisation of legitimate goals to the greatest extent possible.

likely. The second case concerns firms which do not have publicly traded shares. If such a firm obtains a positive return on capital, but a return less than that required by its suppliers of capital, then it is conceivable that those suppliers will withdraw their funds (and/or fail to offer any further capital), with the result that the firm is unable to continue in business. Again, however, it is an empirical question – well outside the scope of this thesis – as to how frequent such an eventuality is in practice. In both cases, of course, it is clear that issues of justice and moral responsibility involve not only those who manage companies but also those who provide capital funds.

Whatever the issues involved in the balancing of different goals for a firm, however, the claim of proposition (A.4) still stands, namely that the unconstrained and sole pursuit of the interests of the owners of capital will tend to produce at least some actions which are incompatible with commutative justice. Advocates of 'business is business' do recognise the need for some constraint, of course: behaviour must be within the law; it must be within the rules of the game. What proposition (A.4) claims, however, is that the types of rule normally accepted by 'business is business' advocates are too loose, if injustices are to be avoided. Consider again the example - used earlier - of the monopolist and the small supplier. The behaviour of the monopolist in that example - using its market power to drive down the price paid to the supplier well below the price paid elsewhere - is within the boundaries of honesty and law-keeping, and it is not fraudulent or deceitful; therefore it is permissible, according to 'business is business' reasoning. As argued earlier, however, it is not compatible with a biblically-rooted understanding of commutative justice. Therefore, unless the accepted rules which constrain behaviour are based solidly upon the norms commanded by God, then the sole pursuit of profit/shareholder wealth maximisation will tend to lead to commutative injustices.[26]

Distributive Justice: Justice in Sharing the Fruits of Economic Endeavour

There is general consent today that the community should arrange for a safety net - normally in the form of monetary payments - for those who are unable to

---

[26]If one wanted to prevent the monopolist - in the example used in the text - from exploiting the small supplier, then it is now clear that more than one strategy is available. One approach would be to make such exploitation illegal - and also (rather more difficult) to enforce such a law. Another approach would be to persuade the monopolist to adopt other goals alongside the interests of the owners of its capital. This chapter does not aim to produce policy proposals - but it is worth noting that policy in the U.K., and elsewhere, has focused largely on the first approach. For a proposal to broaden the stated objectives of business, see George Goyder, *The Just Enterprise* (London: Andre Deutsch, 1987). See also the innovative, though somewhat less radical, discussion in the 'Tomorrow's Company Enquiry', conducted by the RSA: *Tomorrow's Company: The Role of Business In A Changing World* (Aldershot: Gower, 1995).

provide for themselves; and that this safety net should provide at least for basic needs to be met. (It is possible for someone to avoid the safety net if they really do not want it: the general consensus does not, therefore, require the community to meet the needs of everybody *without exception*.) The question is whether a biblical understanding of justice goes any further than this.[27]

A fundamental point to emphasise here is that the principle that 'everyone participates in God's blessing' (a key principle of biblical justice developed in chapter 3) is *not* the same as, or equivalent to, 'everyone participates in the community' or 'everyone participates in production'.[28] The importance of human community is not in question: indeed it is crucial in a biblical framework.[29] Nevertheless, formulations along those lines are inadequate. The point here is not simply that *phrases* such as 'everyone participates in the community', or 'everyone participates in production', are insufficiently theological. More fundamentally, the problem with these claims is that, in terms of their understanding of human life, they effectively place - or at least are in serious danger of doing so - the notion of the *human community* on a pedestal. In that sense they tend to overstate the importance of human community. And, at root, this is a *theological* error, for these claims effectively tend to dethrone God himself.[30]

The nuancing is important here. It is certainly not being denied that community is important. It is certainly not being argued that 'there is no such thing as society'. However, if some people do not receive the material blessings God intends for them, the fundamental problem is not that they do not participate *in the community*, but that they do not participate *in God's blessings*.

---

[27] It is assumed here that the biblical understanding goes at least as far as today's general consensus. The justification for this assumption was given in chapter 3, where the principle was unfolded that justice requires, amongst other things, that all participate in God's blessing. If those unable to provide for themselves do not have even their basic needs met, then this is a *prima facie* case of people not participating in God's blessing, and thus of injustice.

[28] A number of recent treatments of justice offer formulations along those lines. For example, the U.S. Roman Catholic Bishops, in their Pastoral Letter *Economic Justice For All*, argues as follows: 'Basic justice demands the establishment of minimum levels of participation in the life of the human community for all persons' (National Conference of Catholic Bishops, *Economic Justice*, 1986, p39). As is emphasised in the text, such a statement conveys an important truth - but it requires some amendment in order to reflect more fully a biblically-rooted understanding of justice.

[29] As is shown elsewhere in this book.

[30] Such a dethroning is obviously not the intention of, say, the U.S. Roman Catholic Bishops; see *ibid*. Nevertheless, it is vitally important to have an understanding of justice that is theologically well-rooted. One possible consequence of not doing so would be to cede ground to secular humanism - some elements of which would doubtless be happy with justice as 'everyone participates in community' - and thus to lose a critical cutting edge.

The ultimate goodness of human life is not rooted in being in the community, but in living and doing and belonging as God intends. It is a vital truth that *part* of God's intent is for human beings to participate in the life of the community as a whole. Indeed, community is part of God's blessing granted to human beings.[31] But it is God, not the community, who defines life; and it is God who is, indeed, in the person of Christ, the Life.

Given this theological understanding of distributive justice - especially with regard to participation, God's blessings, and community - it is now important to examine in more detail the content of a biblically-rooted understanding of distributive justice: that is, sharing the fruits of economic endeavour. A number of challenges in this regard were discussed in chapter 4, notably those raised by Rawls and - in stark contrast - by Nozick. It should be noted, first, that - as argued in chapter 3 - the biblical understanding of justice makes a significant distinction between, on the one hand, people who find themselves to be relatively dependent upon others, and, on the other hand, people who are relatively able to be independent of the aid of others. (See the material on the OT in chapter 3, especially the discussion of Deuteronomy.)

On a matter of detail, it should be noted that this distinction is not about personal character, but about personal circumstances. It is not being said that some poor are 'deserving' whilst others are 'undeserving' - a contrast not to be found in the Scriptures. (The warning in Proverbs about sloth leading to poverty is not a comment about *desert*, but a warning about the consequences of behaviour.) Rather, the point is that some people are in circumstances where they *cannot* be relatively independent - the widow, orphan, and stranger - whereas others *are* relatively able to provide for themselves. The word 'relatively' is included in order here, incidentally, to avoid making the distinction between the 'dependent' and the 'independent' absolute or excessively large.

Aside from this detail, the central point emphasized here is that justice in regard to those people who are relatively dependent is *not* solely a matter of meeting 'basic needs'. Rather, those people are to participate fully in God's blessings.[32]

A further point to note here concerns diversity: these blessings from God vary both from one community to another, and over time. Economic analysis has never envisaged that economic life is solely about meeting basic needs. Similarly, a full doctrine of creation - as briefly expounded in chapter 3, for example - envisages a degree of flourishing, in material and other terms, that is well in excess of the meeting of basic needs.[33] It has to be recognised immediately, of course, that for many people in the contemporary world, their income is far too *low* to meet even their basic needs. This is cause for total

---

[31]This point is elaborated below.

[32]This has powerful implications in terms of equality, as will be argued below.

[33]By 'basic needs' is meant, essentially, the need for shelter, clothing, food and water.

shame amongst the rich countries. Nevertheless, the point being emphasised here is that God's blessings in material terms are not to be thought of as solely the meeting of basic needs.

There are two aspects here: variety across places, and growth/variety over time. It seems obvious that God's material blessings vary across places. One simple example is that the types of food that people enjoy vary, especially across cultures and climates. In terms of growth/variety over time, a rich doctrine of creation embraces the understanding that, under God's gracious providence, material blessings take new forms as economies continue to develop. This does not mean, of course, that all economic growth is automatically to be approved: indeed, the doctrine of creation itself places restraints on what is appropriate as regards as the use of the earth's resources (see chapter 3). Nevertheless, a suitably balanced doctrine of creation will make room for growth and variety, over time, in what are, at root, *divine* material blessings.

This recognition of diversity in God's material blessings, however, does not in any way, in and of itself, provide a sanction for cases where one person or group has a greater share in God's blessings than another person or group. For someone to have *more* than someone else is logically distinct from them having something different from someone else.[34] Whether any kind of inequality - as opposed to diversity - can ever be compatible with distributive justice is, of course, an issue of central significance, and an issue regarding which Rawls' work (assessed in chapter 4) raises a number of substantial challenges. This is the issue examined in the remainder of this chapter.

Justice, Inequality and Equality

It has already been argued (in chapter 3) that one aspect of justice is that, in the allocation of resources - distributive justice - everyone is to participate in God's blessing. This means not only that no-one is to be missed out, but also that everyone is to participate fully in God's blessing, on the same basis. This formulation does not, however, specify whether 'full participation' means 'numerically equal', or instead permits an allocation that is less than 100% equal. And if the latter is allowed, then this same formulation does not specify how much inequality might be permitted. Given the considerable attention given to these matters in recent discussions of justice, however - by Rawls and Nozick (see chapter 4), amongst many others - then it is extremely important that a biblically-rooted understanding of justice should seek to engage with these matters.[35] As with commutative justice, the argument will be conducted

---

[34]How one might define and measure what is a 'greater share' is examined below. The point here, however, is simply that diversity in blessing is logically distinct from degree of blessing. (The two can, of course, be connected - as is indeed argued below.)

[35]Other significant treatments of these issues include R. H. Tawney, *Equality*, revised

by means of putting forward some particular propositions (in this case, two).

(B.1) Justice - in terms of everyone participating in God's blessing - implies some upper limit to the degree of inequality that is permissible across persons or groups. In other words, inequality that is in excess of that upper limit is not compatible with justice.

(B.2) A just sharing of the growing fruits of economic endeavour *must benefit everyone*; and, unless initial inequality is *less* than the limit set in accordance with (B.1), a just sharing of the growing fruits of economic endeavour *cannot involve greater general inequality over time* - whether of outcome or opportunity.

Proposition (B.1)

This proposition needs some elucidation before its justification can be considered. In particular, the proposition does not require that the upper limit (or upper bound) on inequality has to be measurable in quantitative terms; but, on the other hand, it does require that the upper limit on inequality is something that is *recognisable*. An example from the OT is the narrative account, in the book of Exodus, regarding the LORD's provision of manna for the people of Israel in the desert, following their exodus from Egypt. The text recounts the following words of Moses to the people (Ex.16:16-18; NRSV):

> "This is what the LORD has commanded: 'Gather as much of it as each of you needs, an omer to a person according to the number of persons, all providing for those in their own tents.'" The Israelites did so, some gathering more, some less. But when they measured it with an omer, those who gathered much had nothing over, and those who gathered little had no shortage; they gathered as much as each of them needed.

This account is also referred to by Paul in 2 Corinthians, chapter 8, in support of his appeal to the Corinthians with regard to the collection for the famine-hit Christians in Jerusalem. 'I do not mean that others should be eased and you burdened, but that as a matter of equality [ἰσότητος] your abundance at the present time should supply their want, so that their abundance may supply your want, that there may be equality [ἰσότης]' (vv13-14; RSV).

In neither case can it be said that there was equality in a strict mathematical sense. It is true that the Israelites were instructed to collect 'an omer to a person according to the number of persons' (Ex. 16:16), which is clearly a quantitative measure. The text also explains, however, that 'they gathered as much as each of them needed' (v18). Thus there is a combination of 'no inequality' with

---

2nd ed. (London: George Allen and Unwin, 1931); Amartya Sen, *Inequality Reexamined* (Oxford: Clarendon, 1992); Ellen Frankel Paul *et al* (eds.), *The Just Society* (Cambridge: CUP, 1995) and Jane Franklin (ed.), *Equality* (London: Institute for Public Policy Research, 1997).

'sufficiency for need'.[36] The emphasis of both Moses and Paul is not, therefore, upon mathematical equality but rather upon *both* the avoidance of inequality *and* a plentiful supply for need. This is at least part of what it means for everyone to participate in God's blessings. Paul's appeal to the Corinthians follows from his *recognition* of the present lack of equality between them and their fellow Christians in Jerusalem; and he does not argue simply that the Jerusalem Christians need help, but rather that there may be mutual help, and that there may be equality. Thus the upper limit to inequality does not have to be measurable in quantitative terms, but it is something that is recognisable.[37]

In order to justify proposition (B.1), it is necessary to deal with attacks from two opposing sides. One attack says that (B.1) is too lax with regard to inequality; the other says it is too restrictive.

OBJECTION (a): NO INEQUALITY IS PERMISSIBLE

From one side might come the objection that *no* degree of inequality is defensible. If all are to participate in God's blessing on the same basis, then how can anything less than total equality be acceptable? The basic answer to such an attack is to expose the foundation which typically underlies it. And that foundation is an atomistic understanding of community and therefore an atomistic approach to equality.

The biblical material - as in the passages just discussed - cannot defend an argument for total quantitative equality. But why should anyone think that total equality is desirable? The only possible basis for such an argument is to assert that, since we are all individuals, then no arrangement that ever benefits some individuals more than others is ever permissible. Therefore, all individuals must be treated identically. This is clearly an atomistic framework. Equality is necessary in order to protect individuals.

---

[36]Durham's commentary explains the text as follows: 'No matter how much or how little the men collected, they found themselves when they came to prepare and eat the manna with precisely the amount needed and the amount allowed for the day's food'. So God's specification about the collection of manna was 'miraculously governed' (John I. Durham, *Exodus*, Word Biblical Commentary, Waco, TX: Word, 1987, p225). The equality amongst the people was not a strictly enforced mathematical equality; and yet there was precisely sufficient for everyone's need.

[37]If one were to seek to probe further for clarification of the criteria for such 'recognition', then the basic answer from a biblically-rooted understanding, as argued already in this book, is in terms of discerning God's will on the basis of what his word reveals about his character. Thus there are no hidden quantitative criteria which clever analysis might uncover. Rather, God's justice is such that any humble believer, meditating upon God's word by his Spirit's illumination, can discern what is the just thing to do. The role of specialist analysis is not to offer a better way than that, but rather to support that very process of discernment, through careful attention to the text of God's word, and through critical examination of thought patterns to see where those patterns are not faithful to the text.

The Scriptural critique of such an atomistic conception of community is founded on an entirely different understanding of a human community: an understanding which - inspired by the divine community of the Trinity - recognises that true human community must, as well as being devoted to God, consist of members who know that they belong together. This understanding of persons-in-community is not only in direct opposition to an atomistic conception - which offers no meaningful belonging together at all - but also offers a powerful argument against that conception. For the atomistic view totally fails to make any kind of sense of the immense value of human relationships. The Scriptural view, by contrast - for example, the 'many persons, one body' teaching in 1 Corinthians 12 - rebukes as wrong any idea that individuals can or should isolate themselves from others who are in fact members of their community. Further, the Scriptural teaching is that unity and diversity are to be held together (as, again, in 1 Corinthians 12). It is precisely such diversity that the atomistic framework is unwilling to tolerate. That framework, by insisting on identical treatment, effectively rules out any meaningful diversity, and thus diminishes everyone, forcing them into some identikit mould.[38]

Measurability and Inequality

At this point it is important to highlight an issue which the discussion in the previous paragraphs has not made explicit. The issue concerns the measurability of income (and/or wealth), and the way in which such measurability affects the link between diversity and equality. In a pre-monetary economy - with some kind of barter system operative - the 'incomes' of different people (or households) could not be measured on any common basis, and therefore *comparisons* of income across people (or households) were in general difficult.[39] Whether an arable farmer, for example, was better off, in material terms, than a cattle farmer, would in general be hard to tell.[40] In a

---

[38]If the toleration of diversity were also to tolerate *unfairly* differential treatment of different people, then the concerns which the atomistic framework exhibits might be justified. As is explained below, however, diversity and fairness are held together in a biblically-rooted framework.

[39]The case of the Israelites' manna is the exception which proves this rule: in that unusual (and pre-monetary) context, comparisons were possible, but only because it was so unusual - there was hardly an 'economy' to speak of, only a blanket handout from on high. Once a pre-monetary economy with diverse occupations and diverse goods was underway, comparisons of 'income' would again be, in general, impossible.

[40]In theory, a price for cattle, in terms of arable produce, might exist. However, this exchange price would be known to the two farmers only if they actually conducted such an exchange; and they would know which of them was, in those terms, better off, only if they actually conducted an exchange *between them*. Such stringent conditions would in general not be met. Thus comparisons of income would in general be impossible. (Further details and qualifications could obviously be added, but such a

modern monetary economy, however, income is obviously measured in monetary terms, and therefore inter-personal comparisons of income are easily made. Whether person A is better off than person B can immediately be established. The same is true, in principle, for inter-country comparisons of income, and of income per head (say, in terms of Gross Domestic Product (GDP)).[41]

This measurability (and comparability) of income has the immediate and important consequence that diversity across people, at least in a developed market economy, typically involves differences in incomes across people.[42] Hence the question of inequality is made much more prominent. In a monetary economy, it is obvious whether the arable farmer is better off than the cattle farmer. Let us suppose that the cattle farmer has a higher monetary income. Is it then correct to conclude that there is *inequality* between them? If 'inequality' here carries the connotation that there is something morally unacceptable about such differences in monetary income, then the answer to the question must be in the negative. On the assumption that each farmer has acted in accordance with the norms of commutative justice, and that no other parties involved have acted exploitatively, then the difference in income that emerges cannot be morally unacceptable. The difference in income might result from any combination of a large number of factors;[43] but these factors cannot be regarded as grounds for moral condemnation of the income difference that emerges.[44]

None of this recognition of diversity, however, implies that market outcomes - even given commutative justice - must be accepted as unalterable. For one aspect of justice, in a biblically-rooted conception, is that everyone participates in God's blessings, on the same basis: no-one should be left out. This is why proposition (B.1) states that there is some upper limit on the extent of inequality that is permissible: if it did not do this, then the idea that 'everyone participates in God's blessing' would easily be reduced to a rubber-stamping of whatever outcomes are generated by economic transactions as a whole. Distributive justice, however, requires that careful attention is given by members of the community to ensuring - even given the practice of

---

detailed analysis is well beyond the remit of this book. In any case the general point is clear.)

[41]Clearly such comparisons require a benchmark currency - but the technical issues involved do not require discussion here.

[42]Different employees will tend to receive different wages/salaries, for example, according to the demand and supply conditions for each particular segment of the labour market.

[43]Such as: amounts and quality of investment; levels of entrepreneurial skill; weather, and other factors outside the control of either farmer; and business contacts.

[44]This analysis assumes that there is, in some sense, equality of opportunity for the two farmers. Given that - together with the practice of commutative justice - then equality of outcome is not a moral requirement. The notion of equality of opportunity receives further comment below.

commutative justice - that everyone does participate in God's blessings. This principle receives inspiration from many parts of Scripture, but notably from the range of measures in the OT Law which worked to secure and improve the material position of those who tended to lose out in terms of economic well-being.[45] The teaching of Leviticus 25 is particularly important here, not so much for its 'jubilee' principle of people returning to their own plot of family land (which would happen only in every fiftieth year), but for its *ongoing* provision for the economic well-being of households, especially those that fell upon hard times. Four cases of progressively worse economic circumstances are set out (beginning respectively in verses 25, 29, 35 and 39), and in each case clear provision by the better off for those suffering hardship is prescribed.

In a modern setting, distributive justice requires that, where economic outcomes exhibit inequality in excess of the permissible upper limit, then action is taken to reduce the inequality - in order to ensure that, in a meaningful sense, everyone does participate in God's blessing. The permissible upper limit is not an absolute numerical limit, since no objective criteria are given for establishing such a limit. Nevertheless, in any given community, the above discussion indicates that the permissible upper limit is something *recognizable*: members of the community will be able to acknowledge that a particular degree of inequality clearly exceeds that which is compatible with everyone participating in God's blessings.[46] The appropriate action in such a setting may involve purely voluntary sharing, on the part of those who are better off; it may involve taxation of the incomes of the better off, with the funds used to bring benefits particularly to those who are less well off; and it may involve action to increase the skills and training ('human capital') of the less well off, so that in the future they are likely to receive higher wages/salaries.[47]

OBJECTION (b): ANY DEGREE OF INEQUALITY IS PERMISSIBLE

The argument from the opposite side, rather than saying that proposition (B.1) is insufficiently committed to equality, is that (B.1) allows for too little *in*equality. This argument involves both a claim regarding the importance of merit in economic outcomes, and a warning about the consequences of interfering with economic outcomes. These two aspects - which are related - are examined in turn.

The Place of Merit in Economic Outcomes
The meritocratic idea - the idea that merit should be allowed an important place

---

[45]See chapter 3 for a more detailed treatment of this material.

[46]It follows that all members of a community, however, are responsible for seeking to assess whether - at any given stage in the life of that community - everyone is participating in God's blessings, on the same basis.

[47]This last suggestion is, obviously, one way of achieving a higher degree of equality of opportunity.

in overall economic outcomes - is well-known and is widely held. The use of the very word 'earnings' conveys this sense of merit. And the idea is found in Scripture as well as many other places.[48] The question here is whether merit requires that no upper limit be placed on the degree of inequality in a community or society. The case for unrestrained merit is in part a moral case, namely that people have earned their wages/salaries/bonuses, and that they are entitled to keep them.[49] Conversely, it is said that to take away people's earnings - other than the proportion needed for a safety net - is an act of coercion, a form of theft, a removal of something to which a person is entitled.[50]

A biblically-rooted conception of justice offers a fundamental critique of this approach. First, the meritocratic approach is wrong to regard the resources available to any given person as being under that person's ownership. Instead, the biblical material teaches that human beings are stewards, or trustees, of resources - resources which actually belong to God.[51] It follows that, whilst the idea of a person earning a wage/salary is important, the earnings do not ultimately *belong* to that person: rather, they belong to God. 'The earth is the LORD's, and everything in it' (Ps. 24:1): all resources, indeed, human and otherwise. If, then, God's will is that people who earn far more than others should - by one means or another - share their plenty with others who have far less, then the well-off people have absolutely no grounds for complaint.[52] And a biblically-rooted conception of justice says that such a sharing is indeed part of God's justice.[53]

Secondly, the meritocratic approach fails to come to terms with the biblical understanding of community and relationships. Instead, it regards people solely as individuals, whose earnings can be attributed solely to them as individuals. It is in essence an atomistic approach.[54] In general, such an approach is ill-

---

[48]E.g. 1 Ti. 5:18; 1 Cor. 9:9-14; Mt. 10:10.

[49]Except to the extent that a safety net must be funded for those whose basic needs would otherwise not be met.

[50]Hence Nozick (*Anarchy, State and Utopia*) labels as an 'entitlement' theory his approach to distributive justice, in which merit plays a central role (see chapter 4). As noted earlier, his approach requires that commutative justice - *as he defines it* - is done.

[51]This emphasis was developed in chapter 3.

[52]Note that, if God's will is indeed as here suggested, then taxation might be no less virtuous a means of transferring the plenty than is voluntary giving. It is as much a command of God to pay taxes where due (Rom. 13:7) as to love one's neighbour (the following verse): indeed the former can be understood as part of the latter. Whether taxation is, in the contemporary context, an *appropriate* method for transferring plenty, however, is not established by this reasoning. The role of government in distributive justice is discussed in chapter 6.

[53]Note that such justice is not couched in terms solely of meeting need, but rather of participating in God's blessing. Justice goes beyond a safety net.

[54]It may seem paradoxical that the argument for total *equality* - examined in the previous

equipped to deal with the many ways in which economic endeavour is itself a shared, rather than individual, exercise. This is especially so in a highly industrialised and technological setting where the skills necessary for many occupations can be learnt only with substantial input from other people; and where, for the vast majority of people, their economic contribution can be significant only in combination with contributions from others. The particular problem here, with regard to earnings and merit, is that there are relatively few, if any, people who can say that they alone have the moral entitlement to that which is paid to them as earnings. Each manager, each owner, and each employee in a modern economy owes a substantial moral debt, with regard to their ability to earn, to a significant number of people.

It is not being suggested that earnings should not be paid to individuals. Clearly some such arrangement has to be made. The point is that individuals can have no sovereign right over the earnings paid to them, and hence there is nothing here to provide an argument against some upper limit on income inequality, as put forward in proposition (B.1).

The Consequences of Interfering with Economic Outcomes
The other argument by which proposition (B.1) might be criticised for permitting *too little* inequality is the argument that, through interfering to reduce income inequality, the workings of the economy are badly distorted, so that total GDP turns out to be less than it otherwise would be. There is some validity in this reasoning, in the sense that the economics literature establishes beyond reasonable doubt that, at least in general terms, some trade-off between 'equity' and 'efficiency' exists, so that greater equity (measured in some way or other) can in general be obtained only at the expense of lower efficiency (in the sense of the output of goods and services generated from a given input of resources). The question in the present context, however, is whether this argument is sufficiently significant and strong to render invalid the kind of upper limit to inequality put forward in proposition (B.1).

The discussion here can afford to be somewhat cursory.[55] For example, technical questions regarding the precise size of some upper limit are irrelevant here, since no precise upper limit is either envisaged or proposed.[56] The main

---

section - was also, like its meritocratic opposite here, criticised on the grounds of being atomistic. However, since both approaches arise from Western individualism - especially as found in mainstream neoclassical economics - then their shared commitment to an atomistic framework comes as no surprise.

[55]For a critical review of the welfare economics literature - the locus of the equity/efficiency debates - see Donald Hay, *Economics Today: A Christian Critique* (Leicester: Apollos, 1989), especially pp124-142. The issues involved are far more wide-ranging than can be addressed in this book.

[56]The assessment of whether the extent of income inequality at a particular time is in excess of some upper limit might lead, of course, to the conclusion that inequality ought to be reduced, somehow or other (even though no permanent numerical upper limit need

point, however, is relatively straightforward. Since distributive justice - understood in the sense developed in this chapter - is, according to the argument of this thesis, a central feature of a biblically-rooted conception of justice, then the realisation that the practice of such justice involves less than maximal economic efficiency is simply not an argument against an upper limit on inequality. God's requirement on human beings is not to maximise GDP, but 'to do justice, love kindness, and to walk humbly with your God' (Mic. 6:8).[57]

This argument is not a justification for widespread government interference in economic outcomes. Indeed the question of the most appropriate means for bringing about distributive justice has not yet been addressed in this chapter, and there has been no unqualified advocacy of *government* action. It might conceivably be that widespread government interference forms part of the most appropriate set of means: but the case for that would have to be made.[58] Nevertheless it may be that some, perhaps more limited, role for government, would exist in the quest for a greater measure of distributive justice, given that a lack of such justice had been perceived.[59]

This concludes the current discussion of proposition (B.1). That proposition - as set out and defended above - states that there should be some upper limit to the degree of income inequality in a society or community. The setting for that discussion was effectively a *static* one; it was envisaged that a community would assess, in the light of God's word, whether its current degree of inequality was too great to be compatible with distributive justice. The next proposition considers a more dynamic setting: that is, it considers what distributive justice - sharing the fruits of economic endeavour - requires in a *growing* economy.

Proposition (B.2)

(B.2) states that a just sharing of the growing fruits of economic endeavour

---

be agreed). At this point the technical experts could offer their insight into the likely consequences of such action in terms of economic output; and this insight could be taken into account in the community's decisions about how best to proceed.

[57]It is not being said that the degree of economic efficiency is irrelevant, only that it is not the paramount criterion here. In any case, it has already been argued that some degree of inequality is permissible; and policies that would greatly reduce economic output, for the sake of justice, are not envisaged here.

[58]No such case will be put here. Advocates of widespread government interference would have to deal with the argument that such action is, at least on occasions, counter-productive, even on its own terms. The best way to decide the most appropriate means of bringing some measure of distributive justice might be to consider each situation on its own merits.

[59]More is said in the following chapter on the role of the governing authorities in economic matters.

must benefit everyone;[60] and that, unless initial inequality is *less* than the limit set in accordance with (B.1), a just sharing of the growing fruits of economic endeavour *cannot involve greater general inequality over time* - whether of outcome or opportunity.[61]

The second clause of proposition (B.2) is undoubtedly a radical claim; and it is put in that form of words very deliberately. It is not being said that biblical justice necessarily requires greater equality in all circumstances.[62] But it is being said that biblical justice - in a context of rising general prosperity, and assuming initial inequality is not less than the upper limit set in accordance with (B.1) - prohibits greater general inequality over time.[63] It also follows from both propositions that, if initial inequality exceeds the upper limit, then greater equality is called for.

It is also important to note, before explaining the arguments for this proposition, how that radical claim contrasts with Rawls' difference (maximin) principle.[64] His principle states that any improvement for the better off is permissible *only* if it *maximises* the material well-being of the least well-off. At least two contrasts exist between proposition (B.2) and Rawls' approach. First, the claim being made here has (unlike Rawls' principle) *no* requirement to *maximize* the well-being of the worst-off. Secondly, however, the claim being made here does *prohibit* greater inequality (if general prosperity is rising) - which is not necessarily the case with Rawls' principle. The first contrast

---

[60]The question arises of what happens if some people 'opt out' of meaningful involvement in a community, and therefore do not benefit from the fruits of economic endeavour. The basic answer needs to hold together the responsibility of the community and the responsibility of such individuals: the community must ask how and why such an unacceptable and sad situation has arisen, and what it has done to help bring it about; and yet the responsibility upon individuals to play their part must not be ignored.

[61]The word 'general' in that statement is intended to give recognition to the permissibility of some people doing particularly well, in terms of prosperity, at particular periods of time. And it is certainly not required that all the prosperity of these people be redistributed. What is not permissible is for those who are substantially less well off to be omitted *en masse* from a genuine participation in any growth in prosperity.

[62]Proposition (B.2) is compatible with (B.1) in the sense that, if initial inequality is already less than the upper limit set in accordance with (B.1), then no greater degree of equality is required. If, however, initial inequality *exceeds* that upper limit, then it follows logically that (whether the economy is growing or not) greater equality is required.

[63]How such justice might come about, or be brought about, is a very different matter. For example, it does *not* follow from this claim that action to prevent growth in inequality is required of governments; but nor does it follow, for that matter, that such action is *not* required of governments.

[64]Rawls' approach - developed at length in his *A Theory Of Justice* (Oxford: OUP, 1972/Cambridge, Mass.: Harvard University Press, 1971) - was assessed at length in chapter 4. It assumes, in general, a growing economy, and hence it is discussed here, in the context of proposition (B.2), rather than that of (B.1).

involves the suggestion that Rawls' approach says *too much* - in the sense that, with regard to the well-being of the poorest, it is excessively specific. The second contrast involves the suggestion that Rawls also says *too little* - in the sense that, with regard to inequality, it is insufficiently specific. These suggestions are assessed shortly.

Before that, however, the logic of the argument which underpins proposition (B.2) requires articulation. The essence of the argument is straightforward, and is as follows. In a static setting - as in (B.1) - the requirement that all participate in God's blessing entails an upper limit on the degree of general inequality; therefore, in a dynamic (growth) setting, the same kind of upper limit is also entailed. In particular, since the upper limit in a static setting is *not* determined according to criteria of need, but rather in terms of everyone participating on the same basis, then it follows that the growing fruits of economic endeavour are also to be shared in the same kind of way. This approach rules out, therefore, the idea that, once the basic needs of all have been met, then any kind of distribution across the community is permissible (subject to the practice of commutative justice).[65] Theologically, this approach rests upon a strong doctrine of creation:[66] that is, God's active will for his creation consists of a requirement not only for all to share in having basic needs met, but also for all to share in the full bounty of creation, as human beings successfully work to obtain the material blessings contained in the created order. All this is taught clearly in, for example, 1 Ti. 6:17-19, where those who are rich in this present world are commanded to share generously (v18), and where part of the basis for this command is that God 'richly furnishes us with everything to enjoy' (v17).

Given this articulation of proposition (B.2), it is now appropriate to examine further the contrasts between this proposition and the approach presented by Rawls. The first contrast can be highlighted by noting that Rawls requires that, given an increase in aggregate income, then the income of those who initially are least well-off must be maximised, subject to the condition that no-one becomes worse off.[67] What proposition (B.2) states, by contrast, is that, given an increase in aggregate income, then the income of the least well-off, relative to aggregate income, must not decrease; or, equivalently, that the income of the least well-off increases by at least the same proportion as aggregate income.[68]

---

[65]This approach is thus in direct contrast to that advocated by Robert Nozick (in *Anarchy, State and Utopia*), for whom *any* criteria for the patterning of distribution are illegitimate (see chapter 4).

[66]See also chapter 3.

[67]The particular way in which Rawls specifies 'the least well-off' is highly problematic, as argued in chapter 4. These problems are assumed away in the present discussion, however, since the point at issue concerns more basic principles.

[68]It is assumed throughout this discussion that equality and inequality are measured in percentage terms, rather than in absolute terms. Thus the degree of inequality, given an initial situation where the poorest 10% have, say, 5% of aggregate income, is unchanged

(B.2) does not require that the income of the least well-off be maximised.[69]

It might appear that in this regard proposition (B.2) is morally inferior to Rawls' difference principle. In particular, the theologically-driven advocacy of the 'preferential option for the poor' might seem to be expressed substantially better by Rawls' principle than by proposition (B.2).[70] After all, the difference principle will normally guarantee a higher percentage income growth for the least well-off than will proposition (B.2).[71]

Two responses may be made. First, a biblically-rooted conception of justice, as developed in this thesis, does not appear to require that the incomes of the least well-off be *maximized*. Active concern for the well-being of the poor and needy is evidently a major priority, an essential ingredient of a just community.[72] It is not all clear, however, that maximization of their income - whether or not on the conditions stated by Rawls - is required. This approach says too much. Rawls' difference principle has significant strengths, but there is no reason to regard its particular requirement regarding the least well-off as the best possible encapsulation of the biblical concern for the poor.

The second contrast between proposition (B.2) and Rawls' approach is that, unlike the latter, proposition (B.2) rules out any widening, over time, in the degree of general inequality. The claim here is that Rawls, in this regard, says too little. This may be illustrated by an example, with two different possible growth projections. Suppose that, in one possible projection, (x), the income of

---

if everyone's income over a given period increases by, say, 20%. On an absolute basis, by contrast, the inequality would have risen over that time period. The percentage approach is taken here as preferable, since there is no obvious sense in which a biblically-rooted conception of justice can regard as unjust a situation where everyone receives material blessings that are growing at the same proportionate (=percentage) rate for everyone. The only proviso here is that - as already stated in the text - in the initial situation, the degree of inequality does not exceed the upper limit, as required in proposition (B.1).

[69]Nor does (B.2) - unlike Rawls' difference principle - state that *everyone's* income must not decrease. This is a less significant contrast than that concerning maximisation of the income of the least well-off. It is certainly not required, nor anticipated, by (B.2) that the income of anyone should fall: it is simply the case that the argument for (B.2) does not involve the particular stipulation required by Rawls - a stipulation that, like the above maximisation criterion, arises (see chapter 4) from his contractarian framework.

[70]The preferential option for the poor - advocated by both Roman Catholic social teaching and liberation theology - was discussed in chapter 4. The links between those bodies of teaching and Rawls' approach are discussed by Karen Lebacqz, *Six Theories of Justice* (Minneapolis: Augsburg, 1986).

[71]Exceptions to this can occur, due to Rawls' further stipulation that *no-one* becomes worse off. That stipulation may mean, in certain circumstances, that the aggregate income growth is lower than it would otherwise be, and, in turn, that the maximised income growth for the least well-off is lower than it would otherwise be. These technical matters have no bearing on the matter in hand, however.

[72]Chapter 3 discussed this at some length.

the least well-off will increase by 0.5% p.a., whilst that of everyone else will increase by 2%. Alternatively, in growth projection (y), the income of the least well-off is likely to grow by 1% p.a., the income of the richest tenth of the population will grow by 10%, and the income of everyone else - the middle band - will grow by 5%. In both cases, inequality will increase. However, case (y) evidently entails a substantially larger increase in inequality, compared with case (x). Rawls' difference principle, nevertheless, requires that (y) be chosen - since the maximised income of the least well-off is higher under (y) than under (x).[73] (It should be noted that, despite egalitarian appearances, Rawls' approach will, in certain circumstances, permit outcomes that many egalitarians would consider totally unacceptable.)

Proposition (B.2), by contrast, would disallow both case (x) and case (y), since both involve widening inequality.[74] This would in turn bring a significant challenge to all members of the community, both to ascertain why such a widening of inequality would appear inevitable, and to discover and implement the radical changes necessary for that increase in inequality no longer to be inevitable.[75]

Conclusion

This chapter has begun the task of engaging a biblical conception of economic justice with the challenges posed by the treatments of justice examined in chapter 4. The present chapter has sought to deal with those challenges which relate to justice specifically as a socio-economic conception. In doing so, it has been argued that a biblical conception calls for both commutative justice (justice in producing and exchanging goods and services) and distributive

---

[73]Note that, according to proposition (B.2), neither (x) nor (y) is acceptable. It would follow that further possibilities would have to be considered, even if they are inferior - in terms of aggregate income growth - to both (x) and (y). What would also have to be examined, however, are the structures of power and opportunity that mean that the only two choices apparently on offer each entail widening inequality.

[74]This discussion deliberately avoids any technically sophisticated definition of inequality - primarily on the grounds that such matters are outside the scope of this book. Also, many definitions tend to give as much weight to inequality at the top end of the income scale as the bottom end, whereas the general concern here is that everyone - and especially the poor and needy - participates fully in God's blessings, on the same basis. What is meant in the text by inequality is, it is submitted, sufficiently clear in this regard, without the need for more technical definitions or measurements.

[75]The degree of radicalism required might not be feasible, at least in the short term, especially in a society lacking significant commitment to the gospel of the Lord Jesus Christ. This chapter in general puts to one side the difficulties of applying biblical principles in a secular/pagan setting, in order to focus on the actual content of commutative and distributive justice. The following chapter does seek to address some of those difficulties.

justice (justice in sharing the fruits of economic endeavour). Also, this chapter has argued that a biblical account of each of these aspects is sharply distinct in significant respects from the treatments examined in chapter 4. Further, although the differences between a Rawlsian and a Nozickian approach can be summarized as the difference between, respectively, a primarily distributive and a primarily commutative conception of economic justice (notwithstanding Nozick's adoption of the label 'distributive'), this chapter's argument that *both* aspects are essential is clearly distinctive. In chapter 6, attention is turned to the challenges arising from chapter 4 regarding justice in its moral, political and theological aspects.

CHAPTER 6

God's Demand for Economic Justice: A Biblically-Rooted Conception in Conversation with the U.S. Roman Catholic Bishops' Economic Justice For All

Introduction

This chapter (like chapter 5) aims not only to engage a biblically-rooted conception of economic justice with some of the challenges posed by other treatments (highlighted in chapter 4), but also to articulate further the biblical understanding of economic justice developed in chapters 2 and 3; and the engagement with those challenges is intended to assist in this articulation, and also to demonstrate some of the practical implications of a biblically-rooted conception.[1] The present chapter's material on economic justice focuses on its moral, political and theological dimensions.[2] The analysis is carried out, in part, by means of a conversation between, on the one hand, a biblically-rooted understanding of economic justice and, on the other hand, the approach offered by the U.S. Roman Catholic Bishops in their influential Pastoral Letter, *Economic Justice For All* (1986).[3] Particular attention is given to Chapter II of

---

[1]It is worth emphasising again that there is no claim here that the conception of economic justice presented in these chapters is the final word on what the Bible says about economic justice. Thus the term 'biblically-rooted understanding' as used here means, roughly speaking, 'the conception of economic justice presented and developed in this book, a conception which is intended to be rooted in and faithful to Scripture, but which must itself be subjected - like all theological efforts - to continuing Scriptural scrutiny and critique.

[2]Chapter 5 focused more on economic justice specifically as a socio-economic conception. The two chapters together thus address, at least in outline terms, the four levels at which other treatments of justice raise challenges for a biblically-rooted conception (see the Introduction to chapter 5).

[3]National Conference of Catholic Bishops, *Economic Justice For All: Pastoral Letter on Catholic Social Teaching and the U.S. Economy* (Washington, D.C.: United States Catholic Conference, 1986). The influence of that Letter can be gauged, for example, by the substantial literature it generated (some of it commenting on one or more of the widely circulated first three drafts of the Pastoral, prior to the publication of the final version in November 1986). See, e.g.: John Langan, 'The Pastoral on the Economy:

that Letter ('The Christian Vision of Economic Life').[4]

The first three sections of the chapter focus more on the overall conception of economic justice; and within that overall framework they examine in particular some aspects of justice in its *moral* dimension. The conversation with the Pastoral Letter here is focused mainly on section B of Chapter II ('Ethical Norms for Economic Justice'). The biblically-rooted understanding in this regard is illustrated briefly by means of a couple of concrete examples (there being no absolute divide, of course, between the conception and the practice of economic justice).

The final section of the chapter focuses more specifically on how a biblically-rooted conception of justice applies in contemporary economic life, and on how responsibility for justice is shared within a society. Particular attention is paid to section C of the Pastoral Letter's second chapter ('Working for Greater Justice: Persons and Institutions'). Despite the ontological reality of God's justice, not least in terms of economic life - as depicted, however inadequately, in these chapters - the contemporary world is in many ways at odds with that reality. Economic life, like many other dimensions of life, demonstrates the radical difference between the earthly City and the City of God.[5] However, this observation is not, in a biblical worldview, a justification for inaction on the part of the church of Jesus Christ. Rather, that same Christ

---

From Drafts to Policy', *Theological Studies*, 48, March 1987, 135-156; Douglas B. Rasmussen and James Sterba, *The Catholic Bishops and the Economy: A Debate* (Social Philosophy Policy Center/New Brunswick: Transaction Books, 1987); R. Bruce Douglass, ed., *The Deeper Meaning of Economic Life: Critical Essays on the U.S. Catholic Bishops' Pastoral Letter on the Economy* (Washington, D.C.: Georgetown University Press, 1986); Walter Block, *The U.S. Bishops and Their Critics: An Economic and Ethical Perspective* (Vancouver: Fraser Institute, 1986); Karen Lebacqz, *Six Theories of Justice* (Minneapolis: Augsburg, 1986 - her discussion, and the authors she cites, refer to the first draft of the Letter); Charles P. Lutz, ed., *God, Goods and the Common Good: Eleven Perspectives on Economic Justice in Dialog with the Roman Catholic Bishops' Pastoral Letter* (Minneapolis: Augsburg, 1987); C. Johnston, 'Learning Reformed Theology from the Roman Catholics: the US Pastoral Letter on the Economy' in Robert L. Stivers, ed., *Reformed Faith and Economics* (Lanham, MD: University Press of America, 1989); Charles R. Strain, ed., *Prophetic Visions and Economic Realities: Protestants, Jews and Catholics Confront the Bishops' Letter on the Economy* (Grand Rapids, MI: Eerdmans, 1989).

[4]In the present chapter, the conversation with the Pastoral Letter focuses on seeking to articulate some of the practical aspects of economic justice. By contrast, the discussion of the Letter in chapter 4 of this book concentrated on the extent to which that Letter engaged successfully at the conceptual level with three influential secular treatments of justice. As will be seen below, it is suggested that the Letter makes a considerable contribution regarding the former task, whereas it was somewhat lacking with regard to the latter task.

[5]Augustine, *The City of God.*

sends his people - as he himself was sent by God the Father - into the world.[6] Thus the chapter examines something of what is required in terms of the practice of economic justice now. In the process of this assessment, consideration will be given to economic justice both as a political conception and as a theological conception, in response to the challenges identified in these respects in chapter 4.

Finally, by way of introduction, it should be noted that all of the above matters belong in the wider context of God's *demand* for economic justice.[7] Both the right conception, and the right practice, of justice in economic life are required by God. They are in no sense optional. Recognition of this demand derives from the biblical material presented back in chapter 2, and thus from the theological framework developed there. It was shown in that chapter that righteousness on the part of humanity is demanded by God. Since justice in economic life is one aspect of that righteousness, it follows that economic justice also is demanded by God.

A Biblically-rooted Conception of Economic Justice

Chapters 2 and 3 argued that economic justice, as a biblically-rooted conception, means, in summary form, appropriate treatment of human beings, according to the norms which God has commanded for each particular case - norms which also enable human flourishing - with the context for economic justice usually being a relationship between human beings. This conception was implicit in chapter 5 and its approach to commutative and distributive justice. Thus chapter 5 demonstrated something of the content of these norms commanded by God. The next couple of pages seek to make various aspects of this conception more explicit, and to explain them in a little more detail.

This can be done in part by briefly drawing out some particular facets of the biblically-rooted conception, as stated in summary form in the preceding paragraph. First, the content of economic justice - of what it means to do justice - is derived from particular norms. Whilst the traditional idea of justice as 'to each his due' might also be stated in terms of 'according to norms', a biblically-rooted conception is distinct from that more general type of conception in that it depends - for its content to be meaningful - on the existence of some specified norms, norms which are not humanly created or relativistic but, rather, are in a clear and definite sense *given*.

This point is reinforced by noting a second facet of the above conception, namely that the norms for justice - including economic justice - are commanded *by God*. Thus the origin of economic justice lies outside this world, outside of humanity, and is found instead in the very character and being of God. God, who is not only perfectly just but is also the Creator, is the one who defines the

---

[6]See Jn. 17:11-19.

[7]As highlighted by the title of this chapter.

content of economic justice in his created order. Therefore, what it means to do justice in economic life is not for human beings to define by their own standards, but rather to discern according to God's norms. Further, these norms are not arbitrary, but are appropriate for the world God has created: they are the norms which enable human flourishing.

The third facet of a biblically-rooted conception of economic justice is vital for the first two facets to have practical meaning and value. This third facet is that the norms for justice are *commanded* by God. Supposing that, in God's self-revelation in Scripture and in Christ, God were silent and non-communicative regarding the content and norms of justice, then human beings' knowledge of what it means to do justice would be very limited: it would be limited to what may be known through general revelation, for example by way of human intuition and conscience. In reality, however, God is a speaking God, and by his self-disclosing and revelatory word he has commanded the norms of justice.[8] Thus human beings, if they want to know the norms for economic justice, are to examine God's written word - the Bible - which contains all the words of God necessary for salvation, faith and obedience.[9] And they are to study the Bible Christologically - as Scripture itself requires - since it is Jesus Christ who fulfils the law and the prophets (Matt. 5:17-20; cf. Jn. 5:39) and who, the Word made flesh, is God's final Word (Jn. 1:1-18; Heb. 1:1-4).[10]

In God's commanding the norms of justice, there is a second aspect - in addition, that is, to the communicative aspect explained in the preceding paragraph. For God does not merely state the norms of justice, but *commands* them. This point reinforces what has already been said about the *givenness* of the norms of economic justice. Therefore, to do economic justice, according to these norms, is not an option but an obligation. God demands it.

The fourth facet of a biblically-rooted conception of justice that should be noted here is that justice means *appropriate treatment* of human beings, according to the norms commanded by God. The point here is that justice - including economic justice - is not merely some state of affairs (not even the restoration of a state of affairs), nor some abstract conception, but, rather, is about what is done: specifically, it is about the appropriate treatment of human beings. The biblically-rooted conception of economic justice, then, is neither static nor abstract, but dynamic.

Fifthly and finally, the context for economic justice is, as implied by the previous point, usually that of a relationship between human beings. Thus the biblically-rooted conception of justice is far removed from a conception in

---

[8]The fact that God's command *communicates* is only one aspect of this commanding by God: see below.

[9]A paraphrase of Wayne Grudem's recent formulation of the classic Reformed view of the sufficiency of Scripture (*Systematic Theology: An Introduction to Christian Doctrine*, Leicester: IVP, 1994, p127).

[10]Chapter 3 devoted considerable attention to such a study and examination of Scripture.

which those involved are dispassionate, mere dispensers of a thing called justice. Instead, doing justice in economic life - in a biblical understanding - requires the active involvement of people with one another. This is the case, however large the geographical distance, for example, between the parties to a relationship. This relational context of justice also emphasises - as argued in chapter 3 - that justice is not one-way, but always involves reciprocal obligations.

Some aspects of the nature and content of a biblically-rooted conception of economic justice - as sketched in the above paragraphs - can also be highlighted by comparing that conception with some other conceptions, especially (as indicated in the Introduction) in terms of economic justice in its *moral* dimension . This is the task of the next two short sections, in the first of which the discussion includes some conversation with the Pastoral Letter *Economic Justice For All*.

A Biblically-rooted Conception Compared with Justice Based on Rights [11]

Under the heading 'Ethical Norms for Economic Life', section B of the Pastoral Letter (in its Chapter II) outlines three aspects: first, the duties that all people have to each other and to the whole community; secondly - and corresponding to those duties - the human rights of every person; thirdly the priorities that are entailed by these duties and rights. [12] Of particular importance here is the emphasis on human rights: the Letter argues that 'the obligation to protect the dignity of all demands respect for these rights'. [13]

The duties that all people have are summarized as follows: '*Basic justice demands the establishment of minimum levels of participation in the life of the human community for all persons*'. [14] It is then argued that an account of human rights effectively puts flesh on the bones of this basic justice. Thus the Letter proceeds to say that Catholic social teaching 'spells out the demands of justice in greater detail in the human rights of every person. These fundamental rights are prerequisites for a dignified life in community'. [15] This perspective is rooted

---

[11]There is no intention here to survey in any sense the vast literature on rights, or that on justice conceived in terms of rights. Instead the aim is simply to indicate, in broad strokes, the substantial contrast that exists here between a biblically-rooted conception of justice and a conception founded upon rights. David Miller offers an illuminating examination of rights as a principle of justice, in *Social Justice* (Oxford: Clarendon, 1976), especially chapters I and II.

[12]National Conference of Catholic Bishops, *Economic Justice For All*, p33.

[13]*Ibid*. It is *not* being claimed here that the Pastoral Letter bases justice solely, or even primarily, on human rights. Nevertheless, the prominence of rights in its approach is noteworthy, and the discussion below seeks to tease out some of the strengths and weaknesses of this, in order to illuminate the features of a biblically-rooted conception.

[14]*Ibid*. [emphasis in the original].

[15]*Ibid.*, p40.

in the biblical understanding that each person is sacred, a creature made in the image and likeness of God. Further, the biblical emphasis on covenant and community 'also shows that human dignity can only be realized and protected in solidarity with others. In Catholic social thought, therefore, respect for human rights and a strong sense of both personal and community responsibility are linked, not opposed'.[16] This profound understanding is thoroughly consistent with the account sketched in chapter 3 (above) of a biblical conception of human living.

The Letter goes on to encapsulate its understanding in terms of a concept central to Catholic social teaching, namely the common good. In the words of Vatican II in *Gaudium et Spes*, the common good is 'the sum of those social conditions which allow individuals and groups to achieve their proper purposes more fully and quickly'.[17] Thus, as interdependence 'grows steadily closer and extends to the whole world, the common good...assumes a universal scale and entails rights and duties belonging to the human race as a whole. Any group must take account of the needs and legitimate aspirations of other groups, indeed of the common good of the human family.'[18]

The Letter argues that these conditions for life in community 'include the rights to fulfilment of material needs, a guarantee of fundamental freedoms, and the protection of relationships that are essential to participation in the life of society'.[19] Specifying human rights in more detail, it is argued - in terms very similar to those of the UN Universal Declaration of Human Rights - that human rights include 'the civil and political rights to freedom of speech, worship, and assembly'. Further, and with particular reference to economic life, the Letter continues:

> A number of rights also concern human welfare and are of a specifically economic nature. First among these are the rights to life, food, clothing, shelter, rest, medical care, and basic education... In order to ensure these necessities, all persons have a right to earn a living, which for most people in our economy is through remunerative employment. All persons also have a right to security in the event of sickness, unemployment, and old age. Participation in the life of this

---

[16]*Ibid.*, p41.

[17]Paul VI and the Fathers of the Sacred Council, *Gaudium et Spes*, tr. William Purdy (London: Catholic Truth Society, 1966), #26.

[18]*Ibid.* Christian theology recognises, of course, alongside the importance of such moral exhortations, the reality that the Fall means that groups will sometimes, even often, *not* take account of others as they should. This was discussed in chapter 3 above.
Chapter 4's discussion of the notion of 'the common good' highlighted a weakness as a philosophical foundation, in the context of a fallen world in which that notion and its implications are, in practice, by no means accepted universally. The discussion in the present chapter intends to show, amongst other things, how this weakness can be addressed by a biblical conception of justice.

[19]National Conference of Catholic Bishops, *Economic Justice For All*, p41.

community calls for the protection of this same right to employment, as well as the right to healthful working conditions, to wages, and other benefits sufficient to provide individuals *and their families* with a standard of living in keeping with human dignity, and to the possibility of property ownership.[20]

These are radical teachings: certainly there are few, if any, political parties in the Western world which seriously assert such far-reaching rights, or which advocate policies that would satisfy them. Putting aside the question of how - if at all - these rights might be enacted,[21] it is important to acknowledge not only the scope of these rights (as stated in the previous quotation) but also the fundamental part they play in the framework advocated by the Letter:

These fundamental personal rights - civil and political as well as social and economic - state the *minimum conditions* for social institutions that respect human dignity, social solidarity, and justice. They are all essential to human dignity and to the integral development of both individuals and society... Any denial of these rights harms persons and wounds the human community. Their serious and sustained denial violates individuals and destroys solidarity among persons.[22]

There is considerable similarity between the principles for economic life expressed in the Pastoral Letter and those developed in chapters 3 and 5 above. For example, the claim in chapter 3 that no-one should be excluded from God's blessings - including material blessings - necessarily leads to the same kind of complete intolerance as expressed in the Letter, with regard to any *lack* of means for a household to live adequately. Similarly, the argument in chapter 5 that the remuneration for an employee should normally be sufficient to provide for that person and their household is essentially the same, very radical principle, as that expounded by the U.S. Catholic Bishops.

A difference between the two approaches appears to emerge, however, when the balance is considered between, on the hand, the principles outlined in the last paragraph, and, on the other hand, the principles which relate to the behaviour of others in the economy. The prominent use of rights-language in

---

[20]*Ibid.*, pp41-2 [emphasis added]. The clause 'and their families' is highlighted because it represents a slightly different emphasis from that of *Rerum Novarum*, in which Leo XIII restricted the amount of the 'just wage' to an amount sufficient for the subsistence of an *individual* only. That shift in emphasis in Roman Catholic teaching began in *Quadragesimo Anno*. Kirwan offers a helpful discussion of those two encyclicals in this regard, in his 'Translator's notes' to the 1991 republication of *Rerum Novarum* (Leo XIII, *Rerum Novarum* [1891], tr. Joseph Kirwan, London: Catholic Truth Society, 1991), pp50-65.

[21]The role of the governing authorities in this regard is discussed in the second section of this chapter. For now it is sufficient to note that the Roman Catholic teaching totally rejects a socialist view of government, whereby it is essentially through state action that justice will be attained. Instead the state viewed is much more as an actor of last resort.

[22]National Conference of Catholic Bishops, *Economic Justice For All*, p42.

the Letter raises the question of how, and by whom, these rights are to be met. For example, how is employment for all who seek it to be ensured? And who is to be responsible for ensuring that wages paid are adequate (perhaps in conjunction with other benefits) for an individual and their household? The remaining pages of the same section of the Letter (section B: 'Ethical Norms for Economic Life') argue that responsibility essentially rests upon *everyone*.[23] 'A concerted effort on all levels in our society is needed to meet these basic demands of justice and solidarity'.[24] This includes some kind of responsibility upon companies and employers. Thus the general principle that the 'investment of wealth, talent, and human energy should be specially directed to benefit those who are poor or economically insecure' (p47) is not left purely as a moral exhortation: rather, it leads to 'a strong moral challenge to policies that put large amounts of talent and capital into luxury consumer goods and military technology while failing to invest sufficiently in...the basic infrastructure of society and economic sectors that produce urgently needed jobs, goods, and services'.[25] The point is well made. Nevertheless the Letter falls short, it is argued here, of a clear statement of the specific responsibilities of companies and employers.

Put another way, the weakness in this regard is that the Letter does not provide a framework which can deal fully with all the obligations of *relationships* in economic life. Some duties are laid down, but they are not quite sufficient for the task. This may be demonstrated by the ease with which business enterprises can - and do - effectively bypass the teachings of the Letter. Such companies evidently do put huge amounts of talent and capital into consumer goods - despite the unsatisfied rights (in the Letter's terms) of many people. There may or may not be more socially responsible alternatives for these companies, but - generally speaking - even the possibility of such alternatives is not considered. Why not? Because nowhere is it laid down - whether in current law, or by the Letter, for that matter - that it is their responsibility to do so. The Letter offers only a general appeal, and does not grapple adequately with the relational responsibilities of companies.

This relative lack of emphasis upon the responsibilities of relationship is, it is argued here, linked to the relative prominence of rights-language in the Letter. A comparison here between 'rights' and 'norms' is instructive.[26] For, despite the appearance of the word 'norms' in the heading to section B of the

---

[23]The Letter does *not*, it should again be emphasized, mean that the responsibility rests essentially upon the state.

[24]*Ibid.*, p43.

[25]*Ibid.*, p48.

[26]It is not being claimed here, of course, that the use of one set of terminology or another is itself wholly determinative of the intellectual content of any given framework. Rather, in the present case, the terminology itself reflects differences - somewhat subtle differences, it may be noted - in intellectual content.

Letter, its approach in this regard is significantly different from that developed in chapters 3 and 5 above. According to the present book, the norms for economic life are not only located in the context of the reciprocal obligations of particular relationships, but also hold together to form a picture of what - under the will of the Creator-Redeemer God - economic life is to be like. Thus an appropriate allocation and balancing of responsibilities is *built into* the above framework, from the outset. In particular, for example, the framework offered here states that companies always have very definite responsibilities to employees and the wider community, as well as to their financial shareholders: and, further, these responsibilities would continue even if the 'basic rights' of all had already been met. The Pastoral Letter, in comparison, arrives at its appeal to companies only by derivation from its prior emphasis upon those rights.

The nature and content of the biblically-rooted conception offered here can be highlighted further by examining how it contrasts with approaches which - more fundamentally than that of the Pastoral Letter - are grounded upon the idea of rights.[27]

A rights-based approach to economic justice has to find a way of handling those cases where conflicts exist between the rights of different parties.[28] It was noted in chapter 4 that utilitarianism, in Mill's formulation, responds to this problem by appealing to an aggregate good above and beyond individual rights; it was also noted that utilitarianism's response demonstrates that its implicit conception of justice is *not* based fundamentally on rights, but on general utility. A genuinely rights-based conception of economic justice must therefore adopt some other response. Unless it is asserted that, in a given conflict, the rights of one particular party must take precedence over those of the other party, then the typical solution to such a conflict involves some kind of balancing of the conflicting rights. The difficulty with this balancing approach, however, is that it is not obvious how an appropriate balance is to be found.[29] Appeal might be made to common sense, but this does not actually solve the underlying problem. Common sense might 'work' on certain occasions, but only if the participants share sufficient agreement over the content of 'common sense'. If they do, then it is no longer rights that are fundamental, but rather some view of the wider good. If people do not agree about 'common sense',

---

[27] Thus the criticisms which follow of rights-based approaches do not *necessarily* apply to the Pastoral Letter.

[28] It is evident that human rights tend to be related, fundamentally, to individuals rather than to communities.

[29] In one sense this difficulty is a particular case of a more foundational problem, namely the lack of an adequate philosophical and epistemological basis for any right for any individual party. A rights-based approach requires that rights are in some sense fundamental. The philosophical problem here is that of explaining why such rights can have such foundational importance; the epistemological problem is that of explaining how we can know what those rights (assuming they exist) actually are.

then there is not even an immediate solution. Another possibility is to appeal not only to rights but also - as is increasingly common currently - to responsibilities and duties. Again, however, this succeeds only if there is common agreement concerning the nature and content of such responsibilities; and if there is such agreement, then the approach is no longer rights-based, but is instead based on some wider view of the general good.[30]

The contrast between a rights-based approach and a biblically-rooted conception of economic justice can be seen by considering how the latter handles - in broad terms - the difficulties sketched in the previous two paragraphs. A biblically-rooted conception is based on the understanding that the world in which human beings live is a created order, and that this creation is also a moral order. Thus the norms of economic justice, commanded by God, hold together at a fundamental level. It might be that, in a given situation, the norms relevant to one party conflict with the norms relevant to another party. However, the givenness of the moral order means that such conflicts between norms, even in a fallen world, are open to resolution - although such resolution often necessitates an eschatological perspective. Thus, whilst it may not be possible to achieve a resolution which in this world is perfectly in accord with all the appropriate norms, nevertheless it *is* possible to open up a resolution in which the patterns of behaviour recommended *bear witness to* those norms and to their perfect eschatological fulfilment. An essential aspect of such a resolution is that it itself points ahead to the new world, the eschaton, in which justice is complete. Thus the main point is reinforced, namely that God's norms of economic justice hold together at a fundamental level.

This is undoubtedly a bold claim, no detailed practical justification of which is attempted here.[31] What is offered is a brief account of the kind of approach by which a biblically-rooted conception would address a particular and contemporary 'conflict' setting. The problem to be examined is the conflict between lenders and borrowers: one contemporary case of such conflict concerns international debt;[32] another concerns 'problem debts' owed, in developed Western economies such as the U.K., by households.[33] The aim here

---

[30]There also remains the philosophical problem of explaining why a particular view of the general good is correct, and the epistemological problem of finding out what these responsibilities are. These twin problems also face a rights-based approach (see the previous footnote).

[31]Such a detailed practical justification would require, amongst other things, a thorough analysis of all aspects of a particular socio-economic situation, an analysis well beyond the scope of this book.

[32]'International debt' means debts owed by governments: the problem area concerns debts owed by the governments of less developed countries, especially the highly-indebted poorer countries (HIPCs), debts which - by general consent - are unlikely ever to be repaid in full.

[33]The problem area in this latter case concerns those household (or personal) debts where the borrower is experiencing significant difficulty in servicing and/or repaying the

is not to provide a detailed solution to these difficulties, but rather - and much more simply - to give an indication of the nature and content, in a particular setting, of a biblically-rooted conception of economic justice.

It should be noted from the outset that this setting involves a relationship, between borrower and lender. It has already been argued that, in a biblically-rooted conception of justice, there is usually a relational context. The significance of that in the specific context of a borrower-lender relationship will be brought out below.

Moving to the content of the norms of justice, consider first the borrowers. One central norm of economic justice here is that a borrower should seek to repay the lender in full. This is implicit in the OT teaching, not least the Mosaic law.[34] In a borrower-lender relationship - as any other relationship - obligations are to be met. The resources for repayment are normally to be generated from the borrower's work. For, as shown in chapter 3, self-sufficiency on the part of each household is the normal pattern taught and encouraged by the Scriptures - and there is no biblical support at all for a pattern of repaying one loan by taking out a new loan.

On the part of lenders, one norm is to treat the borrower with dignity (e.g. Lev. 25:35-37; Dt. 24:10-13). Another norm, alongside this, is that there is an *obligation* on the part of the better-off people to provide material assistance for the poor: and one form of this assistance, with regard to those poor who are relatively non-dependent - i.e. who are likely to be able to earn a living - is a compassionate loan.[35] A third norm is that the poor are not to be kept indebted permanently. The Mosaic law prescribed that the poor were to be released from their debts every seven years (Dt. 15:1-2), and that slaves, for whom indebtedness may often have been a principal cause of being sold into slavery,[36] were also to be released every seven years (Ex. 21:1-2; Dt. 15:12-18). Taking the Scriptures as a whole, there is no reason to make an absolute norm out of

---

debt. Attention in the text, with regard to the *contemporary* context, will focus on international debt, not household debt.

[34]For example, in Dt. 15:1-11 the better-off are exhorted to lend, even if the seventh year - the year of cancellation - is near: in which case, as the text says, it is likely that the amount lent will not be returned. By implication, it is likely that, for a loan made early in the 7-year cycle, the amount lent *will* be returned: a likelihood reinforced by the possibility of enslavement (until the same seventh year) for a non-paying debtor - see below. Thus it is clear that borrowers were, in general, expected to repay. Indeed, as chapter 3 argued, the whole purpose of such loans was not to trap the poorer household in debt, but rather to help it back to its feet, i.e. to generate sufficient income that it can both be self-sufficient and repay the loan.

[35]See Dt. 15:1-11. The distinction between the relatively dependent and the relatively non-dependent poor was developed in chapter 3.

[36]Roland De Vaux, *Ancient Israel: Its Life and Institutions*, 2nd ed. (London: Darton, Longman and Todd, 1965), p83.

the time period of 7 years.[37] However, the principle of release from debt for the poor is an important norm of economic justice. This principle embodies both mercy and hope: it expresses mercy towards a borrower who is in severe need; and it ensures hope for such desperate borrowers, the certain expectation that they will soon be released from the stranglehold of debt. That release will in turn enable them to renew their full participation in God's blessings, including material blessings - participation which itself is another principle of economic justice, in a biblically-rooted conception (see chapters 3 and 5).[38]

Given this brief sketch of the norms commanded by God regarding borrowers and lenders, it is now possible to re-examine the contemporary scene with regard, in particular, to international debt, and thereby to contrast the biblical conception with a rights-based approach. A rights-based approach might appeal, first, to the rights of lenders to receive a full return on their loans. On the side of the borrowers, appeal might be made to the right of the poor to have their basic needs met - in terms of food and health, for example - and it might therefore be argued that loans *cannot* be repaid, since repayment could be afforded only if such basic needs were to go unmet. Such appeals to rights are likely, therefore, to result in mutually conflicting conclusions. By contrast, a biblically-rooted conception of economic justice is able to offer some progress. Taking the case of international debt, it is clear that the HIPCs have a responsibility to seek to repay the money lent by creditors. Part of any solution must be a recognition on their part of this responsibility, and a commitment to act, in one way or another, in accord with it. On the other hand, it must be acknowledged by the lenders - in accordance with the norm of release for the indebted poor - that, at least where the debt burden is falling on the poor, then a commitment to cancellation of debt is required.[39]

In a biblically-rooted conception, then, lenders do not have absolute rights, to which they are entitled unconditionally. This does not mean that they have no rights at all, but it does mean that those rights have a place only in the

---

[37]Chapter 3 argued for the Mosaic law to be interpreted in its fulfilled form, i.e. as fulfilled by Christ. There is no NT emphasis upon a specifically seventh-year release. Hence there is no compulsion now to obey the detail of this law. But there is compulsion to adhere to the principles demonstrated by this law (given its interpretation in the light of Scripture as a whole).

[38]A more limited participation was ensured even during the period of indebtedness: debt-slaves were *not* to be treated as *slaves*, nor to be ruled with harshness, but rather treated well as hired servants and sojourners (Lev. 25:39-43). Thus they - and their children - were to be regarded as members of the household, and therefore to participate, albeit in a limited sense, in God's material blessings.

[39]Inevitably there are many practical considerations, which cannot be addressed in any depth here. For example, where loans have been used to strengthen the hand of ruthless dictators in less developed countries, and where debt-cancellation would only serve to strengthen further their grip, then such cancellation would do nothing to bring release to the poor, and would therefore be inappropriate.

context of the norms to which they are to accord in their relationship to the borrowers. As for borrowers, the emphasis of the approach as a whole is as much on their responsibilities as it is on the meeting of their needs. A biblically-rooted conception is thus able, at least in principle, to provide a coherent and just way forward, on the basis of definite norms commanded by God, in the context of the relationship between borrowers and lenders.

A Biblically-rooted Conception Compared both with Purely Deontological and Purely Teleological Conceptions of Justice[40]

The aim in this section is to highlight further the nature of a biblically-rooted conception of economic justice, particularly as an overall moral conception; and to do so by observing the contrasts between, on the one hand, purely deontological and purely teleological conceptions - understood in very broad terms - and, on the other, a biblically-rooted conception.

It should be understood that, in a sense, rights-based approaches to economic justice - discussed in the previous section - are a particular class within the more general deontological category, since these approaches share the perception that morality is based not on some overall good, but rather on doing right. However, rights-based approaches tend to locate 'the right' in the rights of individuals, whereas deontological conceptions, in general terms, focus on the rightness of *actions*.[41]

Returning to the main argument of this section, it might be thought that the biblically-rooted conception of economic justice developed in these pages is in fact a purely deontological conception, given the focus both on *norms* of justice, and on these norms being *commanded* by God. However, this is not the case. The point here is not simply that, in a biblically-rooted conception, consequences matter, as well as actions.[42] Rather, more fundamentally, it is that the nature of the created order as God's moral order means that there is no

---

[40]For convenience, the contrasts with both deontological and teleological conceptions are considered in the same sub-section: given that (as will be argued) a biblically-rooted conception of economic justice is not equivalent to either of those apparently conflicting conceptions, and yet (as again will be argued) contains aspects of both, it is helpful to draw out the contrasts in one place.

[41]This does not mean that the consequences of actions are irrelevant to deontological theories. Rather, as Rawls puts it in outlining the deontological nature of his theory of justice, a deontological theory is 'one that either does not specify the good independently from the right, or does not interpret the right as maximizing the good': in this sense a deontological theory is defined as a non-teleological theory (John Rawls, *A Theory of Justice* Oxford: OUP, 1972/Cambridge, Mass.: Harvard University Press, 1971, p30).

[42]As indicated in the previous footnote, consequences matter to most self-respecting deontological theories. As Rawls puts it: 'All ethical doctrines worth our attention take consequences into account in judging rightness' (*ibid.*).

ultimate dichotomy between right actions and what is good; and therefore it is false to suggest that one of the two - the right (action) and the good - must be defined independently of, or prior to, the other. Instead these are complementary features of morality. Thus, in his discussion of 'deontic' and 'teleological' language, Oliver O'Donovan, whilst acknowledging that to say one 'ought to' do something is different in sense from saying that it is 'good', proceeds to argue in the following manner. Any actual moral claim, he says,

> can be expressed either in terms of obligation or in terms of the good; and it would be merely doctrinaire to insist that in choosing the second form of expression one must fail to appreciate its moral force. What the two languages do is to draw our attention to different and complementary aspects of moral claims as we encounter them.[43]

A biblically-rooted conception of economic justice, therefore, certainly includes deontological aspects - for it requires attention to discerning right actions on the basis of their rightness (not merely their consequences) - but is not a purely deontological conception.[44]

An example of this in terms of economic life would be where a supermarket chain wants to build a new store on, say, the outskirts of a picturesque market town. The chain is convinced that the new store would bring, alongside higher profits for itself, net benefits to the whole community (e.g. lower prices, greater choice, easier parking). However, the public enquiry - required prior to the granting of planning permission - concludes that, for established local shops to be put out of business (which, according to the general consensus, would undoubtedly occur) would simply be wrong.[45] In a biblically-rooted conception of justice, the norms of economic justice will, at least in some situations - such as the above case, perhaps - imply that some economic actions are wrong, whatever the consequences.[46]

An objection here might be that there are no clear criteria, on the basis of

---

[43]Oliver O'Donovan, *Resurrection and Moral Order*, 2nd ed. (Leicester: Apollos, 1994), pp138-9.

[44]O'Donovan - continuing the passage just cited in the text - argues as follows concerning the emphasis of the deontic language: 'We say "ought" when we need to stress the contradiction between this overriding claim [the 'ought'] and what we should otherwise have thought or felt' (*ibid.*, p139).

[45]This example is intended only to illustrate the categories of wrong (or right) action, alongside given outcomes. It is not being said that actions which cause social change are always wrong.

[46]It is important to recognize that, in the above example, the enforced closure of certain businesses is *not* regarded simply as part of the overall set of consequences (with the costs of such closures outweighed, perhaps, by greater benefits to others). Rather, such closures may, at least in some circumstances - such as, perhaps, the long-established nature of those businesses, and the importance of their very presence in that picturesque market town - be wrong in themselves.

Scripture, for saying that, in the above example, the action of the supermarket chain is actually wrong. Thus it might be argued that the biblical material presented in chapter 3, for example, operates at a much higher level of generality than could ever produce clear conclusions in specific cases. In response, however, it can be argued that the Scriptures contain a remarkably rich, and harmonious, amount of material that is, in fact, well able to help people - if they are humble before God and obedient to him - to discern what God's norms of justice are, and what they require in a given situation. With regard to the supermarket/market town example, the Bible places a heavy responsibility on the rich and powerful to defend and respect - and not to oppress - those who are poor and those who lack power.[47] Careful reflection on this material will shape and educate the thinking of the powerful, so that they come to understand what the will of the Lord is. In the OT, the case of Naboth and his vineyard (1 Kings 21) is a poignant illustration here. King Ahab knew full well that that particular vineyard was Naboth's possession under the covenant: it was his share of Israel's inheritance in the promised land. To offer Naboth an alternative piece of land was thus no substitute at all. Yet Ahab (and Jezebel) persisted, using their power to destroy Naboth, rather than to respect his rightful interest. In a similar way - with regard to the market town example - long-established traders, who belong in that community, should in principle have their livelihood and their place in that community respected, rather than destroyed.[48] Note also that this example demonstrates the significance of emphasizing the relational setting for justice: the powerful are in fact in a relationship with those whom they have the power to damage. The question at stake is this: how the powerful will act in that relationship - ruthlessly or respectfully?[49]

The purpose of this example was to demonstrate the claim that a biblically-rooted conception of economic justice, whilst having deontological aspects, is

---

[47]See chapter 3 for a discussion of the Scriptural material on oppression.

[48]Clearly the market town example, as presented here, is no more than a sketch: in practice, there may well be many other details that should be considered. The point to emphasize, however, is that, in a biblically-rooted conception of economic justice, there is a wealth of material to assist those who seek God's justice to be able to discern what that justice requires in a given setting.

[49]A biblically-rooted conception of economic justice, deriving from God's given norms for the created order, is thus clearly distinct here from the communitarian type of understanding presented by, for example, Michael Walzer, in which justice is defined only in a specific community setting. 'A given society is just if its substantive life is lived in a certain way - that is, in a way faithful to the shared understandings of the members... Social meanings...sometimes provide only the intellectual structure within which distributions are debated. But that is a necessary structure. *There are no external or universal principles that can replace it. Every substantive of distributive justice is a local account*' (Michael Walzer, *Spheres of Justice: A Defence of Pluralism and Equality*, New York: Basic Books, 1983, pp313-4; emphasis added.)

not a purely deontological conception. The wrongness of an action, then, is not solely a matter of transgressing some norm - although it includes that - but is also linked to the good; that is, to what is truly good in God's created and moral order. Thus the wrongness of an act by the powerful is linked to the goodness of the existing situation enjoyed by individuals and the community.

It follows that a biblically-rooted conception of economic justice contains not only deontological aspects but also *teleological* aspects. O'Donovan's encapsulation is again helpful here:

> 'Teleological' ethics...derives from the ontological conception of God as the *summum bonum*, in which it was the task of moral reasoning to recognize and respond to the ordered structures of being and good. 'Teleological' is not meant to be understood narrowly, as speaking only of a calculating, consequentialist morality, but in the way that we ourselves have used it, pointing to any kind of propriety or order within the world.[50]

With regard to justice in economic life, this means that it is not only the rightness of economic behaviour that matters, but also the goodness of the purpose of that behaviour: that is, the goal of justice, towards the fulfilment of which it is to be directed. Thus the eschatological hope - the certain expectation - of the coming of the kingdom of God is a vital and indispensable part of a biblically-rooted conception of economic justice. Even the best present efforts at justice, in this fallen world, are contaminated by sin. Nevertheless, the knowledge of that coming and visible rule of God - founded on Jesus Christ's horrific yet victorious atoning death, and his vindicating resurrection - ensures that justice in economic actions can now have this teleological dimension.[51]

Whilst a biblically-rooted conception of economic justice has teleological aspects, it is not - as already demonstrated - a purely teleological conception. The rightness of economic actions does matter, as well as the goodness to which they are directed. O'Donovan expresses the tension between deontic and teleological emphases in these words:

We may say, then, that the tension between the two moral languages reflects a necessary dialectic in the perceptions of moral agents for whom moral insight is still a task and not yet an achieved fact. In moments of grace we may be given the perception that our duty and our fulfilment are one and the same, and we may speak of that unity in hope and faith; but we cannot ask that we should

---

[50]O'Donovan, *Resurrection and Moral Order*, p138.

[51]The helpfulness of teleological language - alongside deontic language - is again brought out by O'Donovan. Whereas the force of the 'ought' - as already noted - is to stimulate us to think critically, 'the teleological language draws attention to the rationality of moral and divine authority. It drives us to express, as best we can, the meaning of that authority within the ordered universe, even when that expression is the expression of a hope for a resolution that we cannot yet comprehend' (O'Donovan, *Resurrection and Moral Order*, p139).

never be challenged to further thought and conscientious struggle by an awareness of the divergence of inclination and duty.[52]

Achieving Economic Justice: Who is Responsible?

Some of the contemporary demands laid upon human beings in *practical* terms, as regards economic justice, provide the particular focus of this section.[53] The aim here is to highlight some specific implications - especially in conversation with some of the practical proposals in the U.S. Roman Catholic Bishops' Pastoral Letter - and thus to indicate further something of the distinctive character of a biblically-rooted understanding of economic justice.

The Pastoral Letter makes no attempt to disguise the extremely radical nature of its vision for economic life. This inevitably raises the question of how such a vision is to be implemented, and this is addressed in some detail in section C of chapter II - a section entitled 'Working for Greater Justice: Persons and Institutions'. As that title suggests, the Letter argues that economic justice is the responsibility of all people in the society; and, in addition, that *all* human institutions and associations - not only national government - bear responsibility. As noted earlier, the Letter robustly rejects both Socialism and free-market capitalism, and so it is incumbent upon the Bishops to offer some kind of alternative to those philosophies.[54]

The problem that the Pastoral faces here, however, is the reality that persons and human associations do not in fact bring about justice. Indeed the empirical starting point for the Letter is precisely that.[55] The question thus arises of the role of the state in attaining economic justice; and the Letter has to find a way of ensuring that it does *not* in practice put forward the state as the chief actor for economic justice. If it cannot ensure that, then the Letter cannot avoid becoming little more than yet one more call for greater government intervention in free markets.[56] One of the Letter's chief arguments here, in resisting those

---

[52]*Ibid.*, p139.

[53]Although some practical aspects have already been touched upon in the previous, more conceptual, section.

[54]Robert A. Destro argues that the Bishops tried to be much more specific in their alternative than was either wise or productive. He argues that papal teaching has always, and rightly, held back from such detail; he also argues that the Bishops wrongly interpreted *Laborem Exercens* as inviting the specification of more detailed moral norms than had hitherto been offered. See his article, '*Laborem Exercens*', in George Weigel and Robert Royal, eds., *A Century of Catholic Social Thought: Essays on* Rerum Novarum *and Nine other Key Documents* (Washington, D.C.: Ethics and Public Policy Center, 1991).

[55]National Conference of Catholic Bishops, *Economic Justice For All*, pp6ff.

[56]Commentators from the political right argued that the Letter failed to avoid such an outcome. See, e.g., Walter Block, *The U.S. Bishops and Their Critics: An Economic and Ethical Perspective* (Vancouver: Fraser Institute, 1986). Such critics do not have to

pressures, involves the principle of *subsidiarity*.

Subsidiarity

This principle, a long-standing component of Roman Catholic social teaching, requires 'vital contributions from different human associations - ranging in size from the family to government'.[57] The Letter cites here Pius XI's encyclical *Quadragesimo Anno*, a document which states the principle of subsidiarity as follows:

> ...just as it is wrong to withdraw from the individual and commit to the community at large what private enterprise and industry can accomplish by their own initiative and industry and give it to the community, so too it is an injustice, a grave evil and a disturbance of right order for a larger and higher organization to arrogate to itself functions which can be performed efficiently by smaller and lower bodies... Of its nature the true aim of all social activity should be to *help* individual members of the social body, but never to destroy and absorb them.[58]

The following pages of the Letter (pp52-59) apply this principle, not only with a number of detailed statements of the respective roles and responsibilities of, for example, trades unions and companies in the attainment of economic justice, but also - the point to emphasize here - with a noticeable *lack* of emphasis on government action. The Letter evidently seeks to put subsidiarity into practice.

One requirement that is made of government in those pages relates to the responsibilities of companies. The Letter argues for a regulatory role for the state, at least with regard to certain matters:

> Businesses have a right to an institutional framework that does not penalize enterprises that act responsibly. Governments must provide regulations and a system of taxation which encourage firms to preserve the environment, employ disadvantaged workers, and create jobs in depressed areas. Managers and stockholders should not be torn between their responsibilities to their organizations and their responsibilities toward society as a whole.[59]

The Letter then moves on from that statement - clearly intended to assist companies in *their* responsibilities, rather than delineate in detail the

---

argue that the Letter is a Socialist wolf in Roman Catholic clothing, only that its case is effectively no different from, and no more workable than, that put forward by existing centre-left proponents.

[57]National Conference of Catholic Bishops, *Economic Justice For All*, pp50-51.

[58]Pius XI, *Quadragesimo Anno* (London: Catholic Truth Society, 1931), p37 [emphasis added]. The term 'help' is the translation offered of *subsidium*.

[59]National Conference of Catholic Bishops, *Economic Justice For All*, p59 [emphasis added].

responsibilities of government - to address the roles of citizens and government. Every citizen has some responsibility here, it is argued, including the poor, who have obligations 'to work together as individuals and families to build up their communities by acts of social solidarity and justice'.[60] It is also argued that every group within the community has responsibilities here. 'We have just outlined some of the duties of labor unions and business and financial enterprises. These must be supplemented by initiatives by local community groups , professional associations, churches, and synagogues. *All the groups that give life to this society have important roles to play in the pursuit of economic justice.*' Thus every citizen 'has the responsibility to work to secure justice and human rights through an organized social response.'[61]

All these applications of the powerful principle of subsidiarity exhibit substantial common ground at this point between the teaching of the Pastoral Letter and the biblically-rooted conception of economic justice outlined in this book. Indeed, the Letter may be regarded here as effectively elaborating in some detail - and much more so than has been attempted here - the obligations that individuals and groups have in their relationships with others. So, although the Letter rarely uses the language of relationships (unlike this book), it offers some very helpful material on contemporary relational obligations, not least on the reciprocal nature of these obligations.[62]

Subsidiarity and the Role of the Government in Economic Justice

Notwithstanding all this emphasis on *everyone's* duties with regard to economic justice, the Letter does advocate a significant role for the state. Here, as indicated earlier, the Letter has to face the reality of economic *injustice*, and here it has provoked much comment. The Bishops conclude their account of the widespread social responsibilities regarding justice with these words: 'All the groups that give life to this society have important roles to play in the pursuit of economic justice'. Then they proceed to say:

> For this reason, it is all the more significant that the teachings of the Church insist that *government has a moral function: protecting human rights and securing basic justice for all the members of the commonwealth.*[63] Society as a whole and in all its diversity is responsible for building up the common good. But it is

---

[60]National Conference of Catholic Bishops, *Economic Justice For All*, p60.

[61]National Conference of Catholic Bishops, *Economic Justice For All*, p60 [emphasis added].

[62]In the same way that chapter 3 (above) emphasized reciprocity in relationships, so does the Letter: as, for example, in its reference (cited earlier) to the responsibilities of the poor to work for justice.

[63]Emphasis in the original.

government's role to guarantee the minimum conditions that make this rich social activity possible, namely, human rights and justice.[64]

The Letter continues (p61):

More specifically, it is the responsibility of all citizens, acting through their government, to assist and empower the poor, the disadvantaged, the handicapped, and the unemployed. Government should assume a positive role in generating employment and establishing fair labour practices, in guaranteeing the provision and maintenance of the economy's infrastructure... It should regulate trade and commerce in the interest of fairness...[65]

The Letter is careful to reaffirm that this is not intended to leave all responsibility for economic justice in the hands of the state. 'The primary norm for determining the scope and limits of governmental intervention is the "principle of subsidiarity" cited above... Government should not replace or destroy smaller communities and individual initiative. Rather it should help them to contribute more effectively to social well-being and supplement their activity when the demands of justice exceed their capacities.'[66]

As the literature on this Letter and on other pieces of Roman Catholic social teaching indicates, this kind of delineation of the principle of subsidiarity by no means resolves all the questions regarding the precise scope and functions of government in its involvement in economic life - and it may well not have been intended to resolve those questions. Nevertheless it is a valuable and carefully-balanced approach to the role of government, and it seems highly compatible with the emphases already offered here, in a biblically-rooted understanding of economic justice, on reciprocal obligations to follow the norms given by God.

What appears to be lacking, however, is an adequate account of the role of the state with regard to the responsibilities, in particular, of business enterprises.[67] The nature and scope of the responsibilities of businesses, in a biblically-rooted conception, were indicated in the previous chapter, in its section on commutative justice. When business enterprises significantly fail to act in accord with the principles of economic justice, one vitally important role

---

[64]National Conference of Catholic Bishops, *Economic Justice For All*, pp60-61. The 'minimum conditions' referred to here must be those specified earlier in the Letter (pp41-42), and cited earlier in this chapter.

[65]The Letter here refers (footnote 74) to Leo XIII's *Rerum Novarum* for 'the basic norm that determines when government intervention is called for': "If, therefore, any injury has been done to or threatens either the common good or the interests of individual groups, which injury cannot in any other way be repaired or prevented, it is necessary for public authority to intervene" (Leo XIII, *Rerum Novarum*, #52).

[66]National Conference of Catholic Bishops, *Economic Justice For All*, p62.

[67]Section 2 of this chapter argued that the Letter does not state adequately what the responsibilities of business enterprises are. The argument in the present section is that the role of the state itself, with regard to businesses, also requires elucidation.

of the governing authorities is to bring them to book for their wrongdoing. Not only is this an appropriate role for the state, but it is sometimes the only body with sufficient means to deal adequately with the enormous power of large and often multinational companies. The state cannot guarantee that all economic behaviour will be in line with the norms given and commanded by God. But it can, at least in the more serious cases, act to bring business enterprises back into line.

Conclusion

This chapter has continued to demonstrate, together with the previous one, that the biblical conception of economic justice, developed earlier in the book, is able to engage seriously with the challenges posed by other approaches, and thus to make an incisive contribution regarding justice in contemporary economic life. The present chapter has argued that a biblically-rooted conception of economic justice is clearly distinct from a rights-based approach, and also that it *combines* deontological and teleological aspects. In the process, it has been shown how a biblically-rooted conception opens up new territory for thought with regard, for example, to issues involving debt - especially international debt - and the responsibilities of both borrowers and lenders. In addition, whilst justice is required of all persons and institutions, this chapter has again argued strongly that business enterprises in particular have serious responsibilities to act justly towards others in their economic behaviour; and also that, where they significantly fail to do so, then the state must call them to account.

CHAPTER 7

Conclusion

The main question tackled in this book has been the following: what would it be for an account of economic justice to take the Bible seriously? In other words, if we were to root our conception or understanding of economic justice in the Scriptures – as opposed to any other foundation – then what would that conception consist of? What kind of character and shape would it have? The book has also sought to sharpen such a conception by means of critical engagement with other understandings of economic justice – some secular, some from within the Christian tradition – and thus to develop a biblically-rooted conception of justice which can be applied with relevance and rigour to the challenges of contemporary economic life.

With regard to the basic character and shape of a Scripturally-rooted conception of economic justice, a counter-argument – which has of necessity been addressed in these pages – is that the biblical material lacks both the depth and the coherence to speak with any cogency on matters of justice in economic life. This counter-argument, however, has been shown to be weak. Thus one major achievement of this book (primarily in chapters 2 and 3) is its demonstration that the Scriptures – in the context of God's saving work in Christ – provide a substantial and harmonious treatment of justice in economic life; and its development of a theological framework for, and a biblical conception of, economic justice. At the foundation of this theological framework is the righteousness of God – that is, God's acts of faithfulness to his own justice and mercy in his relationship with humanity, and his gift to believers of righteousness in Christ. This righteousness in Christ secures Christian believers in a right relationship with God, and it is received by faith. But this righteousness is to be worked out in practice, in terms of loving obedience. It is here that this theological framework locates the place of human justice: actions which work for righteousness in human relationships, conforming in general to the norm of appropriate treatment, and conforming in particular to the norms appropriate, within God's created order, to each given relationship. These norms are commanded and set by the Creator-Redeemer God who himself is a God of justice.

Thus the underlying shape of economic justice involves appropriate treatment of people in terms of economic behaviour, according to the norms which God has commanded, and which enable human flourishing. Moreover, justice in economic life is something that God *demands* of humanity.

This biblically-rooted conception of economic justice was developed in detail in chapter 3, and it was shown that four elements must be included in such a conception. First, justice means appropriate treatment, according to the norms commanded by God for each particular case – norms built into the moral order of creation. Secondly, God's justice, in terms of economic life, involves justice to the needy. Thirdly, economic justice is not only about how resources are allocated, but also concerns the quality of relationships. Fourthly, justice in the allocation of resources means that everyone participates in God's blessing.

A second achievement of this book concerns its appraisal – in the light of the biblical conception – of other treatments of justice in economic life (chapter 4). This appraisal exposes serious inadequacies and mutual incompatibilities in these treatments. A fundamental problem with utilitarianism is that social utility is unable to bear the weight of being a foundation of justice. It follows that neither variant of utilitarianism can underpin our search for economic justice: rule-utilitarianism is incoherent, in that it fails to provide any of the rigorous rules which it claims to offer; and act-utilitarianism is inadequate due its total exclusion of any meaningful notion of justice from its methodology.

As for the contractarian approach offered in Rawls' *A Theory of Justice*, its two fundamental problems are that (like utilitarianism, which is similarly individualist) it says little or nothing about relationships, and that it has an inadequate view of the person. There are also severe practical problems with this conception of justice: for example, the people who are actually worst off in a society may not be bettered at all by the application of Rawls' principles; and, more generally, these principles seem ill-equipped to cope with the complex distributive problems posed in modern societies.

The third conception of justice considered here – the libertarian approach advocated by Nozick – also has fundamental flaws. Although this conception starts out as a riposte to that of Rawls, the lack of rigour in Nozick's principles for justice mean not only that they offer at best solutions which are very messy, but also that a key pragmatic criterion to deal with the mess is this: maximise the position of whatever group in society ends up least well-off – yet this is what Rawls says! Thus the libertarian approach to justice fails.

As well as each having fundamental flaws, these three secular conceptions of economic justice are mutually incompatible. Thus debates about contentious economic and social issues cannot be resolved by appealing to some shared notion of 'justice', for there is no such shared notion. For example, rights, deserts and need are sometimes put forward as principles of justice; and yet it can easily be shown that these give rise to conclusions which are fundamentally incompatible. Moreover, with regard to the three specific conceptions of justice discussed here, the utilitarian approach would never approve of the kind of social contract proposed by Rawls, whilst the libertarian conception points in principle in a very different direction to either of the others. There is no shared understanding of economic justice.

This appraisal of secular conceptions of economic justice is not solely critical, however: it also highlights some major challenges they pose if the biblical conception is to grapple adequately with contemporary issues regarding economic justice. For example, the utilitarian framework poses serious challenges: What is the appropriate shape of justice? Is it aggregative or distributive? Is it based on rights, or on the general good? The Rawlsian approach also raises major questions. Is something like the maximin (difference) principle a necessary ingredient of justice? Those who perceive in Scripture a 'bias to the poor' clearly answer 'yes', but is this so? Does a biblically-rooted conception of justice have anything to say about the extent to which justice is egalitarian? If so, is it more egalitarian, or less egalitarian, than Rawls' conception? And does it – with Rawls – dismiss a meritocratic emphasis? If it has nothing to say on this, it can hardly claim with any conviction to have relevance to contemporary debates. As for Nozick's libertarian conception of justice, it poses two major sets of challenges. First, what rights, if any, are involved in relation to the ownership and/or use of property, and how does liberty in this area relate to justice? Secondly, in what ways, if any, can state-enforced transfers of income, wealth and property be justified? Even though Nozick has not successfully made a positive libertarian case, his negative critique of standard assumptions about the legitimacy of government socio-political action is extremely important, and needs a response.

As well as highlighting these challenges raised by secular approaches, it has been shown that existing treatments of economic justice from Christian quarters have not dealt adequately with them. This is an extremely serious weakness in contemporary Christianity. Thus in Roman Catholic social teaching, whilst there is a clear attempt to articulate what a 'preferential option for the poor' means in practice – which may be seen as, at least implicitly, a response to Rawls' maximin/difference principle – the philosophical underpinnings of the teachings seem very limited. Although it is claimed that human rights are God-given, and grounded in the nature and dignity of being human, the detailing of these rights appears to be a matter of assertion rather than argument. Also, the reliance on 'the common good', despite the strengths of this approach, has some serious limitations in practice, at least to the extent that others in society do not share a similar commitment to the common good. Finally, the emphasis on *participation in production* cannot by itself succeed in providing a solid philosophical basis for justice.

A key weakness of the work of Reinhold Niebuhr in this area concerns his deliberate unwillingness to define or even pin down what justice actually is. He offers a list of criteria for justice, but these come entirely out of the secular world, and no attempt at all is made to derive them from any theological-biblical principle(s). Thus he has not provided an adequate response, in theological terms, to the challenges posed by secular conceptions of justice.

As for liberation theology, its primary area of weakness here concerns the definition of justice. There is a strong tendency to accept uncritically a class-based conception of socio-economic oppression, injustice and liberation – with the correlate that all non-Marxist perspectives are on the capitalist side of the class struggle. Thus liberation theology renders itself unable to engage meaningfully with other conceptions of justice. In particular, liberation theology is unable to provide any kind of adequate response to the serious challenges posed by utilitarianism, Rawls and Nozick.

Despite the weaknesses of these three Christian sets of approaches to economic justice, they also pose further challenges to the quest for a biblically-rooted conception of justice in economic life. Putting these together with those posed by secular treatments, a fourfold set of challenges can be identified. The first of these concerns justice as a moral conception – such as the question, raised by utilitarianism, of whether justice is to be conceived in terms of rights or in terms of the general good. A second type of challenge concerns justice as a political conception or theory – such as Nozick's argument about the notion of justice with respect to the ownership and use of property, and hence the question of how state-enforced transfers of property could ever be justified. A third type of challenge concerns justice as a socio-economic conception – such as the broadly egalitarian challenge posed (in different ways) by Rawls, Roman Catholic social teaching, and liberation theology. A final type of challenge concerns justice as a theological conception - such as Niebuhr's question concerning whether the pursuit of justice may be regarded as some kind of 'social sanctification'.

The third major achievement of the book (in chapters 5 and 6) is its response to these challenges, in the light of the biblical conception of economic justice developed earlier, and thus its demonstration of the power and contemporary relevance of a biblical understanding of justice in economic life. With regard to justice specifically as a socio-economic conception (chapter 5), it is argued that a biblical conception calls for both commutative justice (justice in producing and exchanging goods and services) and distributive justice (justice in sharing the fruits of economic endeavour). A number of specific propositions are put forward regarding each of these aspects, and it is argued that a biblical account of them is sharply distinct in significant respects from the treatments examined in chapter 4. It is shown, for example, that the unconstrained and sole pursuit of the interests of the owners of capital will tend to produce at least some actions which are incompatible with commutative justice. In other words, the types of rule normally accepted by 'business is business' advocates are too loose, if injustices are to be avoided. For example, a monopolist company may behave exploitatively, and yet this is permissible, according to 'business is business' reasoning. However, it is not compatible with a biblically-rooted understanding of commutative justice. Therefore, unless the accepted rules which constrain behaviour are based solidly upon the norms commanded by God, then the sole pursuit of profit/shareholder wealth maximisation will tend to lead to commutative injustices.

As for distributive justice, it is argued that a biblically-rooted conception of justice in economic life will require a significant degree of sharing in the fruits of economic endeavour, within a community or society, and that this implies some kind of upper limit, other things being equal, on the extent of inequality. Beyond some point, therefore, any widening of inequality will challenge that community or society to examine both why it is occurring, and how it may be altered.

A further conclusion is that, although the differences between a Rawlsian and a Nozickian approach can be summarized as the difference between, respectively, a primarily distributive and a primarily commutative conception of economic justice (notwithstanding Nozick's adoption of the label 'distributive'), the argument that *both* aspects are essential is clearly distinctive. Underlying this distinctiveness is a fundamental conviction that an atomistic conception of human beings is utterly inadequate. Human life is, foundationally, about relationships, and this gives rise to the centrality of both commutative and distributive justice.

The radical, distinctive and coherent nature of a biblically-rooted conception of economic justice was developed further in chapter 6, especially in its moral, political and theological dimensions. With regard to the moral dimension, it is argued – in common with recent Roman Catholic social thought – that respect for human rights and a strong sense of both personal and community responsibility hold together, and are central. Further, since no-one should be excluded from God's blessings, then it is intolerable if a household is unable to live adequately. In addition, the remuneration for an employee should normally be sufficient to provide for that person and their household. However, the relative prominence of rights-language in recent Roman Catholic social thought is not a wholly adequate basis for a conception of economic justice. A biblically-rooted conception, by contrast, lays emphasis both upon the God-given *norms* for human behaviour, and upon the way those norms hold together in the context of *relationships*. (This is the broad thrust of the response to the challenge regarding whether justice is about rights or about the general good.) As an example, Chapter 6 demonstrated the application of this twofold emphasis to the case of lenders and borrowers and the relationship between them. Given the vital importance of credit and debt in the contemporary world, both within Western countries and for less-developed countries in relation to the West, this is a very powerful demonstration of the power and relevance of a biblical conception of economic justice.

The final point to make concerns the theological dimension of justice. The origin of economic justice, according to this biblical conception, lies outside this world, outside of humanity, and is found instead in the very character and being of God. And it is God who commands the norms for justice – the guiding rules for appropriate treatment of human beings – and who makes his will known in his written word of Scripture and his Word made flesh, Jesus Christ. It is in confessing him that new life and the power for sanctification are to be found, through the enabling of the Holy Spirit. Here, and here alone, is the underlying theological basis for a biblical conception of justice in economic life.

Bibliography

Allen, Leslie C., *Psalms 101-150*, Word Biblical Commentary (Waco, TX: Word, 1983).

Anchor Bible Dictionary, vol.3, D. N. Freedman, ed. (New York: Doubleday, 1992).

Andersen, F. I., and D. N. Freedman, *Amos*, The Anchor Bible, 24A (New York: Doubleday, 1989).

Aristotle, *The Nicomachean Ethics*, tr. J. A. K. Thompson (Harmondsworth: Penguin, 1955).

Arrow, Kenneth, *Social Choice and Individual Welfare* (New York: Wiley, 1963).

Atkinson, D.J., and D. H. Field, eds., *New Dictionary of Christian Ethics and Pastoral Theology* (Leicester: IVP, 1995).

Augustine, *The City of God*, Everyman's Library, 2 vols., tr. John Healey, ed. R. V. G. Tasker (London: Dent, 1945).

Austin, J. L., *How To Do Things With Words*, 2nd ed. (Cambridge, MA: Harvard University Press, 1985).

Bahnsen, Greg, *Theonomy in Christian Ethics* (Nutley, NJ: Craig Press, 1977).

Barr, James, *The Semantics of Biblical Language* (Oxford: OUP, 1961).

Barry, Brian, *The Liberal Theory of Justice: A Critical Examination of the Principal Doctrines in* A Theory of Justice *by John Rawls* (Oxford: Clarendon, 1973).

Barth, Karl, *Church Dogmatics* (eds.) G. W. Bromiley and T. F. Torrance, tr. G. W. Bromiley *et al* (Edinburgh: T&T Clark, 1957), II:1.

Bernbaum, John A., ed., *Economic Justice and the State: A Debate Between Ronald H. Nash and Eric H. Beversluis* (Grand Rapids, MI: Baker, 1986).

Blaug, Mark, *Economic Theory in Retrospect*, 4th ed. (Cambridge: CUP, 1985).

Block, Walter, *The U.S. Bishops and Their Critics: An Economic and Ethical Perspective* (Vancouver: Fraser Institute, 1986).

Brueggemann, Walter, *The Land: Place as Gift, Promise and Challenge in Biblical Faith* (London: SPCK, 1978).

Brueggemann, Walter A., 'The Epistemological Crisis of Israel's Two Histories (Jer.9:22-23)' in John G. Gammie *et al* (eds.), *Israelite Wisdom: Theological and Literary Essays in Honour of Samuel Terrien*, Missoula, MT: Scholars Press, 1978). Reprinted in Walter Brueggemann, *Old Testament Theology*, ed. Patrick D. Miller (1992).

Brunner, Emil, *Justice and the Social Order*, tr. Mary Hottinger (London: Harper, 1945).

Calvin, John, *Commentary on the Four Last Books of Moses Arranged in the Form of a Harmony Vols I-IV*, tr. C. W. Bingham (Edinburgh: Calvin Translation Society, 1852-55).

Carson, D. A., *Matthew*, The Expositor's Bible Commentary, Vol. 8 (Grand Rapids, MI: 1984).

Carson, D. A., and John D. Woodbridge (eds.), *Scripture and Truth* (Grand Rapids, MI: Zondervan, 1983; repr. Grand Rapids, MI: Baker/Carlisle: Paternoster, 1995).

____, *Hermeneutics, Authority and Canon* (Grand Rapids, MI: Zondervan, 1986; repr.

Grand Rapids, MI: Baker/Carlisle: Paternoster, 1995).

Catechism of the Catholic Church (London: Geoffrey Chapman, 1994).

Ceresko, Anthony R., *Introduction to the Old Testament: A Liberation Perspective* (London: Geoffrey Chapman/Maryknoll, NY: Orbis, 1992).

Childs, Brevard S., *Introduction to the Old Testament as Scripture* (Philadelphia: Fortress, 1979).

Corlett, J. Angelo (ed.), *Equality and Liberty: Analyzing Rawls and Nozick*, (Houndmills, Basingstoke: Macmillan, 1991).

Cranfield, Charles E. B., *A Critical and Exegetical Commentary on the Epistle to the Romans*, The International Critical Commentary series, 2 vols., (Edinburgh: T & T Clark, 1975).

Destro, Robert A., 'Laborem Exercens' in George Weigel and Robert Royal, (eds.), *A Century of Catholic Social Thought: Essays on* Rerum Novarum *and Nine other Key Documents* (Washington, DC: Ethics and Public Policy Center, 1991).

De Vaux, Roland, *Ancient Israel: Its Life and Institutions*, 2nd ed. (London: Darton, Longman and Todd, 1965).

Dillard, Raymond B., and Tremper Longman III, *An Introduction to the Old Testament* (Leicester: Apollos, 1995).

Dorr, Donal, *Option for the Poor: A Hundred Years of Catholic Social Teaching*, rev. ed. (Maryknoll, NY: Orbis), 1992.

Douglass, R. Bruce, ed., *The Deeper Meaning of Economic Life: Critical Essays on the U.S. Catholic Bishops' Pastoral Letter on the Economy* (Washington, D.C.: Georgetown University Press, 1986).

Dunn, James D. G., *Romans 1-8*, Word Biblical Commentary (Dallas, TX: Word, 1988).

Durham, John I., *Exodus*, Word Biblical Commentary (Waco, TX: Word, 1987).

Fee, Gordon D., *The First Epistle to the Corinthians*, Grand Rapids, MI: Eerdmans, 1987.

Forrester, Duncan, *Christian Justice and Public Policy* (Cambridge: CUP, 1997).

Franklin, Jane (ed.), *Equality* (London: Institute for Public Policy Research, 1997).

Friedman, Milton, *Capitalism and Freedom* (Chicago: University of Chicago Press, 1962).

Goldingay, John, *After Eating the Apricot* (Carlisle: Solway, 1996).

Gonzalez, Justo L., *Faith and Wealth: A History of Early Christian Ideas on the Origin, Significance and Use of Money* (San Francisco: Harper & Row, 1990).

Goyder, George, *The Just Enterprise* (London: Andre Deutsch, 1987).

Grudem, Wayne, *Systematic Theology: An Introduction to Christian Doctrine*, Leicester: IVP, 1994.

Harrison, R. K., *Numbers*, Wycliffe Exegetical Commentary (Chicago: Moody, 1990).

Hauerwas, Stanley, *Dispatches From The Front* (Durham, NC: Duke University Press, 1994).

Hausman, Daniel M., and Michael S. McPherson, *Economic Analaysis and Moral Philosophy* (Cambridge: CUP, 1996).

Hay, Donald, *Economics Today: A Christian Critique* (Leicester: Apollos, 1989).

Hayek, F. A., *The Mirage of Social Justice* [1976]; Vol. 2 of F. A. Hayek, *Law, Legislation and Liberty: A new statement of the liberal principles of justice and political economy* (London: Routledge and Kegan Paul, 1982).

Hays, Richard B., *The Moral Vision of the New Testament* (Edinburgh: T&T Clark, 1996).

Helm, Paul, *The Providence of God* (Leicester: IVP, 1993).

Hill, David, *Greek Words and Hebrew Meanings: Studies in the Semantics of Soteriological Terms*, Society for the New Testament Studies, Monograph series, no.5 (Cambridge: CUP, 1967).

Hollenbach, David, 'Modern Catholic Teachings Concerning Justice' in John C. Haughey (ed.), *The Faith That Does Justice: Examining the Christian Sources for Social Change* (New York: Paulist Press, 1977).

Hubbard, D. A., *Joel and Amos*, Tyndale Old Testament Commentaries, (Leicester: IVP, 1989),

John Paul II, *Laborem Exercens* (London: Catholic Truth Society, 1981).

____, *Centesimus Annus* (London: Catholic Truth Society, 1991).

Johnston, C., 'Learning Reformed Theology from the Roman Catholics: the US Pastoral Letter on the Economy' in Robert L. Stivers, ed., *Reformed Faith and Economics* (Lanham, MD: University Press of America, 1989).

Kaiser, Walter, *Toward an Old Testament Theology* (Grand Rapids, MI: Zondervan, 1978).

Käsemann, Ernst, '"The Righteousness of God" in Paul', in *New Testament Questions of Today* (Philadelphia: Fortress, 1969).

Kaye, B. N., and G. J. Wenham, eds., *Law, Morality and the Bible: A Symposium* (Leicester: IVP, 1978)

Kidner, Derek, *Proverbs*, Tyndale Old Testament Commentaries (Leicester: IVP, 1964).

Kidner, Derek, *Genesis*, Tyndale Old Testament Commentaries (Leicester: IVP, 1967).

Kidner, Derek, *Psalms 73-150*, Tyndale Old Testament Commentaries (Leicester: IVP, 1975).

Kukathas, Chandran, and Philip Pettit, *Rawls: A Theory of Justice and its Critics* (Cambridge: Polity, 1990).

Langan, John, 'The Pastoral on the Economy: From Drafts to Policy', *Theological Studies*, 48, March 1987, 135-156.

Lebacqz, Karen, *Six Theories of Justice* (Minneapolis: Augsburg, 1986).

Leo XIII, *Rerum Novarum* [1891], tr. Joseph Kirwan (London: Catholic Truth Society, 1991).

Lohfink, Norbert, *The Laws of Deuteronomy: A Utopian Project For a World Without any Poor?* The 1995 Lattey Lecture (Cambridge: Von Hugel Institute, 1996).

Lovin, Robin W., *Reinhold Niebuhr and Christian Realism* (Cambridge: CUP, 1995).

Lutz, Charles P., ed., *God, Goods and the Common Good: Eleven Perspectives on Economic Justice in Dialog with the Roman Catholic Bishops' Pastoral Letter* (Minneapolis: Augsburg, 1987).

MacIntyre, Alasdair, *Whose Justice? Which Rationality?* (London: Duckworth, 1988).

McCann, Dennis P., 'The Church and Wall Street', *America*, 158, Jan.1988, 85-94; repr. in Max L. Stackhouse *et al* (eds.), *On Moral Business: Classical and Contemporary Resources for Ethics in Economic Life*, (Grand Rapids, MI: Eerdmans, 1995).

Mason, John D., 'Assistance Programmes in the Bible', *Transformation*, 4, April/June 1987, 1-14.

Meeks, M. Douglas, *God The Economist: The Doctrine of God and Political Economy* (Minneapolis: Fortress, 1989).

Mill, John Stuart, *Utilitarianism* [1861]; (reprinted, with an introduction by A. D. Lindsay, in John Stuart Mill, *Utilitarianism, Liberty and Representative Government*, London: Dent [Everyman's Library], 1910).

Miller, David, *Social Justice* (Oxford: Clarendon, 1976; repr. 1998).

Moo, Douglas, 'The Law of Christ as the Fulfilment of the Law of Moses', in Wayne Strickland (ed.), *Five Views on Law and Gospel* [previously titled *The Law, The Gospel and the Modern Christian*] (Grand Rapids, MI: Zondervan, 1996).

Motyer, Alec, *The Prophecy of Isaiah* (Leicester: IVP, 1993).

National Conference of Catholic Bishops, *Economic Justice For All: Pastoral Letter on Catholic Social Teaching and the U.S. Economy* (Washington, DC: United States Catholic Conference, 1986).

Ng, Y.-K., *Welfare Economics* (London: Macmillan, 1979).

Niebuhr, Reinhold, *Moral Man and Immoral Society* (London: SCM, 1963).

North, Gary, *Leviticus: An Economic Commentary* (Tyler, TX: Institute for Christian Economics, 1994).

Nozick, Robert, *Anarchy, State and Utopia* (Oxford: Blackwell, 1974).

O'Donovan, Oliver, *Resurrection and Moral Order*, 2nd ed. (Leicester: Apollos, 1994).

Patterson, Bob E., *Reinhold Niebuhr* (Waco, TX: Word, 1977).

Paul VI, *Evangelii Nuntiandi* [1976] (London: Catholic Truth Society, 1990).

Paul VI and the Fathers of the Sacred Council [Second Vatican Council: Pastoral Constitution on the Church in the World of Today], *Gaudium et Spes*, tr. William Purdy (London: Catholic Truth Society, 1966).

Paul, Ellen Frankel *et al* (eds.), *The Just Society* (Cambridge: CUP, 1995).

Pius XI, *Quadragesimo Anno* (London: Catholic Truth Society, 1931).

Posner, R., 'A Theory of Primitive Society, with Special Reference to Law', *Journal of Law and Economics*, 23, April 1980, 1-53.

Poythress, Vern S., *The Shadow of Christ in the Law of Moses* (Phillipsburg, NJ: P&R Publishing, 1991).

Przybylski, Benno, *Righteousness in Matthew and His World of Thought* (Cambridge: CUP, 1980).

Ramsey, Paul, *Basic Christian Ethics* (London: SCM, 1950).

Rasmussen, Douglas B., and James Sterba, *The Catholic Bishops and the Economy: A Debate* (Social Philosophy Policy Center/New Brunswick: Transaction Books, 1987).

Rauschenbusch, Walter, *Christianity and the Social Crisis* (New York: Macmillan, 1907; repr. Louisville, Kentucky: Westminster/John Knox, 1991).

Rawls, John, *A Theory of Justice* (Cambridge, MA: Harvard University Press, 1971/ Oxford: OUP, 1972).

Rawls, John, 'Kantian Constructivism in Moral Theory', *The Journal of Philosophy*, 1980, 88, 515-72.

Rawls, John, 'The Basic Liberties and Their Priority', in S. MacMurrin (ed.), *The Tanner Lectures on Human Values* (Cambridge: CUP, 1982).

Richardson, David J., 'Frontiers in Economics and Christian Scholarship', *Christian Scholar's Review*, 17, 1988, 381-400.

RSA, *Tomorrow's Company: The Role of Business In A Changing World* (Aldershot: Gower, 1995).

Sanders, E. P., *Paul and Palestinian Judaism: A Comparison of Patterns of Religion* (Philadelphia: Fortress, 1977).

Scarre, Geoffrey, *Utilitarianism* (London: Routledge, 1996).

Scheffler, Samuel (ed.), *Consequentialism and Its Critics* (Oxford: OUP, 1988).

Schlossberg, Herbert, *et al*, eds., *Christianity and Economics in the Post-Cold War Era: The Oxford Declaration and Beyond* (Grand Rapids, MI: Eerdmans, 1994).

Segundo, Juan Luis, *Liberation of Theology*, tr. John Drury (Dublin: Gill and Macmillan, 1977).

Seifrid, Mark A., *Christ, our Righteousness: Paul's Theology of Justification* (Leicester: Apollos, 2000).

Sen, Amartya, *Inequality Reexamined* (Oxford: Clarendon, 1992).

Silva, Moises, *Biblical Words and Their Meaning: An Introduction to Lexical Semantics*, revised and expanded edition (Grand Rapids, MI: Zondervan, 1994).

Smart, J. J. C., and Bernard Williams, *Utilitarianism: For and Against* (Cambridge: CUP, 1973).

Smart, J. J. C., 'An Outline of a System of Utilitarian Ethics' in J. J. C. Smart and Bernard Williams, *Utilitarianism: For and Against* (Cambridge: CUP, 1973).

Smith, Adam, *The Theory of Moral Sentiments* [1759], in D. D. Raphael and A. L. Macfie (eds.), *The Glasgow Edition of the Works and Correspondence of Adam Smith*, Vol. I (Oxford: OUP, 1976).

_____, *An Inquiry into the Nature and Causes of the Wealth of Nations* [1776] (London: Methuen, 1961).

Stackhouse, Max L. *et al* (eds.), *On Moral Business: Classical and Contemporary Resources for Ethics in Economic Life*, (Grand Rapids, MI: Eerdmans, 1995).

Sternberg, Elaine, *Just Business: Business Ethics in Action* (London: Little, Brown and Company, 1994).

Stibbs, A. M., *The Meaning of the Word 'Blood' in Scripture* (London: Tyndale Press, c.1948).

Stiglitz, Joseph E., *Economics of the Public Sector*, 3rd ed. (New York/London: Norton, 2000).

Storkey, Alan, *Transforming Economics: A Christian Way to Employment* (London: SPCK, 1986).

Strain, Charles R., (ed.), *Prophetic Visions and Economic Realities: Protestants, Jews and Catholics Confront the Bishops' Letter on the Economy* (Grand Rapids, MI: Eerdmans, 1989).

Strickland, Wayne, (ed.), *Five Views on Law and Gospel* (Grand Rapids, MI: Zondervan, 1996) = *The Law, The Gospel and the Modern Christian* (Grand Rapids, MI: Zondervan, 1993).

Tawney, R. H., *Equality*, rev. 2nd ed. (London: George Allen and Unwin, 1931).

The New Brown-Driver-Briggs-Gesenius Hebrew and English Lexicon (Peabody, MA: Hendrickson, 1979).

Thiselton, Anthony C., *New Horizons in Hermeneutics: The Theory and Practice of Transforming Bible Reading* (London: HarperCollins, 1992).

VanGemeren, Willem A. ed., *New International Dictionary of Old Testament Theology and Exegesis*, (Carlisle: Paternoster, 1997).

Vanhoozer, Kevin J., *Is There a Meaning in This Text? The Bible, the Reader and the Morality of Literary Knowledge* (Leicester: Apollos, 1998).

Von Rad, Gerhard, *Genesis*, Old Testament Library, rev. ed. (London: SCM, 1972).

Vos, Geerhardus, *Biblical Theology: Old and New Testaments* (Edinburgh: Banner of Truth, 1975).

Walzer, Michael, *Spheres of Justice: A Defence of Pluralism and Equality* (New York: Basic Books, 1983).

Ward, Timothy, *Word and Supplement: Speech Acts, Biblical Texts, and the Sufficiency of Scripture* (Oxford: OUP, 2002).

Watson, Francis, *Text and Truth: Redefining Biblical Theology* (Edinburgh: T&T Clark, 1997).

Wenham, Gordon, 'Law and the Legal System in the Old Testament', in B. N. Kaye and G. J. Wenham (eds.) *Law, Morality and the Bible: A Symposium* (Leicester: IVP, 1978).

Wenham, Gordon J., *Numbers*, Tyndale Old Testament Commentaries (Leicester: IVP, 1981).

Wenham, Gordon, *Genesis 1-15*, Word Biblical Commentary (Milton Keynes: Word, 1991).

Wenham, J. W., 'Large Numbers in the Old Testament', *Tyndale Bulletin*, 18 (1967), 19-53.

Whybray, R. N., *Wealth and Poverty in the Book of Proverbs*, Journal for the Study of the Old Testament Supplement Series, 99 (Sheffield: JSOT Press, 1990).

Williams, Bernard, 'A Critique of Utilitarianism' in J. J. C. Smart and Bernard Williams, *Utilitarianism: For and Against* (Cambridge: CUP, 1973).

Williams, Bernard, *Morality: An Introduction to Ethics* (Harmondsworth: Penguin, 1973).

Williams, Sam K.,'The "Righteousness of God" in Romans', *Journal of Biblical Literature*, 99, 1980, 241-290.

Wolff, Jonathan, *Robert Nozick: Property, Justice and the Minimal State* (Cambridge: Polity Press, 1991).

Wolterstorff, Nicholas, *Divine Discourse: Philosophical Reflections on the Claim that God Speaks* (Cambridge: CUP, 1995).

Woodhead, Linda, 'Love and Justice', *Studies in Christian Ethics*, 5, 1992, 44-61.

Wright, C. J. H., *Living as the People of God: The Relevance of Old Testament Ethics* (Leicester: IVP, 1983).

Wright, C. J. H., *God's People in God's Land: Family, Land and Property in the Old Testament* (Exeter: Paternoster, 1990).

Yri, Norvald, 'Seek God's Righteousness: Righteousness in the Gospel of Matthew', in D. A. Carson (ed), *Right With God: Justification in the Bible and in the World* (Carlisle: Paternoster, 1992).

Index

Paternoster Biblical Monographs

(All titles uniform with this volume)
Dates in bold are of projected publication

Joseph Abraham
Eve: Accused or Acquitted?
A Reconsideration of Feminist Readings of the Creation Narrative Texts in Genesis 1–3
Two contrary views dominate contemporary feminist biblical scholarship. One finds in the Bible an unequivocal equality between the sexes from the very creation of humanity, whilst the other sees the biblical text as irredeemably patriarchal and androcentric. Dr Abraham enters into dialogue with both camps as well as introducing his own method of approach. An invaluable tool for any one who is interested in this contemporary debate.
2002 / 0-85364-971-5 / xxiv + 272pp

Octavian D. Baban
Mimesis and Luke's on the Road Encounters in Luke-Acts
Luke's Theology of the Way and its Literary Representation
The book argues on theological and literary (mimetic) grounds that Luke's on-the-road encounters, especially those belonging to the post-Easter period, are part of his complex theology of the Way. Jesus' teaching and that of the apostles is presented by Luke as a challenging answer to the Hellenistic reader's thirst for adventure, good literature, and existential paradigms.
2005 */ 1-84227-253-5 / approx. 374pp*

Paul Barker
The Triumph of Grace in Deuteronomy
This book is a textual and theological analysis of the interaction between the sin and faithlessness of Israel and the grace of Yahweh in response, looking especially at Deuteronomy chapters 1–3, 8–10 and 29–30. The author argues that the grace of Yahweh is determinative for the ongoing relationship between Yahweh and Israel and that Deuteronomy anticipates and fully expects Israel to be faithless.
2004 / 1-84227-226-8 / xxii + 270pp

Jonathan F. Bayes
The Weakness of the Law
God's Law and the Christian in New Testament Perspective
A study of the four New Testament books which refer to the law as weak (Acts, Romans, Galatians, Hebrews) leads to a defence of the third use in the Reformed debate about the law in the life of the believer.
2000 / 0-85364-957-X / xii + 244pp

Mark Bonnington
The Antioch Episode of Galatians 2:11-14 in Historical and Cultural Context
The Galatians 2 'incident' in Antioch over table-fellowship suggests significant disagreement between the leading apostles. This book analyses the background to the disagreement by locating the incident within the dynamics of social interaction between Jews and Gentiles. It proposes a new way of understanding the relationship between the individuals and issues involved.

2005 / 1-84227-050-8 / approx. 350pp

David Bostock
A Portrayal of Trust
The Theme of Faith in the Hezekiah Narratives
This study provides detailed and sensitive readings of the Hezekiah narratives (2 Kings 18–20 and Isaiah 36–39) from a theological perspective. It concentrates on the theme of faith, using narrative criticism as its methodology. Attention is paid especially to setting, plot, point of view and characterization within the narratives. A largely positive portrayal of Hezekiah emerges that underlines the importance and relevance of scripture.

2005 / 1-84227-314-0 / approx. 300pp

Mark Bredin
Jesus, Revolutionary of Peace
A Non-violent Christology in the Book of Revelation
This book aims to demonstrate that the figure of Jesus in the Book of Revelation can best be understood as an active non-violent revolutionary.

2003 / 1-84227-153-9 / xviii + 262pp

Robinson Butarbutar
Paul and Conflict Resolution
An Exegetical Study of Paul's Apostolic Paradigm in 1 Corinthians 9
The author sees the apostolic paradigm in 1 Corinthians 9 as part of Paul's unified arguments in 1 Corinthians 8–10 in which he seeks to mediate in the dispute over the issue of food offered to idols. The book also sees its relevance for dispute-resolution today, taking the conflict within the author's church as an example.

2006 / 1-84227-315-9 / approx. 280pp

Daniel J-S Chae
Paul as Apostle to the Gentiles
*His Apostolic Self-awareness and its Influence on the Soteriological Argument
in Romans*
Opposing 'the post-Holocaust interpretation of Romans', Daniel Chae competently demonstrates that Paul argues for the equality of Jew and Gentile in Romans. Chae's fresh exegetical interpretation is academically outstanding and spiritually encouraging.
1997 / 0-85364-829-8 / xiv + 378pp

Luke L. Cheung
The Genre, Composition and Hermeneutics of the Epistle of James
The present work examines the employment of the wisdom genre with a certain compositional structure and the interpretation of the law through the Jesus tradition of the double love command by the author of the Epistle of James to serve his purpose in promoting perfection and warning against doubleness among the eschatologically renewed people of God in the Diaspora.
2003 / 1-84227-062-1 / xvi + 372pp

Youngmo Cho
Spirit and Kingdom in the Writings of Luke and Paul
The relationship between Spirit and Kingdom is a relatively unexplored area in Lukan and Pauline studies. This book offers a fresh perspective of two biblical writers on the subject. It explores the difference between Luke's and Paul's understanding of the Spirit by examining the specific question of the relationship of the concept of the Spirit to the concept of the Kingdom of God in each writer.
2005 / 1-84227-316-7 / approx. 270pp

Andrew C. Clark
Parallel Lives
The Relation of Paul to the Apostles in the Lucan Perspective
This study of the Peter-Paul parallels in Acts argues that their purpose was to emphasize the themes of continuity in salvation history and the unity of the Jewish and Gentile missions. New light is shed on Luke's literary techniques, partly through a comparison with Plutarch.
2001 / 1-84227-035-4 / xviii + 386pp

Andrew D. Clarke
Secular and Christian Leadership in Corinth
A Socio-Historical and Exegetical Study of 1 Corinthians 1–6
This volume is an investigation into the leadership structures and dynamics of first-century Roman Corinth. These are compared with the practice of leadership in the Corinthian Christian community which are reflected in 1 Corinthians 1–6, and contrasted with Paul's own principles of Christian leadership.
2005 / 1-84227-229-2 / 200pp

Stephen Finamore
God, Order and Chaos
René Girard and the Apocalypse
Readers are often disturbed by the images of destruction in the book of Revelation and unsure why they are unleashed after the exaltation of Jesus. This book examines past approaches to these texts and uses René Girard's theories to revive some old ideas and propose some new ones.
2005 / 1-84227-197-0 / approx. 344pp

David G. Firth
Surrendering Retribution in the Psalms
Responses to Violence in the Individual Complaints
In *Surrendering Retribution in the Psalms*, David Firth examines the ways in which the book of Psalms inculcates a model response to violence through the repetition of standard patterns of prayer. Rather than seeking justification for retributive violence, Psalms encourages not only a surrender of the right of retribution to Yahweh, but also sets limits on the retribution that can be sought in imprecations. Arising initially from the author's experience in South Africa, the possibilities of this model to a particular context of violence is then briefly explored.
2005 / 1-84227-337-X / xviii + 154pp

Scott J. Hafemann
Suffering and Ministry in the Spirit
Paul's Defence of His Ministry in II Corinthians 2:14–3:3
Shedding new light on the way Paul defended his apostleship, the author offers a careful, detailed study of 2 Corinthians 2:14–3:3 linked with other key passages throughout 1 and 2 Corinthians. Demonstrating the unity and coherence of Paul's argument in this passage, the author shows that Paul's suffering served as the vehicle for revealing God's power and glory through the Spirit.
2000 / 0-85364-967-7 / xiv + 262pp

Scott J. Hafemann
Paul, Moses and the History of Israel
The Letter/Spirit Contrast and the Argument from Scripture in 2 Corinthians 3
An exegetical study of the call of Moses, the second giving of the Law (Exodus 32–34), the new covenant, and the prophetic understanding of the history of Israel in 2 Corinthians 3. Hafemann's work demonstrates Paul's contextual use of the Old Testament and the essential unity between the Law and the Gospel within the context of the distinctive ministries of Moses and Paul.
2005 / 1-84227-317-5 / xii + 498pp

Douglas S. McComiskey
Lukan Theology in the Light of the Gospel's Literary Structure
Luke's Gospel was purposefully written with theology embedded in its patterned literary structure. A critical analysis of this cyclical structure provides new windows into Luke's interpretation of the individual pericopes comprising the Gospel and illuminates several of his theological interests.
2004 / 1-84227-148-2 / xviii + 388pp

Stephen Motyer
Your Father the Devil?
A New Approach to John and 'The Jews'
Who are 'the Jews' in John's Gospel? Defending John against the charge of antisemitism, Motyer argues that, far from demonising the Jews, the Gospel seeks to present Jesus as 'Good News for Jews' in a late first century setting.
1997 / 0-85364-832-8 / xiv + 260pp

Esther Ng
Reconstructing Christian Origins?
The Feminist Theology of Elizabeth Schüssler Fiorenza: An Evaluation
In a detailed evaluation, the author challenges Elizabeth Schüssler Fiorenza's reconstruction of early Christian origins and her underlying presuppositions. The author also presents her own views on women's roles both then and now.
2002 / 1-84227-055-9 / xxiv + 468pp

Robin Parry
Old Testament Story and Christian Ethics
The Rape of Dinah as a Case Study
What is the role of story in ethics and, more particularly, what is the role of Old Testament story in Christian ethics? This book, drawing on the work of contemporary philosophers, argues that narrative is crucial in the ethical shaping of people and, drawing on the work of contemporary Old Testament scholars, that story plays a key role in Old Testament ethics. Parry then argues that when situated in canonical context Old Testament stories can be reappropriated by Christian readers in their own ethical formation. The shocking story of the rape of Dinah and the massacre of the Shechemites provides a fascinating case study for exploring the parameters within which Christian ethical appropriations of Old Testament stories can live.
2004 / 1-84227-210-1 / xx + 350pp

Ian Paul
Power to See the World Anew
The Value of Paul Ricoeur's Hermeneutic of Metaphor in Interpreting the Symbolism of Revelation 12 and 13
This book is a study of the hermeneutics of metaphor of Paul Ricoeur, one of the most important writers on hermeneutics and metaphor of the last century. It sets out the key points of his theory, important criticisms of his work, and how his approach, modified in the light of these criticisms, offers a methodological framework for reading apocalyptic texts.
2006 / 1-84227-056-7 / approx. 350pp

Robert L. Plummer
Paul's Understanding of the Church's Mission
Did the Apostle Paul Expect the Early Christian Communities to Evangelize?
This book engages in a careful study of Paul's letters to determine if the apostle expected the communities to which he wrote to engage in missionary activity. It helpfully summarizes the discussion on this debated issue, judiciously handling contested texts, and provides a way forward in addressing this critical question. While admitting that Paul rarely explicitly commands the communities he founded to evangelize, Plummer amasses significant incidental data to provide a convincing case that Paul did indeed expect his churches to engage in mission activity. Throughout the study, Plummer progressively builds a theological basis for the church's mission that is both distinctively Pauline and compelling.
2006 / 1-84227-333-7 / approx. 324pp

David Powys
'Hell': A Hard Look at a Hard Question
The Fate of the Unrighteous in New Testament Thought
This comprehensive treatment seeks to unlock the original meaning of terms and phrases long thought to support the traditional doctrine of hell. It concludes that there is an alternative—one which is more biblical, and which can positively revive the rationale for Christian mission.
1997 / 0-85364-831-X / xxii + 478pp

Sorin Sabou
Between Horror and Hope
Paul's Metaphorical Language of Death in Romans 6.1-11
This book argues that Paul's metaphorical language of death in Romans 6.1-11 conveys two aspects: horror and hope. The 'horror' aspect is conveyed by the 'crucifixion' language, and the 'hope' aspect by 'burial' language. The life of the Christian believer is understood, as relationship with sin is concerned ('death to sin'), between these two realities: horror and hope.
2005 / 1-84227-322-1 / approx. 224pp

Rosalind Selby
The Comical Doctrine
The Epistemology of New Testament Hermeneutics
This book argues that the gospel breaks through postmodernity's critique of truth and the referential possibilities of textuality with its gift of grace. With a rigorous, philosophical challenge to modernist and postmodernist assumptions, Selby offers an alternative epistemology to all who would still read with faith *and* with academic credibility.
2005 / 1-84227-212-8 / approx. 350pp

Kiwoong Son
Zion Symbolism in Hebrews
Hebrews 12.18-24 as a Hermeneutical Key to the Epistle
This book challenges the general tendency of understanding the Epistle to the Hebrews against a Hellenistic background and suggests that the Epistle should be understood in the light of the Jewish apocalyptic tradition. The author especially argues for the importance of the theological symbolism of Sinai and Zion (Heb. 12:18-24) as it provides the Epistle's theological background as well as the rhetorical basis of the superiority motif of Jesus throughout the Epistle.
2005 / 1-84227-368-X / approx. 280pp

Kevin Walton
Thou Traveller Unknown
The Presence and Absence of God in the Jacob Narrative
The author offers a fresh reading of the story of Jacob in the book of Genesis through the paradox of divine presence and absence. The work also seeks to make a contribution to Pentateuchal studies by bringing together a close reading of the final text with historical critical insights, doing justice to the text's historical depth, final form and canonical status.
2003 / 1-84227-059-1 / xvi + 238pp

George M. Wieland
The Significance of Salvation
A Study of Salvation Language in the Pastoral Epistles
The language and ideas of salvation pervade the three Pastoral Epistles. This study offers a close examination of their soteriological statements. In all three letters the idea of salvation is found to play a vital paraenetic role, but each also exhibits distinctive soteriological emphases. The results challenge common assumptions about the Pastoral Epistles as a corpus.
2005 / 1-84227-257-8 / approx. 324pp

Alistair Wilson
When Will These Things Happen?
A Study of Jesus as Judge in Matthew 21–25
This study seeks to allow Matthew's carefully constructed presentation of Jesus to be given full weight in the modern evaluation of Jesus' eschatology. Careful analysis of the text of Matthew 21–25 reveals Jesus to be standing firmly in the Jewish prophetic and wisdom traditions as he proclaims and enacts imminent judgement on the Jewish authorities then boldly claims the central role in the final and universal judgement.
2004 / 1-84227-146-6 / xxii + 272pp

Lindsay Wilson
Joseph Wise and Otherwise
The Intersection of Covenant and Wisdom in Genesis 37–50
This book offers a careful literary reading of Genesis 37–50 that argues that the Joseph story contains both strong covenant themes and many wisdom-like elements. The connections between the two helps to explore how covenant and wisdom might intersect in an integrated biblical theology.
2004 / 1-84227-140-7 / xvi + 340pp

Stephen I. Wright
The Voice of Jesus
Studies in the Interpretation of Six Gospel Parables
This literary study considers how the 'voice' of Jesus has been heard in different periods of parable interpretation, and how the categories of figure and trope may help us towards a sensitive reading of the parables today.
2000 / 0-85364-975-8 / xiv + 280pp

Paternoster
9 Holdom Avenue,
Bletchley,
Milton Keynes MK1 1QR,
United Kingdom
Web: www.authenticmedia.co.uk/paternoster

July 2005

Paternoster Theological Monographs

(All titles uniform with this volume)
Dates in bold are of projected publication

Emil Bartos
Deification in Eastern Orthodox Theology
An Evaluation and Critique of the Theology of Dumitru Staniloae
Bartos studies a fundamental yet neglected aspect of Orthodox theology: deification. By examining the doctrines of anthropology, christology, soteriology and ecclesiology as they relate to deification, he provides an important contribution to contemporary dialogue between Eastern and Western theologians.

1999 / 0-85364-956-1 / xii + 370pp

Graham Buxton
The Trinity, Creation and Pastoral Ministry
Imaging the Perichoretic God
In this book the author proposes a three-way conversation between theology, science and pastoral ministry. His approach draws on a Trinitarian understanding of God as a relational being of love, whose life 'spills over' into all created reality, human and non-human. By locating human meaning and purpose within God's 'creation-community' this book offers the possibility of a transforming engagement between those in pastoral ministry and the scientific community.

***2005** / 1-84227-369-8 / approx. 380 pp*

Iain D. Campbell
Fixing the Indemnity
The Life and Work of George Adam Smith
When Old Testament scholar George Adam Smith (1856–1942) delivered the Lyman Beecher lectures at Yale University in 1899, he confidently declared that 'modern criticism has won its war against traditional theories. It only remains to fix the amount of the indemnity.' In this biography, Iain D. Campbell assesses Smith's critical approach to the Old Testament and evaluates its consequences, showing that Smith's life and work still raises questions about the relationship between biblical scholarship and evangelical faith.

2004 / 1-84227-228-4 / xx + 256pp

Tim Chester
Mission and the Coming of God
Eschatology, the Trinity and Mission in the Theology of Jürgen Moltmann
This book explores the theology and missiology of the influential contemporary theologian, Jürgen Moltmann. It highlights the important contribution Moltmann has made while offering a critique of his thought from an evangelical perspective. In so doing, it touches on pertinent issues for evangelical missiology. The conclusion takes Calvin as a starting point, proposing 'an eschatology of the cross' which offers a critique of the over-realised eschatologies in liberation theology and certain forms of evangelicalism.
2006 / 1-84227-320-5 / approx. 224pp

Sylvia Wilkey Collinson
Making Disciples
The Significance of Jesus' Educational Strategy for Today's Church
This study examines the biblical practice of discipling, formulates a definition, and makes comparisons with modern models of education. A recommendation is made for greater attention to its practice today.
2004 / 1-84227-116-4 / xiv + 278pp

Darrell Cosden
A Theology of Work
Work and the New Creation
Through dialogue with Moltmann, Pope John Paul II and others, this book develops a genitive 'theology of work', presenting a theological definition of work and a model for a theological ethics of work that shows work's nature, value and meaning now and eschatologically. Work is shown to be a transformative activity consisting of three dynamically inter-related dimensions: the instrumental, relational and ontological.
2005 / 1-84227-332-9 / xvi + 208pp

Stephen M. Dunning
The Crisis and the Quest
A Kierkegaardian Reading of Charles Williams
Employing Kierkegaardian categories and analysis, this study investigates both the central crisis in Charles Williams's authorship between hermetism and Christianity (Kierkegaard's Religions A and B), and the quest to resolve this crisis, a quest that ultimately presses the bounds of orthodoxy.
2000 / 0-85364-985-5 / xxiv + 254pp

Keith Ferdinando
The Triumph of Christ in African Perspective
A Study of Demonology and Redemption in the African Context
The book explores the implications of the gospel for traditional African fears of occult aggression. It analyses such traditional approaches to suffering and biblical responses to fears of demonic evil, concluding with an evaluation of African beliefs from the perspective of the gospel.
1999 / 0-85364-830-1 / xviii + 450pp

Andrew Goddard
Living the Word, Resisting the World
The Life and Thought of Jacques Ellul
This work offers a definitive study of both the life and thought of the French Reformed thinker Jacques Ellul (1912-1994). It will prove an indispensable resource for those interested in this influential theologian and sociologist and for Christian ethics and political thought generally.
2002 / 1-84227-053-2 / xxiv + 378pp

David Hilborn
The Words of our Lips
Language-Use in Free Church Worship
Studies of liturgical language have tended to focus on the written canons of Roman Catholic and Anglican communities. By contrast, David Hilborn analyses the more extemporary approach of English Nonconformity. Drawing on recent developments in linguistic pragmatics, he explores similarities and differences between 'fixed' and 'free' worship, and argues for the interdependence of each.
***2006** / 0-85364-977-4 / approx. 350pp*

Roger Hitching
The Church and Deaf People
A Study of Identity, Communication and Relationships with Special Reference to the Ecclesiology of Jürgen Moltmann
In *The Church and Deaf People* Roger Hitching sensitively examines the history and present experience of deaf people and finds similarities between aspects of sign language and Moltmann's theological method that 'open up' new ways of understanding theological concepts.
2003 / 1-84227-222-5 / xxii + 236pp

John G. Kelly
One God, One People
The Differentiated Unity of the People of God in the Theology of
Jürgen Moltmann
The author expounds and critiques Moltmann's doctrine of God and highlights
the systematic connections between it and Moltmann's influential discussion of
Israel. He then proposes a fresh approach to Jewish–Christian relations building
on Moltmann's work using insights from Habermas and Rawls.
2005 / 0-85346-969-3 / approx. 350pp

Mark F.W. Lovatt
Confronting the Will-to-Power
A Reconsideration of the Theology of Reinhold Niebuhr
Confronting the Will-to-Power is an analysis of the theology of Reinhold
Niebuhr, arguing that his work is an attempt to identify, and provide a practical
theological answer to, the existence and nature of human evil.
2001 / 1-84227-054-0 / xviii + 216pp

Neil B. MacDonald
Karl Barth and the Strange New World within the Bible
Barth, Wittgenstein, and the Metadilemmas of the Enlightenment
Barth's discovery of the strange new world within the Bible is examined in the
context of Kant, Hume, Overbeck, and, most importantly, Wittgenstein.
MacDonald covers some fundamental issues in theology today: epistemology,
the final form of the text and biblical truth-claims.
2000 / 0-85364-970-7 / xxvi + 374pp

Keith A. Mascord
Alvin Plantinga and Christian Apologetics
This book draws together the contributions of the philosopher Alvin Plantinga to
the major contemporary challenges to Christian belief, highlighting in particular
his ground-breaking work in epistemology and the problem of evil. Plantinga's
theory that both theistic and Christian belief is warrantedly basic is explored and
critiqued, and an assessment offered as to the significance of his work for
apologetic theory and practice.
2005 / 1-84227-256-X / approx. 304pp

Gillian McCulloch
The Deconstruction of Dualism in Theology
With Reference to Ecofeminist Theology and New Age Spirituality
This book challenges eco-theological anti-dualism in Christian theology, arguing that dualism has a twofold function in Christian religious discourse. Firstly, it enables us to express the discontinuities and divisions that are part of the process of reality. Secondly, dualistic language allows us to express the mysteries of divine transcendence/immanence and the survival of the soul without collapsing into monism and materialism, both of which are problematic for Christian epistemology.
2002 / 1-84227-044-3 / xii + 282pp

Leslie McCurdy
Attributes and Atonement
The Holy Love of God in the Theology of P.T. Forsyth
Attributes and Atonement is an intriguing full-length study of P.T. Forsyth's doctrine of the cross as it relates particularly to God's holy love. It includes an unparalleled bibliography of both primary and secondary material relating to Forsyth.
1999 / 0-85364-833-6 / xiv + 328pp

Nozomu Miyahira
Towards a Theology of the Concord of God
A Japanese Perspective on the Trinity
This book introduces a new Japanese theology and a unique Trinitarian formula based on the Japanese intellectual climate: three betweennesses and one concord. It also presents a new interpretation of the Trinity, a co-subordinationism, which is in line with orthodox Trinitarianism; each single person of the Trinity is eternally and equally subordinate (or serviceable) to the other persons, so that they retain the mutual dynamic equality.
2000 / 0-85364-863-8 / xiv + 256pp

Eddy José Muskus
The Origins and Early Development of Liberation Theology in Latin America
With Particular Reference to Gustavo Gutiérrez
This work challenges the fundamental premise of Liberation Theology, 'opting for the poor', and its claim that Christ is found in them. It also argues that Liberation Theology emerged as a direct result of the failure of the Roman Catholic Church in Latin America.
2002 / 0-85364-974-X / xiv + 296pp

Jim Purves
The Triune God and the Charismatic Movement
A Critical Appraisal from a Scottish Perspective
All emotion and no theology? Or a fundamental challenge to reappraise and realign our trinitarian theology in the light of Christian experience? This study of charismatic renewal as it found expression within Scotland at the end of the twentieth century evaluates the use of Patristic, Reformed and contemporary models of the Trinity in explaining the workings of the Holy Spirit.
2004 / 1-84227-321-3 / xxiv + 246pp

Anna Robbins
Methods in the Madness
Diversity in Twentieth-Century Christian Social Ethics
The author compares the ethical methods of Walter Rauschenbusch, Reinhold Niebuhr and others. She argues that unless Christians are clear about the ways that theology and philosophy are expressed practically they may lose the ability to discuss social ethics across contexts, let alone reach effective agreements.
2004 / 1-84227-211-X / xx + 294pp

Ed Rybarczyk
Beyond Salvation
Eastern Orthodoxy and Classical Pentecostalism on Becoming Like Christ
At first glance eastern Orthodoxy and classical Pentecostalism seem quite distinct. This ground-breaking study shows they share much in common, especially as it concerns the experiential elements of following Christ. Both traditions assert that authentic Christianity transcends the wooden categories of modernism.
2004 / 1-84227-144-X / xii + 356pp

Signe Sandsmark
Is World View Neutral Education Possible and Desirable?
A Christian Response to Liberal Arguments
(Published jointly with The Stapleford Centre)
This book discusses reasons for belief in world view neutrality, and argues that 'neutral' education will have a hidden, but strong world view influence. It discusses the place for Christian education in the common school.
2000 / 0-85364-973-1 / xiv + 182pp

Hazel Sherman
Reading Zechariah
The Allegorical Tradition of Biblical Interpretation through the Commentary of Didymus the Blind and Theodore of Mopsuestia
A close reading of the commentary on Zechariah by Didymus the Blind alongside that of Theodore of Mopsuestia suggests that popular categorising of Antiochene and Alexandrian biblical exegesis as 'historical' or 'allegorical' is inadequate and misleading.
2005 / 1-84227-213-6 / approx. 280pp

Andrew Sloane
On Being a Christian in the Academy
Nicholas Wolterstorff and the Practice of Christian Scholarship
An exposition and critical appraisal of Nicholas Wolterstorff's epistemology in the light of the philosophy of science, and an application of his thought to the practice of Christian scholarship.
2003 / 1-84227-058-3 / xvi + 274pp

Damon W.K. So
Jesus' Revelation of His Father
A Narrative-Conceptual Study of the Trinity with Special Reference to Karl Barth
This book explores the trinitarian dynamics in the context of Jesus' revelation of his Father in his earthly ministry with references to key passages in Matthew's Gospel. It develops from the exegeses of these passages a non-linear concept of revelation which links Jesus' communion with his Father to his revelatory words and actions through a nuanced understanding of the Holy Spirit, with references to K. Barth, G.W.H. Lampe, J.D.G. Dunn and E. Irving.
2005 / 1-84227-323-X / approx. 380pp

Daniel Strange
The Possibility of Salvation Among the Unevangelised
An Analysis of Inclusivism in Recent Evangelical Theology
For evangelical theologians the 'fate of the unevangelised' impinges upon fundamental tenets of evangelical identity. The position known as 'inclusivism', defined by the belief that the unevangelised can be ontologically saved by Christ whilst being epistemologically unaware of him, has been defended most vigorously by the Canadian evangelical Clark H. Pinnock. Through a detailed analysis and critique of Pinnock's work, this book examines a cluster of issues surrounding the unevangelised and its implications for christology, soteriology and the doctrine of revelation.
2002 / 1-84227-047-8 / xviii + 362pp

Scott Swain
God According to the Gospel
Biblical Narrative and the Identity of God in the Theology of Robert W. Jenson
Robert W. Jenson is one of the leading voices in contemporary Trinitarian theology. His boldest contribution in this area concerns his use of biblical narrative both to ground and explicate the Christian doctrine of God. *God According to the Gospel* critically examines Jenson's proposal and suggests an alternative way of reading the biblical portrayal of the triune God.
2006 / 1-84227-258-6 / approx. 180pp

Justyn Terry
The Justifying Judgement of God
A Reassessment of the Place of Judgement in the Saving Work of Christ
The argument of this book is that judgement, understood as the whole process of bringing justice, is the primary metaphor of atonement, with others, such as victory, redemption and sacrifice, subordinate to it. Judgement also provides the proper context for understanding penal substitution and the call to repentance, baptism, eucharist and holiness.
2005 / 1-84227-370-1 / approx. 274 pp

Graham Tomlin
The Power of the Cross
Theology and the Death of Christ in Paul, Luther and Pascal
This book explores the theology of the cross in St Paul, Luther and Pascal. It offers new perspectives on the theology of each, and some implications for the nature of power, apologetics, theology and church life in a postmodern context.
1999 / 0-85364-984-7 / xiv + 344pp

Adonis Vidu
Postliberal Theological Method
A Critical Study
The postliberal theology of Hans Frei, George Lindbeck, Ronald Thiemann, John Milbank and others is one of the more influential contemporary options. This book focuses on several aspects pertaining to its theological method, specifically its understanding of background, hermeneutics, epistemic justification, ontology, the nature of doctrine and, finally, Christological method.
2005 / 1-84227-395-7 / approx. 324pp

Graham J. Watts
Revelation and the Spirit
*A Comparative Study of the Relationship between the Doctrine of Revelation
and Pneumatology in the Theology of Eberhard Jüngel and of
Wolfhart Pannenberg*
The relationship between revelation and pneumatology is relatively unexplored.
This approach offers a fresh angle on two important twentieth century
theologians and raises pneumatological questions which are theologically crucial
and relevant to mission in a postmodern culture.
2005 / 1-84227-104-0 / xxii + 232pp

Nigel G. Wright
Disavowing Constantine
*Mission, Church and the Social Order in the Theologies of John Howard Yoder
and Jürgen Moltmann*
This book is a timely restatement of a radical theology of church and state in the
Anabaptist and Baptist tradition. Dr Wright constructs his argument in dialogue
and debate with Yoder and Moltmann, major contributors to a free church
perspective.
2000 / 0-85364-978-2 / xvi + 252pp

Paternoster:
thinking faith

Paternoster
9 Holdom Avenue,
Bletchley,
Milton Keynes MK1 1QR,
United Kingdom
Web: www.authenticmedia.co.uk/paternoster

July 2005